The Practical Application of Medical and Dental
HYPNOSIS

Milton H. Erickson, M.D.
Past President and Co-founder, ASCH

Seymour Hershman, M.D.
Past President and Co-founder, ASCH

Irving I. Secter, D.D.S.
Past President and Historian, ASCH

BRUNNER/MAZEL *Publishers* • New York

Library of Congress Cataloging-in-Publication Data

Erickson, Milton H.
    The practical application of medical and dental hypnosis / Milton
H. Erickson, Seymour Hershman, Irving I. Secter.
        p.   cm.
    Includes bibliographical references.
    ISBN 0-87630-570-2
    1. Hypnotism—Therapeutic use. 2. Hypnotism. I. Hershman,
Seymour. II. Secter, Irving I. III. Title.
RC495.E725,   1989
615.8'512—dc20   89-23918
                                                                          CIP

Published by
BRUNNER/MAZEL, INC.
19 Union Square
New York, New York 10003

Manufactured in the United States of America

10 9 8 7 6 5 4 3 2 1

Foreword

The history of twentieth century hypnosis primarily reflects the contributions of the late psychiatric genius Milton H. Erickson, M.D. If one were to list the important historical figures in hypnosis, in the eighteenth century one would name Mesmer; in the nineteenth century, Braid, Esdaile, Liébault, Bernheim, and Charcot; and in the twentieth century, Erickson. Erickson dominated modern hypnosis and almost single-handedly legitimized it and brought hypnosis into a state of respectability in the professional community. In the process, he revolutionized its practice.

Previous to Erickson, the practice of hypnosis was regarded as an authoritarian, operator-based model where direct suggestions were "implanted" into a passive subject. Erickson developed a patient-based model of tailoring indirect hypnotherapy to elicit strengths (dormant resources) that could be utilized in strategic steps. Thereby, he changed the direction of hypnosis. In traditional practice, hypnosis was directed from the outside in, that is, hypnosis was conducted as a series of commands dictated from the operator to the subject. Erickson's work was from the inside out: indirect methods were used to elicit strengths *from* the patient rather than force-feeding suggestions into the passive subject. Erickson formulated the central concepts of modern hypnosis. His contributions seem to have sprung de novo; he did not build on the work of predecessors.

However, there were many junior colleagues and students of Erickson who followed his lead and built the application of his methods in far-reaching ways. Early protégés were the co-authors of this book, Seymour Hershman, M.D., a physician in general practice, and Irving I. Secter, D.D.S., M.A., a dentist and Master's level psychologist. These three were the backbone of the Seminars on Hypnosis Foundation, a group who traveled the country in the early and mid-1950s to teach workshops on clinical hypnosis to professionals. In 1957 the practitioners who taught for the Seminars on Hypnosis Foundation were instrumental in forming the American Society of Clinical Hypnosis (ASCH), and the Seminars on Hypnosis Foundation eventually merged into the educational arm of the ASCH. Other notable lecturers of the Seminars on Hypnosis group included William Kroger, M.D., Edward E. Aston, D.D.S., David Cheek, M.D., and Leslie LeCron.

In the 1950s the attendees at these seminars were mostly physicians and dentists, and this book was directed to that audience. Currently, hypnotic practice has shifted and become the purview of psychotherapists such as psychologists and Master's level mental health professionals. The teaching of the Seminars on Hypnosis Foundation group on the Ericksonian/indirect approach to hypnosis is, however, valuable for all medical, dental, and psychotherapeutic clinicians.

In this book you will encounter fundamental principles of Ericksonian hypnosis of which I have listed ten important postulates:

1. *Use indirection.*

Consider the following passage:

> In contrasting [direct and indirect approaches], one might employ the following direct approach to the production of hypnotic deafness: "When I count to ten, you will find yourself getting more and more deaf, until finally, at the count of ten, you will be unable to hear anything at all."
>
> On the other hand, the indirect approach might proceed in this fashion: "I wonder how it feels to a person who is about to lose his hearing. I wonder if he notices the fact that sounds seem to grow very, very slightly less distinct at first, if he finds that they seem to be fading off into the distance? And I wonder if the person then sits in his chair, leaning forward toward the sound. . . ."
> (pp. 274–275)

This indirect method may stand as the greatest contribution that Erickson made to the field of hypnosis and psychotherapy. It deserves careful study by practitioners in all health fields.

2. *Make hypnosis interactional.*

Milton Erickson invented the interactional trance. It continues to be the case that the vast majority of practitioners of hypnosis, even those using the indirect method, carry out their work on patients who are essentially passive. To Erickson, trance was bilateral communication. Hypnotized patients would have extensive ongoing dialogue with Erickson. It was presupposed that this dialogue would enhance the trance and in no way interfere with the development of even somnambulistic (deep trance) states. In this book you will find transcripts that elucidate the interactional trance that was one of the hallmarks of Erickson's formal induction technique. A distinction between the master practitioner and the journeyman is that the master uses interactional trance, whereas the journeyman continues to work with a relatively quiescent patient.

3. *Move in small, directed steps.*

Reading Erickson's cases is often like reading O. Henry short stories: there is a discrete denouement and suddenly the symptom is resolved. However, Erickson was more akin to a master craftsman—he worked meticulously in small steps. By building in a directed fashion, he asked patients to do tasks that were eminently possible. After doing these minor tasks, the patient would "suddenly" realize major change.

4. *Focus on the symptom.*

Hypnosis is a symptomatic therapy. However, it is not a superficial approach. People benefit immeasurably by gaining control of their symptoms. There can be a snowballing effect even from a small salutory change in a symptom.

5. *Have respect for the patient.*

As a humanist, Erickson recognized the fact that the therapy should focus on the patient, not on the therapist. He admonished therapists to think, "What does my patient want to do next?" rather than to think, "What shall I, the therapist, do next?" At the same time, Erickson was supremely confident. He wanted his patients to know that they *could* do things, such as develop anaesthesias. Erickson's confidence and interest in the patients' ability to succeed was communicated verbally and nonverbally.

6. *Recognize that hypnosis is cooperation.*

The induction of hypnosis is primarily the induction of cooperation. It is a way in which therapist and patient join forces to surmount the patient's difficulty. Hypnosis secures the attention of the patient to maximize constructive collaboration with the therapist.

7. *Communicate precisely.*

Erickson admonished his students that "the hypnotist must be constantly aware of just what he is saying to the subject" (p. 59). Erickson used communication with the precision of a surgeon using a scalpel. He focused the words, the implication of the words, the nonverbal behavior, and the implication of the nonverbal behavior.

8. *Utilize the symptoms.*

Erickson advised his students to utilize symptoms. Carefully consider the case reported on page 326 of a child who regularly made squeaking noises. Rather than challenging the symptom, Erickson sent the boy to his room until the boy could increase the frequency of the sound. That new frequency could be continued for a full day. Subsequently, it was indirectly suggested that the squeaking behavior could be increased even more. Within a week's time, the boy discarded the habit when he realized, to his own credit, how cumbersome it would be to maintain.

9. *Tailor the hypnotherapy.*

By studying Erickson's transcripts in this book, it will be apparent that he worked hard to individualize his approach. He assiduously avoided cookbook approaches by championing the importance of individual differences: Erickson created free-form hypnosis and therapy to fit the values and the styles of the individuals with whom he worked.

10. *Point the therapy to the future.*

Erickson's approach to psychiatry was practical. He set about helping patients to secure the best possibilities for living effectively. Promoting change took precedence over acquiring insight into an unchangeable past. Consider the following quote: "One of the purposes hypnosis and hypnotherapy should accomplish is to make plain to the patient that he has not only a past that is highly important to him; he also has a present that is more important, and a future even more so than the present or the past" (p. 324).

The Practical Application of Medical and Dental Hypnosis is interesting from a historical perspective. One can see how hypnosis has evolved in the almost thirty years since the original publication of this text. While the vast majority of information contained herein is refreshingly up-to-date and eminently useful, some concepts are antiquated. For example, hypnosis is operationally defined as an increased susceptibility to suggestion. In his later work, Erickson de-emphasized the importance of suggestion as a central concept in hypnosis. As Erickson progressed, he promoted the importance of identifying, accessing, developing, and utilizing strengths. Also, in some of the induction transcripts, the practitioners suggest that patients go "deeply asleep." Modern practitioners rarely use this metaphor.

This book contains a wealth of practical information. There are commonsense tips on working with all types of clinical problems. Through actual transcripts, one can see how Erickson conducted hypnosis and taught students. Practitioners from all fields will learn not only important methods of hypnosis, but also ways to communicate with patients more effectively.

October 1989

JEFFREY K. ZEIG, Ph.D.
Director
The Milton H. Erickson Foundation

Contents

CONTENTS

Preface

The material in this book has been adapted from that presented in seminars throughout the country during the past several years. These seminars are conducted at the post-doctoral level, for physicians, dentists, and psychologists. To avoid the verbosity of the spoken word, some revisions have been made. For inductions and other techniques, the full flow of conversation has been preserved as transcribed from tapes, so that the reader may capture the entire sequence and interplay of events.

Each of the co-authors is engaged in the active practice of his specialty. This fact is important because of the assurance it gives that cases presented, techniques demonstrated, and theoretical discussions are all based on day-to-day experience rather than on any purely academic approach to topics or secondhand access to clinical material and problems.

It is impossible to put into book form the full give and take that exists in an actual teaching situation. A good many of the considerations that will occur to the reader have been taken into account, however, in the various question and answer periods, which have served as a basis for supplementing the individual approaches of the co-authors. There is no adequate substitute for actual participation in an active interpersonal training situation. This book is not intended as a substitute and it will have limited usefulness when employed alone. As a supplement to and preparation for actual training, it does serve important needs, not the least of which is that students can be relieved of the need for taking notes, and feel free to participate fully and actively in the training situation.

Seminars and texts can serve only as beginnings in the training of individuals for the employment of hypnosis in their specialties. Beyond that point, it is essential for each student to practice, analyze, discuss with others, and gain as extensive and intensive experience as possible. Where two or more students are close enough to meet occasionally, the interaction of experiences and outlooks will help to provide continuing training and advice, either formally or through informal groups.

Clearly, no seminar or single text can provide basic training for the internist, obstetrician, gynecologist, anesthesiologist, dentist, oral surgeon, psychologist, or psychiatrist. It is necessary to assume that each specialist has his basic training and then to demonstrate methods and approaches by which he can apply his special training to the areas benefited by the employment of hypnosis. Inevitably, the various discussions of problems in any given specialty have overtones that also apply to others. Each specialist who seeks to employ hypnosis is dealing with people and with the problems of human nature. Regardless of the specialty involved, people are people and certain general lessons are applicable in many fields.

Since hypnosis is a psychologic technique, the more experience and knowledge its practitioners have of human nature and the psychodynamics of human behavior, the more effectively they will use it. A good deal of attention has therefore been paid to the nuances of psychodynamic interaction. In the long run, everyone using hypnosis in the healing arts will find that he needs to gain a good deal of familiarity and facility in this area. If he observes the psychologic processes that are activated when he employs hypnosis, he will achieve definite gains on that basis alone. How much further he can go depends on personal incentives and supplementary study of psychologic and psychiatric literature.

1

Outline of History and Theories of Hypnosis

Hypnotism is as old as time and probably originated when man first crawled out of the primeval mud. It has been employed for centuries in one form or another in all parts of the world. Primitive societies still use the "beat-beat-beat of the tom-tom" and ritualistic dances and tribal rites to induce a trancelike state similar to hypnosis. There are even several hundred references to the apparent use of hypnotic-like methods in the Bible. For instance, the laying on of hands to obtain cures was well known during the time of Christ.

The king's "royal touch" or divine healing during the Middle Ages is another form of hypnosis. Receptive and suggestible individuals eagerly sought to have the godlike figure touch them and the hypnotic state was induced in a matter of seconds. In the Orient, yoga is still another form of hypnosis. Yoga uses breathing and postural exercises to effect physiologic responses in the body. The Greek and Egyptian priests used hypnosis over two thousand years ago in the treatment of various ailments.

Modern history

The modern history of hypnosis began with Franz Mesmer in 1773. Mesmer worked with the Jesuit priest, Maximilian Hell, who was the royal astronomer in Vienna. They used magnets in the treatment of several cases of hysteria. Hell thought that the magnet cured because of its physical properties, while Mesmer believed that the cures were produced by a redistribution of some sort of fluid, which he called animal magnetism to distinguish it from *mineral* magnetism. Later he abandoned the use of magnets, since his doctrine was continually misunderstood. Many people thought that he attributed his cures to mineral magnetism.

Mesmer later observed Father Gassner obtain cures by the laying on of hands and by making passes over the subject's body. In 1775, Mesmer expressed the opinion that Gassner was using animal magnetism without knowing it. Gassner's bishop soon forbade any further manipulation of this kind.

Mesmer then elaborated on Gassner's technique. He postulated that a fluid circulating in the body was influenced by the magnetic forces originating from astral bodies. The theory sounded scientific at the time. It coincided with the discovery of electricity and advances in astronomy. Mesmer later contended that he, himself, had this force and that patients could be cured when the magnetic rays flowed from his fingers.

Public pressure forced him to leave Vienna, and he moved to Paris in about 1778. There, he developed a bath-like structure, or "bacquet," lined with iron filings and magnets. When a patient entered the bath, he "recovered" from his ailment. Neurotics, neglected by their well-meaning physicians, flocked to Mesmer's salon from all over Europe. He developed a large following with a very high percentage of cures. He also established a tremendous reputation that incurred the animosity of his colleagues. In 1784, the French Academy appointed a committee consisting of Benjamin Franklin, Lavoisier the chemist, Dr. Guillotin, the inventor of the guillotine, and others to investigate Mesmer.

The commission found that certain persons, supposedly very sensitive to animal magnetism and capable of experiencing convulsive reactions when they touched trees that had been magnetized by stroking, could not tell which trees in an orchard had been magnetized unless they saw the magnetizing performed. If they were told that a tree had been magnetized, they could have convulsions when they touched it. The commission declared that the effects attributed to animal magnetism were the results of imagination and denounced Mesmer as a fraud. He subsequently fell into disrepute. These scientists failed to recognize, however, that suggestion resulting in strong rapport was actually responsible for the so-called cures. Though Mesmer was discredited, he actually laid the foundation for modern dynamic psychiatry. His investigations led to a better understanding of the relationship of suggestion to psychotherapy.

Interest in Mesmerism was revived by Dr. Elliotson, Professor of Medicine at University College, London, the physician who, in 1838, introduced the stethoscope to England. Dr. Elliotson was asked to resign from his college and hospital appointments because of his profound interest in Mesmeric phenomena. After his resignation, he and others carried on their research on Mesmerism. They published their findings in a journal entitled *Zoist*.

In 1841, another English physician, James Braid, who had originally opposed Mesmerism, became interested in the subject. He stated that animal magnetism was not involved in the cures; that they were due to suggestion. He developed the eye-fixation technique of inducing relaxation and called it "hypnosis." Since he initially thought that hypnosis was identical with sleep, he used the term *hypnos* from the Greek word for "sleep." Later, after he recognized his error, he tried to change the name to *monoeidism*, meaning concentration on one idea. The term "hypnosis" has persisted despite the fact that it is technically a misnomer.

In 1845 James Esdaile, a surgeon, working in the back woods of India, performed hundreds of major and minor surgical procedures on natives under Mesmeric anesthesia. Esdaile's book, *Mesmerism in India*,[1] published in 1850,

1 Esdaile, James, *Hypnosis in Medicine and Surgery:* Originally entitled *Mesmerism in India.* New York: Julian Press, Inc., 1957.

describes over two hundred and fifty surgical operations, many of them extremely formidable ones, such as amputations of the leg, removal of huge scrotal tumors weighing from eighty to a hundred and twenty pounds, amputation of the penis, and other comparable surgery. He accurately described many of the phenomena of hypnosis as we know them. Even today this volume is a valuable scientific document. Like present-day investigators, he noted the diminution of surgical shock in his hypnotic patients. He or his native assistants mesmerized the subjects early in the morning and left them in a cataleptic state. Esdaile then went about his business, later returning and swiftly operating. His cases were all documented and observed by local dignitaries and physicians. When Esdaile returned to England and related his experiences, however, he was ridiculed and ostracized by his colleagues. He went to Scotland and eventually reported many more surgical successes. It is interesting to note that he remarked in his beautifully written book that it was difficult both to convince people of the validity of his work and to fight public opinion. These words are equally true today.

Concurrently, in Nancy, France, Dr. Ambroise-Auguste Liébault, a French physician, read about Braid's work and became interested in hypnosis. In order to avoid being branded a charlatan, he worked without financial remuneration. His results were noticed by Hippolyte Bernheim, a famous neurologist, who taught at the medical school. Bernheim sent Liébault a patient suffering from sciatica, whom he had unsuccessfully treated for over six years. Liébault cured him with several sessions of hypnosis. This interested

Bernheim in Liébault's work and together they treated over ten thousand patients. Bernheim wrote the first scientific treatise on hypnosis, *Suggestive Therapeutics,* in 1886. This belongs on any reading list dealing with the historical development of hypnotism.

In France, hypnosis encountered a very serious obstacle in the person of Charcot, another French neurologist, who disagreed with Bernheim's and Liébault's ideas that suggestion was the important factor in hypnosis. Charcot contended that hypnosis was just another manifestation of hysteria. In a decade, he found only a dozen cases of "major hypnotism." His experiments were performed mainly on three subjects who were hysterics. Charcot revived Mesmer's theory of animal magnetism and a bitter controversy raged between the two schools of thought. History has proved that Charcot was wrong and Bernheim and Liébault correct. At this time many other famous scientists such as Broca, Heidenhain, Krafft-Ebing, and others became interested in the subject of hypnotism.

Freud heard of Liébault's and Bernheim's work and in 1890 came to Nancy. He had employed hypnosis with Breuer, a physician who was interested in using this technique on mentally disturbed individuals. Freud wanted to develop his own hypnotic techniques; he studied with Charcot and Bernheim. For his purposes, he found the cures too superficial and therefore abandoned the method. Freud's rejection of hypnosis unfortunately retarded this field for over fifty years. There is some basis for the belief, however, that Freud developed his penetrating insights into human behavior and the workings of the mind from his early work with hypnosis. He found, too, that hypnotism was a very helpful tool for recovering buried memories.

Because of the tremendous incidence of shellshock among soldiers during World War I, Ernst Simmel, a German psychoanalyst, became interested in using hypnosis for the treatment of war neuroses. He developed a technique that he called hypnoanalysis. Here for the first time the use of hypnosis was combined with psychodynamic techniques. Hadfield and Horsley, working independently, and later Grinker and Spiegel during World War II, used barbiturates to induce a state of drug hypnosis (narcosynthesis) in order to bring traumatic material to the surface. During the last war hypnosis played a prominent part in the treatment of combat fatigue and other neuroses.

The merger of hypnotic techniques with psychoanalysis was one of the most important medical developments to come out of World Wars I and II. World War I revived a great deal of interest in hypnosis in the United States. Hull, a psychology professor at Yale, became interested in the experimental aspects of hypnosis. His data and observations are described in his book, *Hypnosis and Suggestibility*.[1] Since then many books have appeared on this subject and at present hypnosis is on the march. Several schools such as the University of California, Long Island University, Roosevelt University, Tufts University, and others are teaching hypnosis in this country. These are not enough, but at least a start has been made. It is gratifying that more physicians and dentists are becoming interested in this age-old science. Recently the British Medical Associa-

[1] Hull, C. L. *Hypnosis and Suggestibility.* New York: D. Appleton-Century, 1933.

tion, after a thorough investigation of hypnosis, decided that all medical students and physicians should be well grounded in the fundamentals of hypnotherapy, that hypnotherapy is a very valuable technique in the treatment of neuroses and for anesthesia in obstetrics and surgery. Similarly, the American Medical Association has recently endorsed the use of hypnosis by qualified medical practitioners.

Current developments

In 1956 a committee of the American Medical Association met to consider how hypnosis could be integrated into medical teaching and reported their findings in the *Journal* of September 13, 1958.[2] A number of other leading medical journals have also published articles on hypnosis. There are now several journals devoted exclusively to the experimental and clinical applications of hypnosis, (1) *The Amer-*

[2] General practitioners, medical specialists, and dentists might find hypnosis valuable as a therapeutic adjunct within the specific field of their professional competence. It should be stressed that all those who use hypnosis need to be aware of the complex nature of the phenomena involved.

Teaching related to hypnosis should be under responsible medical or dental direction, and integrated teaching programs should include not only the techniques of induction but also the indications and limitations for its use within the specific area involved. Instruction limited to induction techniques alone should be discouraged.

Certain aspects of hypnosis still remain unknown and controversial, as is true in many other areas of medicine and the psychological sciences. Therefore, active participation in high-level research by members of the medical and dental professions is to be encouraged. The use of hypnosis for entertainment purposes is vigorously condemned.

ican Journal of Clinical Hypnosis, (2) *British Journal of Medical Hypnotism,* and (3) *The Journal of Clinical and Experimental Hypnosis,* and two journals in Spanish.

It is interesting to note that from time immemorial hypnosis has masqueraded under a multiplicity of labels. At the turn of the century there was the Janet method of relaxation, the Pierce method, and the DuBois method. More recently, there was Jacobson's progressive relaxation. At present, autoconditioning and autogenic training are very popular in Germany. Other convenient labels for hypnoanesthesia are the Russian Psychoprophylactic Relaxation and Read's Natural Childbirth.

It is believed that the approach of the faith healer embodies various forms of hypnotic suggestions. References to this method of relaxation are noted in the literature.

Theories

Some brief mention should be made concerning the various theories of hypnosis. In an operational definition, hypnosis may be viewed as an increased susceptibility to suggestion, as a result of which sensory and motor capacities are altered in order to initiate appropriate behavior. The difficulty with most theories is that they do not separate the trance induction process from the actual phenomena resulting from the hypnotic state. They are different entities. In hypnosis, the concern is with a segment or phenomenon of behavior that cannot be separated from the total realm of human behavior.

Whether done consciously or unconsciously, man has used suggestion and/or hypnosis long before he was ever aware of it. Hypnosis is a part of everyday life. Many persons have been hypnotized thousands of times, although they may not have recognized this fact. For example, a fisherman sitting in his boat and fishing for several hours may find that the shimmering and dancing of the water lulls him into a sort of reverielike state. A man may glance at his watch and make the statement, "My goodness, have I been here for six or eight hours? Why, it seemed like only three or four to me." Any repetitious visual, auditory, tactile, olfactory, or gustatory sensation can induce a state of increased susceptibility to suggestion. Verbal and nonverbal stimuli can readily produce relaxation when the stimulus is repetitiously maintained. Many a person has memories of sitting in a classroom while the professor droned monotonously on and on. He may recall that there were times when his eyes got very heavy and his head began to nod, and he actually went into a hypnoidal state. This often merged into actual sleep. Awareness can fluctuate up and down the entire broad spectrum of consciousness.

Hypnosis and susceptibility to suggestion play an important role in everyone's life, especially in advertising. A radio or TV commercial, repeated over and over again, can eventually become a conditioned stimulus ultimately affecting behavior toward the desired response.

In some individuals, the hypnotic state may be an atavism, analogous to the inanimate state of catalepsy commonly observed in frightened animals when they "freeze to the landscape" in order to escape detection. The presence of a highly evolved cortex in the human now makes unnecessary the various instinctive defense mechanisms, unless the individual is subjected to inordinate fear or danger. In some the atavistic tendency is closer to the surface than in others. It accounts for the fact that some individuals are readily hypnotizable while others are not.

Schneck likewise believes that the state of hypnosis is a return to a very primitive level of psychophysiologic functioning and is present in all living animals, especially the human.

Hypnosis can be observed throughout the animal kingdom. A snake hypnotizes a bird by its sinuous movements. In turn a snake can be hypnotized by stroking. Strangely enough, snakes are deaf. All of us have seen pictures of or heard about the flute player who "charms" the snake into a sort of hypnotic-like state. Actually, it is his to-and-fro motions that cause the induction of a hypnotic-like state in the snake. Animal hypnosis has been well described. Anyone who has ever been on a farm knows that he can place a chicken on the ground and draw a line next to the eye closest to the ground, and the chicken will develop a tonic immobility of the limbs. A butcher who puts a chicken's head under its wing can observe the immediate extensor rigidity of the chicken's limbs. The chicken lies immobile. This is a form of animal hypnosis.

It is important to emphasize that hypnosis is not a state of sleep. This is evidenced by electroencephalographic studies and tests of reflexes, circulation time, and blood pressure, which reveal themselves as identical to the waking state but different from the sleep state of the same individual. Both hypnosis and sleep are altered states of awareness. One may merge into the other. The closing of the eyes, often associated with hypnosis, is used to blot out visual stimulation; as a result, there is concentration on the operator's verbalizations. This is a common phenomenon. Music lovers at a concert who wish to concentrate put their heads back and close their eyes to hear better.

At present, conditioned reflexology, which is yet another term for hypnosis, is very popular in the Soviet Union. Pavlov, the great Russian physiologist, is probably as well known to the Russian scientists for his research on hypnosis as he is for his work on conditioned reflexes. Pavlov says it is true that words and ideas acquire a conditioned meaning for us. Conditioning is only a part of hypnosis, however, and both this concept and Pavlov's idea of cortical inhibition are really too simple to explain the hypnotic phenomenon. Pavlov also erred in his assumption that hypnosis was a modified form of sleep.

Another theory propounded by Ferenczi, the psychoanalyst, was that hypnosis was a regression to infancy. Where one used a permissive technique, this was called a maternal type of hypnosis. Ferenczi believed that the individual being hypnotized was merely regressing to infancy in a sort of dependent child-parent relationship. This theory is not tenable, as was pointed out by McDougall.[3] If it were true, a woman could be expected to hypnotize only those who resembled her mother and a man only those resembling his father. Hypnosis does not work that way.

[3] McDougall, William. *Outline of Abnormal Psychology*. New York: Charles Scribner's Sons, 1926, pp. 132-34.

Robert White thinks that the subject in hypnosis acts as the hypnotized person thinks he should act. He refers to this as "meaningful goal-directed striving." For the induction of the trance, this might be true to some extent, but it does not explain how a child, who knows nothing about meaningful experiences, can go into a hypnotic state and manifest most of the phenomena of hypnosis. Nor does it explain how an adult can be regressed to infancy or even to the age of one or two. The validity of the regression can be substantiated by elicitation of the Babinski reflex, which occurs only during the first year of life.[4]

Still another theory is Janet's, in which he contends that a part of the personality is split off to produce dissociation. This, too, fails to explain other types of behavior manifested in hypnotic subjects. Not all individuals are dissociated. Hypnosis can be induced by sensory modalities other than words, namely, by nonverbal, extraverbal, and intraverbal stimuli or communication processes. Anyone listening to a speaker is in two-way communication with the speaker, evaluating the intonation of his voice, his gestures, his demeanor, and the listener's own response to all these. "Analyzers" in the brain are constantly predicting or assessing what we feel, see, or hear. These "analyzers" correct or overcorrect stimuli from without and within. They are, as in electronics, known as feed-back mechanisms. There is a continual process of communication going on at all times between individuals and with the total environment. Words and gestures and other stimuli can be interpreted only

[4] Gidro-Frank, L., and Bowersbuch, M. K.: "A Study of the Plantar Response in Hypnotic Age Regression," *J. Nerv. & Ment. Dis. 107:* 443, 1948.

in terms of past memory experiences. Actually, hypnosis, which facilitates learning processes, becomes a very powerful control mechanism in the presence of good rapport, for it enables suggestions to be accepted uncritically. This affects responses in the organism.

Finally, the basis for understanding the very nature of hypnotic responses certainly requires a knowledge of human nature. We are interested in explanations of hypnosis itself, but we are concerned even more with an understanding of how it fits into the framework of all human behavior.

2

Suggestion and Hypnotizability

The preceding material has been leading to the practical applications of hypnosis. Before this matter can be considered, an understanding of the relationship of suggestion and hypnotizability will be required. Pertinent in this regard is a paragraph from an article written by Heron of the University of Minnesota, entitled "Principles of Hypnosis," published in the *Southern Medical Journal*. In this he says, in essence, that everyone, whether as a layman or as a professional man, spends a good portion of his waking time endeavoring to control certain segments of the behavior of other persons. For example, physicians and dentists are concerned with those aspects of the behavior of their patients that have to do with their health. Do their patients look upon them in a friendly manner? Do they accept surgery when advised? Do they follow directions on the prescriptions that are written? Do they take more rest and sleep when they need it?

There are only a few ways in which control of behavior can be attained: by mechanical means, by the use of drugs, by the use of rewards, by the use of punishment, by the use of reason and, very importantly, by the use of suggestion. It is suggestion that is basic in hypnosis.

Many attempts have been made to define hypnosis, both in terms of phenomena involved and in terms of possible causal mechanisms, but no definition has yet satisfactorily answered all the questions raised by the subject matter. Bernheim advanced the concept that suggestion is the basic factor in producing and in utilizing hypnosis. Suggestions need not be of a verbal nature only. They can occur at any sensory level. These include, of course, the olfactory, the gustatory, the auditory, the tactile, the visual, and many others.

Suggestion and hypnotizability are very highly correlated. In hypnosis, repetition is an important factor, as it is in many things, especially in learning. Initially, suggestion and repetition can be considered of basic importance. If asked for a capsule definition of hypnosis, one might say: suggestion and repetition. Everything else that the student learns will be modification, amplification, variation, and explanation of these two basic ingredients.

To these may be added monoedism, concentration on one idea to the exclusion of all others, as suggested by Braid, or in other words the elimination of all external stimuli except those needed to initiate the desired behavior. To this we may add expectant desire, imagination, visualization, and the prestige of the operator. All these play an important part in the initial induction of hypnosis. Any one or any combination of these factors may be involved in producing the hypnotic state.

Bernheim pointed out that there is really no marked difference between normal acts carried out in the hypnotic state and those carried out in the normal, waking state. The term "normal state" might give the impression that hypnosis is an abnormal state. Actually, it is a continuum from the ordinary state of wakefulness.

Furthermore, all the phenomena of the trance state can be demonstrated in at least a minor form in the waking state. If this is accepted, then hypnosis can be considered as the control of behavior (speaking of behavior in terms of thought and action) through suggestion. It is sometimes necessary to influence patients for their own welfare, and suggestion does this very well. The suggestions can include a variety of activity, such as the behavior or suggestions involved in a mother's singing her baby to sleep: the monotonous, mellifluous, repetitious sound of the lullaby, producing a soporific effect on the child.

Repetitions of direct statements in advertising—Buy Bonds, Buy Bonds; Drink Sparkling Pop, Drink Sparkling Pop—are effective in producing the desired behavior by virtue of their repetition. In regard to one soft drink, this method of advertising has been so effective that it is one of the most widely consumed beverages in the world, not excepting water.

Propaganda advanced by government agencies and others to influence behavior falls within this category. Dentists and physicians occasionally use placebos. They give them to their patients and say, "Take *this* and it will make you well," and the patient does take the placebo and it does make him well. But is it the innocuous medication that has accomplished this? No, it is the suggestive therapy that has been previously mentioned.

At this point it would be well to advance some common definition of the word "suggestion." Webster defines suggestion as the presentation of an idea, impulse, or belief to the mind. However, a psychologically effective suggestion must not only be presented; it must also be accepted uncritically—not uncritically in the sense of being without any evaluation of any kind, but uncritically in the sense that it is reacted to favorably, and leads to initiation of appropriate behavior. To be effective, the suggestion must be acted upon by the subject or patient, even if there are no logical grounds for his acceptance of the suggestion. Thus this definition of suggestion can be reached: Suggestion is an idea that one accepts uncritically and favorably, resulting in the initiation of appropriate behavior.

Before considering a few of the psychologic principles connected with suggestion, it would be desirable to demonstrate one physiologic phenomenon that gives a rationale for accepting a number of the psychologic phenomena. This is the Kohnstamm Phenomenon.

Demonstration 1: **KOHNSTAMM PHENOMENON**

DOCTOR A (*demonstrating*)

Doctor K has agreed to help us. Doctor, will you please stand up, facing parallel to the wall and about a foot away from it? Feet together, heels together, toes together, shoulders back, chest out, stomach in, at the position of attention. With your left hand, press it against the wall as if you were going to push a hole in the wall. Push hard so that you can feel the tension building up in your arms, your upper arm, your shoulder muscles. In twenty seconds, at the count of three, take a giant step away from the wall. (*Lapse of twenty seconds.*) One—two—three. (*Subject steps away from wall and his left arm rises of its own accord.*) There is a perseveration of muscular activity in the arm which caused that to happen. Did you voluntarily help the arm go up?

DOCTOR K (*subject*)

No.

DOCTOR A (*demonstrating*)

Thank you very much, Doctor K.

DOCTOR A (*demonstrating*)

The foregoing demonstrated an entirely physiological response. This may furnish a rationale for accepting the fact that such things do happen psychogenically.

Psychological principles

Many of the devices used to help patients psychologically involve the same mechanism, except that it occurs on a psychologic basis. This leads directly into the first psychologic principle, the law of concentrated attention.

THE LAW OF CONCENTRATED ATTENTION

This principle states that when spontaneous attention is concentrated on an idea, the idea tends to realize itself. When the idea involves muscular or other motor activity, it is known as ideomotor activity. When the sense organs are involved, as in feeling, temperature change, and so on, we speak of ideosensory activity. If a person holds his arm out to the side, stiffly and rigidly, with his eyes closed, and thinks to himself that there is a rope tied to his wrist, upon which someone is pulling harder and harder to force it in front of him, the arm will gradually move toward the front without any conscious effort. The arm moves, and it is on a psychologic basis, without any voluntary activity. That is ideomotor activity. When sensations are involved, such as those related to temperature change and anesthesia, the process is known as ideosensory activity. These activities combine to form a neuropsychophysiologic reorientation and reintegration within the person, with the resultant sensory and/or motor changes described.

THE LAW OF REVERSED EFFECT

The second important psychologic principle involved in suggestion is Coué's "law of reversed effort," which is sometimes known as his law of reversed effect. It says this: When the will and the imagination come into conflict, the imagination always wins. When one thinks that he would like to do something but feels he cannot, then the more he tries the more difficult it becomes. If a person were asked to walk along a twelve-foot plank placed on the floor, he would have no difficulty in doing so. But if the plank were placed on two chairs about twenty or twenty-four inches from the floor, he might have some difficulty traversing the plank from one end to the other. Then if the plank were placed across a courtyard at the twelfth story between two office buildings, what motivation would he need to have to induce him to cross that plank? What happens to him? He gets up there and notices the distance from the ground. Then he thinks to himself, "I might fall," and then, "I might not get across." The harder he tries to traverse that plank, the more difficult it becomes for him. This principle will be used over and over in hypnotic induction procedures.

THE LAW OF DOMINANT EFFECT

The third principle is the law of dominant effect. Here we learn that attaching an emotion to a suggestion makes it more effective. Furthermore, a stronger emotion tends to repress or eliminate a weaker one. For example, if two students are studying and one does not feel like studying any more, he may suggest to his friend, "Let's go to a movie." He may follow this with the reminder, "You remember the last time you studied hard before an exam you flunked?" The chances are that his friend will then put his books aside and say, "Well, let's go."

Suggestibility

Suggestibility has been described as the degree with which one readily accepts suggestions. This must be distinguished from gullibility, which involves the use of deceit. Erickson has described suggestibility further as a capacity, or indication of one's capacity, to respond to ideas, which is normal. Suggestibility is a function of normal behavior. All of us who are normal are suggestible. If that were not so, we would spend all our time analyzing the suggestions made to us: "What does he mean by that?" and we would have no time left for normal, ordinary responses.

Hypnotizability

Who is hypnotizable? And who is not hypnotizable? Generally speaking, although there is no statistically significant correlation between intelligence and hypnotizability, clinical experience does seem to indicate that the more intelligent, the more extroverted, and the stronger willed the person is, the more likely he is to be a good hypnotic subject. When persons say, "I can't be hypnotized," a reasonable response to that statement is, "Well, that's very interesting, but I certainly wouldn't brag about it." Why not brag about it? Because those who make the poorest subjects, generally speaking, are children under the age of six, psychotics, morons, and others of low-grade intelligence. Why should this be? These persons have difficulty with monoedism, concentrating on one idea. The mind of the child wanders, as does the mind of the moron or the psychotic. They can't hold onto just one idea. Thus they find it difficult to cooperate. This is not to intimate that if a person is unable to go into hypnosis, there may not be another reason for the failure. Such reasons will be discussed later. Certainly, however, inability to enter hypnosis is not something in which to take particular pride.

Tests

There are various hypnotizability or suggestibility tests and the important ones will be described. It is important to note at this point that the longer one uses hypnosis and the more expert he becomes in it, the less he will use tests merely for the purpose of testing. Tests do not really tell very much. When the reactions of an individual are positive to any of the tests, there is a likelihood that he will be a good hypnotic subject; if the response is a negative, all that can be inferred is that the patient has not responded to that particular test and that particular tester at that particular time. There is nothing to indicate that the same individual would not respond to that test at another time, or to that test with another tester, or to a different tester with a different test and a different time and a different place. Many hypnotists believe that every normal person is hypnotizable under proper conditions by a skilled operator. Generally speaking, therefore, the experienced hypnotist does not bother with tests. Of course, any one of the tests may be used as the initial procedure for inducing the early stages of hypnosis, but ordinarily it is just as well to start with the actual induction of hypnosis and gauge the progress of the patient without the use of formal tests. Until he has gained confidence, the beginner can initiate hypnosis under the guise of testing, and then deepen positive responses until hypnosis is effected. If a negative response is obtained, for whatever reason, the operator can tell the patient, "Well, this time you did not respond to this test," and he can use his own judgment about the value of continuing with that patient at that particular time. When this procedure succeeds, hypnosis has become an extreme of positive response to suggestion.

HAND CLASP TEST

One of the commonest tests is the hand clasp. It is frequently used by the stage hypnotist, who is concerned with discovering very rapidly those who are likely to respond. At this point it is worth mentioning that the stage hypnotist deliberately sets up the misconception that he has a special power and with this power imposes his will on the individual. Any experienced hypnotist will know that this is utter nonsense. No one hypnotizes anyone else. All that is possible for anyone to accomplish, in spite of or regardless of the staging of the process, is to lead or guide the subject into the hypnotic state. If the subject is unwilling or if the subject is unable, there will be no hypnosis. There can be hypnosis without an operator, but there can not be hypnosis without a willing, able, and cooperative subject.

When a patient is wearing a ring or other jewelry with sharp edges, there is potential danger of injury. It is wise to have the ornament removed first. With this precaution, if one wishes to use the test, the procedure is roughly as follows:

> Clasp your hands together, interlocking the fingers. Squeeze the palms of your hands together. Close your eyes, so that you are not visually distracted and so that you can pay all your attention to these instructions that I am giving you. Now: press the palms of your hands together and try to exclude all the air that is between your hands. Press the fingers tightly together against the backs of your hands, so that you can bring the palms of your hands tighter, tighter together. Feel the tips of your fingers as they press against the backs of your hands, blanching them. Your hands become so tightly clasped that you cannot tell one hand from the other. The harder you press, the tighter locked they become. As a matter of fact, when you try to get your hands apart, you

> won't be able to. And the harder you try (*Law of Reversed Effect*)—the harder you try, the tighter shut they will be. At the count of three you will try, but you won't be able to. One—two—three. Try, but you can't.—Stop trying.—Now, though, you can do it.

Of course, the same processes are involved here as with the hand against the wall. It is a physiologic and a psychologic phenomenon. When a patient has no difficulty, it is because he has just relaxed his hands and deliberately tried to get them apart. If he has cooperated fully, however, the same thing will happen as happened with the arm muscles in the demonstration of the Kohnstamm Phenomenon. There is an enlargement of the knuckles, so that there is an actual physical difficulty in movement and a time lag is involved before the patient can get his hands apart. But to the patient who does not know this physiologic factor, psychologic suggestion makes it seem that the instructions have enabled him to accomplish this. And having accepted the simpler instructions enables him to accept the more difficult ones, until in progression he is able to accept more complicated instructions, such as anesthesia, age regression, negative hallucinations, automatic writing, and the like.

EYEBALL SET TEST

In the same category of tests is the eyeball set test. The instructions are as follows:

> Sit comfortably in your chair, close your eyes and, without moving your head, look upward at a point above eye level

as if you had a coin or an object placed at your hairline. Now, with your eyes focused straight ahead, let your eyeballs tilt up to where they are looking at that point at the junction of your forehead and your hairline. Next, close your eyelids tighter and tighter shut, as if I had glued them together with cement, as if I had sutured them together with surgical thread. So tightly shut that you cannot get them apart. One—two—three, try, but you can't get them open. Stop trying.—Now you can do it.

While the patient's eyeballs are rolled up, it is physically impossible for him to open his eyelids. He doesn't know this. In order for him to open his eyes, he is compelled to drop his eyes and then his eyelids can come apart. Through this test, a hypnotist can find out just how cooperative his patient is.

With any of these tests, it is advisable to watch the patient very carefully. If it seems obvious that he is not following suggestions and will succeed in unclasping his hands, opening his eyes, or meeting whatever challenge has been made, the operator says immediately, "Stop trying," or "Now you can do it." In this way, the patient finds himself following the operator's suggestion rather than opposing it.

A major objection to the use of these tests is that the myth of the hypnotist's "power" is thus perpetuated. The implication here is that hypnosis necessarily involves a dominance-submission relationship. The fact is that anxieties arising from such a misconception may actually contribute to a patient's resistance to the induction process.

RELAXATION TEST

Because the application of hypnotic techniques to dentistry is based on the scientific principle that associates tension with lowering of the pain threshold and relaxation with raising of the pain threshold, relaxation is one of the most important accomplishments in dentistry. It is also important for the medical man. Too often, the patient with hypertension, with emotional involvements, is told, "You must relax," but he is never shown how. The following demonstration will show a means of relaxation that will serve several purposes: (1) to relax the patient; (2) to increase the pain threshold; (3) to gain cooperation for other things, and (4) as a steppingstone to hypnosis.

Demonstration 2: RELAXATION TEST WITH FOUR VOLUNTEER DENTISTS

DOCTOR B (*demonstrating*)

We are not going to use this demonstration as a stepping stone to hypnosis. When I use hypnosis, you are the ones who are going to produce it. I'll tell you when, so just don't worry about it.

A patient may come to the dental office manifesting great fear and anxiety. The dentist can speak as follows: "You're doing the very things that make it possible for you to feel pain. The more tense one is, the more easily one feels pain. But the more relaxed one is, the harder it is to feel pain. Physicians can teach their patients how to relax so perfectly that many of them have their babies without pain, and dentists can teach their patients to relax so perfectly that a great many of them can have dentistry done without pain, even without using drugs. Wouldn't you like me to show you how to relax, so that you may more easily eliminate pain?" It is seldom that one gets a "No" to that particular question, for everyone wants to learn how to relax and in this manner patients are supplied with the motivation.

(*To volunteers*)

> Let us all get into a comfortable position. Relax as well as you can with your feet flat on the floor and your hands in your lap. It's pretty hard to teach you how to relax your whole body all at one time, so you are going to be shown how to relax the various parts of your body one at a time. Once you learn how, you're going to be able to relax the entire body quickly. I'd like each of you to find a spot on the ceiling. Find a spot to look at, keep your eyes fixed on it, and do not remove your eyes from the spot until the exercise is over.

This will take about two minutes at the most in your offices. Next, you give the patient a rationale for keeping his eyes on the spot.

> I'm asking you to keep your eyes on the spot, so that you won't be distracted by other visual things and you can pay attention mentally to all the things I'm going to ask you to do here and now.

(*to volunteer 1*)

> I want you to relax your arm as well as you can, so that it just hangs heavy and limp there, so that when I lift it, it will

be as if you were a rag doll. A rag doll can't lift its arm. Fine, you've paid attention.

This patient doesn't have much to learn. His arm is quite limp. He is already relaxed.

(*to volunteer 2*)

Just let yourself go real limp. Now, there was a little lag there; did you notice it? There are tensions that are keeping that arm up. Just let your arm get so heavy now, really heavy. Do nothing at all to help me. That's much better. Do you notice the difference? Fine!

If you can accomplish it that quickly, fine. If not, let it go.

(*to volunteer 3*)

There is a definite tension there; if there weren't tension, you wouldn't be able to keep your arm up. So keep your eyes on that spot. Let your arm get really heavy. Do nothing about it. Make no effort to help it. Just let it be limp. Think of your arm as being a rag doll's arm and do nothing at all. You feel me working but you want to help me. You are helping me, but you are exercising tensions. Relaxation consists of doing nothing. So do nothing. Just let your arm hang heavy now. Drop it on your lap now. That's it! Let it drop and stay dropped. Just let it drop. Do nothing about it. O.K. Just relax as well as you can.

(*to volunteer 4*)

Pretty good, pretty good, but there's tension there, Doctor. Just let your arm drop. That's much better! That's pretty good now; not bad at all. No, you see you're lifting your arm. Let me lift it. Now let it drop. O.K.

There are various degrees of response. In working with a group we have the advantage of being able to see the various responses individuals can make.

(*to volunteers*)

> Keep your feet flat on the floor. But while your eyes are glued on that one spot, I would like you to take a slow, deep breath and then let it out very slowly. As you let it out, become aware of the feeling of comfort that there is in your abdomen. Learn how to breathe properly. Now, take another slow, deep breath and hold it until I count to five before you let it out. Hold it now. One—two—three—four —five. Now, let it out very slowly and really enjoy that nice sensation of comfort that enters your abdomen and your chest and you'll begin to appreciate what relaxation actually means. It's so pleasant, so comfortable. With relaxation comes a feeling of heaviness, of a heaviness as in sleep. As you become more and more relaxed, you become more and more aware of that feeling of heaviness. While your eyes are visually occupied, pay mental attention to the soles of your feet and as you relax more and more, you become aware of the feeling of heaviness in the soles of your feet. You can think to yourself, "My feet are becoming heavier and heavier." As you think about it, they *do* become h-e-a-v-i-e-r and so you feel it and enjoy it.

Allow the patients about ten seconds between each of the following suggestions as they are made, so that the patients can begin to feel and sense these things. One of the common errors is to rush the suggestions.

(*to volunteers*)

> Now you can become aware, as you increase your relaxation, of that heaviness creeping up into your ankles and in time

into your lower limbs. Then that heaviness may creep up into your entire lower body and into the abdomen. Your whole body from the waist down may become h-e-a-v-y with relaxation, so pleasant, so comfortable. That heaviness may creep up into your hands and arms, up your chest, into your neck, your whole body from the neck down feeling very heavy. Now, let this relaxation enter your jaws. You know that the proper position of the jaw at rest is with the teeth apart. An intermaxillary space is formed. If you have difficulty in keeping the jaws apart, you may wet your lips and that will help you keep them apart.

Now some of you have been blinking as a means of defending yourselves against eye fatigue. That's good. That's the way the body defends itself against eye fatigue. It takes tensions to keep your eyes open and it is more comfortable for you when there are no tensions. Don't do anything to maintain those tensions. Don't fight to keep your eyes open. It will be more comfortable to keep them closed. If they want to close, just let them close. That's fine. Once they are closed, keep them closed. Very, very good. Don't fight to keep your eyes open. They really want to close; you'll be more comfortable with them closed. Let them close. That's fine.

You don't have to spend too much time on the eye closing. If the response is too slow, just ask the patients to close their eyes.

(to volunteers)
Now, while your eyes are closed, visualize the color black or the color gray, or any color so that you can empty your minds of thoughts. Think of nothing. Do nothing. That's

the secret of relaxation, doing nothing and thinking of nothing. Just visualize a blankness so that you can relax in mind as well as in body. That's fine, just r-e-l-a-x a-l-l o-v-e-r, in mind and in body. That's fine. Enjoy it, breathe slowly and deeply. Now with each breath that you take, you'll begin to feel yourself getting more and more deeply relaxed. It's so comfortable. It's such a desirable state to be in, deeply relaxed, as close to sleep as it's possible to get; yet, remain conscious, hear the sound of my voice, follow my instructions and enjoy this relaxation. Now continue that breathing slowly and deeply while I talk to the members of the audience. And you can listen, but pay no attention because you will remember this anyway.

Many dentists are satisfied to carry their relaxation or hypnosis no further than this. What has the dentist accomplished if he has used this procedure up to this point? *First,* with the subject's eyes closed, he has removed from the patient's visual range an entire host of negative suggestions which, up to this point, have made dental visits very uncomfortable to the patient. When the patient's eyes are open, he looks at the syringe and it disturbs him. He sees the rotary instruments and wonders, "What's he going to do with that?" or, "Is it going to hurt?" or, "I haven't seen that before—that is just terrible." What he does not see does not disturb him. The dentist removes all those negative suggestions by having the patient close his eyes.

Second, by relaxing the patient, the dentist has raised his pain threshold until it becomes more difficult for him to appreciate as pain those ordinary stimuli that are regarded as painful. At this point, with a patient who has previously refused a local anesthetic, it is possible to gain his acceptance of that procedure by careful technique. When the patient can go into very deep hypnosis and can develop his own anesthesia, then no chemical anesthesia will be needed.

The dentist can advise his patients that every time they come to his office they can relax as they are now relaxed. They will be able to follow his instructions and distract their minds from the situation in any way that is pleasant for them. It is helpful to give them something else to think about, such as a pleasurable scene of their own choosing in which they are participants, so that they are psychologically away from the office. Now, what has happened if the patient can depersonalize himself from the situation? The patient who has gone to the seashore or the patient who has gone to the opera and is listening to the music with his head and feet somewhere else is not there with the body that is experiencing the tooth grinding and the surgical procedure. He will find dentistry an enjoyable experience, enjoyable as he has never previously felt possible. The dentist will find patients coming to his office to relax and enjoy themselves. At home they have the children, the menu, the budget, and other problems, but in his office they can forget everything and everyone.

In asking patients to alert themselves, one should instruct them to do it slowly. "I'm going to count to four, and I want you to orient yourself so that you are wide awake and alert, and feel comfortable and happy, having enjoyed this nice rest. Every time you come here you will be able to relax at my request or suggestion, much as you are relaxed now. Every time you come here you will be able to do it more quickly. You will be able to relax more deeply, to do it better, and you will find dentistry more and more enjoyable. You will not need to find it fearful at all. You will find it pleasant and comfortable."

The reason for taking one's time is this: A sudden awakening from a reverie, or nap, may cause one to awaken with a headachy feeling. If the patient is given a chance to reorient himself, he usually wakens with a wide-awake, rested feeling.

(to volunteers)

> Gentlemen, you feel pleasant and comfortable. Before I ask you to alert yourselves, I'm going to test your relaxation. Make no attempt to help me, because if you help me one iota you are taking away from your relaxation. Don't do anything to change the way you feel. Do nothing to take away from your relaxation.

(to volunteer 1)

> When I test you here, let me do it. You do nothing about it.

Of course, this fellow was pretty well relaxed to begin with. The only thing that keeps his arm up is the fact that I've got hold of his sleeve. When I let it go there was no tension at all there.

(to volunteer 2)

> Do nothing about it. *I'll* do what is necessary. Fine. Just stay relaxed now. Doing wonderful, wonderful.

And this gentleman, too, was very good to begin with, but maybe he will tell you what he has accomplished by way of learning to relax still more.

(to volunteer 3)

> Do nothing about it. Just stay deeply and comfortably relaxed. Deeply and comfortably relaxed. Let me do everything. Don't do a thing now. You see, you want to help me,

but don't. Let me do the work. If you help me the least bit, you are taking away from your relaxation. You don't want to do anything to change the way you feel. Let your arm feel heavy like a lump of lead, so that it is so heavy that you cannot lift it. Let it feel that way. Now you see, you are doing the work, and that takes away from the way you feel. Drop your arm on your leg. That's it! Let it stay there. Just let it stay there, feeling heavy. That's it; you've got the idea now. Do you feel the difference? Let it stay heavy now. Do nothing at all. I manipulate it. You do nothing at all—much better, much better. Wonderful, wonderful.

Compliment your patient on whatever degree of success he has been able to accomplish.

(*to volunteer 4*)
Very fine! Enjoy the situation; enjoy the feeling of heaviness. Deeply relaxed, breathe slowly and deeply, slowly and deeply.

This individual really learned something, because there is an obvious difference in the response that he made now and the previous response. He did very, very well. That's real relaxation; you can feel the difference. When there is heaviness, it is obvious; when there is tension, one can feel the tension.

In a group demonstration it is possible to observe the individual differences. If we had used the first volunteer alone, we would not have learned very much, because he didn't have to learn very much. He already knew quite a bit about relaxing.

(*to volunteers*)
Gentlemen, I think you should all be pleased with yourselves. You've done very well to be able to continue to learn

more and more. Each time you do it, you will do it more quickly, more easily, and relax more deeply. Any time you want to, gentlemen, you can arouse yourselves—I'll help by counting to four. One—two—three—four.

Here is an important fact. Unless suggestions are given to the contrary, no matter how deeply you are hypnotized, you always know what is going on. A person in the deepest somnambulistic state may act and behave as though he were perfectly wide awake. You'll have difficulty sometimes in knowing when the patient is in a trance and when he is not.

Even in the deepest hypnosis, one is no more unconscious than were our volunteers. Even in the deepest hypnosis, the subject could terminate the situation when he desired it as easily as could our volunteers. Hypnosis is different in almost every way from sleep. If anything, the patient is more alert, more able to cooperate in activities, mental or physical, than the so-called wide-awake person.

3

The Phenomena of Hypnosis

In any adequate orientation to hypnosis, it is essential to clear up the various misconceptions that are prevalent. Unfortunately, some of these misconceptions are held by experienced hypnotists. This state of affairs is hardly surprising in view of the mystical and confused attitudes of the early workers, beginning with Mesmer. As with any other scientific discipline, the weeding out of errors and misconceptions is a long-term process. Ever since Braid, there have been workers who showed an excellent grasp of hypnotic processes and phenomena. It was the insights provided by Freud, however, that have made it possible to develop clearer and more adequate bases for evaluating hypnosis and its applications.

At the present stage of psychologic and psychiatric knowledge, there is still substantial resistance to the insights of dynamic psychology. Within the realm of a dynamic orientation, the field, of course, is still subject to revision.

Misconceptions about hypnosis

Not all the misconceptions about hypnosis can or need to be presented here. Those will be discussed which most often seem to concern prospective subjects and patients, or which serve as sources of difficulty during the induction process. Much of this material can thus be used in the orientation of new subjects.

THAT MEDICAL OR DENTAL HYPNOSIS CAN BE LEARNED FROM A STAGE HYPNOTIST

The first misconception has to do with the belief that medical or dental hypnosis can be learned from a stage hypnotist. One can learn hypnosis in that manner for work on the stage. If the purpose is medical, dental, or psychological work, however, one cannot learn from the stage hypnotist. A great deal of professional study and earnest, sincere effort are primary requisites. The knowledge of hypnosis here is oriented about a patient's needs and reactions rather than audience entertainment.

THAT HYPNOTISTS HAVE SPECIAL POWERS

Another misconception is to the effect that anyone who uses hypnosis must have very special powers, special knowledge, special ability. Actually, hypnosis is a common phenomenon in all human living. Anybody who can communicate with anyone else can learn to use hypnosis.

THAT HYPNOSIS WORKS MIRACLES

A third mistaken idea, prevalent among lay persons, is that hypnosis works miracles. Hypnosis does not work miracles. It is genuine, honest, and earnest discipline of learning and effort. Anything that is accomplished depends upon work and attention given to the task in hand.

THAT HYPNOSIS MEANS UNCONSCIOUSNESS

Many persons believe that to become hypnotized one must become unconscious. That impression is a very serious error. The subject does not need to be unconscious. Hypnosis requires him to utilize his ability to hear, to see, to think, to understand, and to feel in a certain directed way, but it does not require unconsciousness. The hypnotic subject is a responsive creature and the operator who employs hypnosis is a responsive creature. No unconsciousness is required.

THAT HYPNOSIS INVOLVES SURRENDER OF THE WILL

There is no surrender of the will. Hypnosis is a dual effort, with cooperation between the subject and the operator. One does not necessarily surrender his will when he lets someone else drive his car, but there can be cooperation and there can be permission given for someone else to drive the car. It is a matter of assignment of roles in a given situation.

THAT HYPNOSIS WEAKENS THE MIND

There is no question of hypnosis weakening the mind any more than there can be a weakening of the mind from ordinary everyday living. The operator lacks the power, as an operator or practitioner of hypnosis, to reach into the skull of his subject and alter the brain cells in such manner that the mind becomes weakened. One can only effect a stimulation of the subject's thinking and his feeling, enabling him to function more adequately or less adequately, as the situation demands.

THAT HYPNOTIZABILITY MEANS GULLIBILITY

There is a common confusion between hypnotizability and gullibility. Suggestibility may be defined as the uncritical acceptance of an idea. By "uncritical" is not meant any abandonment of an intelligently critical attitude. Suggestibility may be further defined as the capacity of a person to respond to ideas. In the individual's capacity to respond there is necessarily the implication that he is utilizing all his understandings, both critical and associative.

THAT A HYPNOTIZED PERSON WILL TELL HIS SECRETS

Another misconception is that one will talk and tell secrets, as with drugs. Hypnosis, as already noted, is a cooperative venture. There is no undue or miraculous disclosure of secrets. Anybody who has had practice with hypnosis in psychotherapy knows how extremely difficult it is to get the patient who comes seeking therapy, who "wants to tell you everything," to overcome his reluctance to tell it. Hypnosis can aid him in telling what he needs to tell, but hypnosis cannot force him to tell anything that he does not wish to tell. There is a general lay misconception about the hypnotic subject being at the mercy of the operator. This is most certainly incorrect.

FEAR OF NOT AWAKENING FROM THE HYPNOTIC TRANCE

One should again bear in mind the fact that hypnosis is a cooperative venture. Two persons are involved, two persons with perhaps divergent purposes. The subject goes into a trance state. That subject has purposes known to that personality, or perhaps not known to that personality. There will be no difficulty in awakening, because the trance is contingent upon the achieving of purposes and that includes awakening as an integral part.

One may encounter the possibility that a given subject is unwilling to awaken from the trance, but that is the patient's own choice. Patients who want to remain in the trance may sometimes attempt to defy the hypnotist to awaken them. In cases of such recalcitrant subjects, one simply reverses the technique of trance induction. This matter will be discussed in greater detail in the section on "Maintaining the Trance."

WORRY ABOUT THE HYPNOTIST DROPPING DEAD

The question has been asked many times: "Suppose you hypnotize someone and have him in a deep trance and then you drop dead of heart failure. What would happen?" Actually, of course, if the hypnotist were to drop dead, that would terminate any cooperative, interpersonal relationship between the subject and the operator, and that would eliminate the entire situation. The subject would probably awaken to find out why the hypnotist was not more attentive.

Defining hypnosis

It is important to note first of all that, in everyday life, all persons evidence some types of hypnotic phenomena: the reverie, the abstraction, the absorption in an idea, the forgetting of many things. Many an individual, while listening to a lecture or a symphony, becomes so absorbed in what he is hearing that he becomes temporarily unaware of his surroundings or of some part of his surroundings: he may forget that he is sitting on a chair; he may forget that he is wearing shoes, but if this is drawn to his attention, he begins to feel his feet. Actually, he was capable of feeling his feet before this fact was mentioned, but he was not consciously aware of them. In ordinary consciousness one has a certain relationship to externalities and the total reality in which he lives. In hypnosis there is also a certain awareness of things, but it is much more channeled and concentrated.

The primary mark of the hypnotic trance is the capacity of the person to limit his thinking and feeling to his conceptual life, to memory images, visual images, auditory-sensory images of all sorts. It is his conceptual life, his experiential life with which he tends to deal, rather than irrelevant realities existing in his general environment.

THE TRANCE

It has already been indicated that hypnosis is not physiologic sleep. What is a trance? The word "trance" is a very handy term. It should be emphasized that a trance is a certain psychologic state of awareness that one can learn to recognize, and that it differs from the ordinary state of conscious awareness.

There are light, medium, and deep trances. The kind of trance needed is one that serves the purpose for the particular patient. If the purpose is to work on some profound physiologic problem, it might be best to seek a very deep, stuporous trance. Likewise, when working on a profound psychotherapeutic problem, a very deep trance might be desirable. Ordinarily, for other purposes, light or medium trances will be sufficient.

A major difficulty for the beginner will be to recognize and accept the fact that the phenomena of hypnosis appear in light trances, medium trances, and deep trances in rather disorderly fashion, depending on the capacity of the subject to respond. Thus, one subject will display the phenomena typical of a deep trance in what is actually a light trance, while another subject in a deep trance will show many of the phenomena of the light trance. The only kind of a trance to seek is the one that serves the purposes of the particular patient or the experimental subject. The beginner need not be disappointed if he has a light trance, or a medium trance, but never has a deep trance; he may obtain deep trances without recognizing them until he has had more experience.

Separateness of trance induction and trance state

If a man takes a trip somewhere, whatever develops at his destination is independent of the trip itself. The trip was one thing; his activity at the completion of the trip is another. Similarly, the induction of a trance is one thing, but the trance state itself and the utilization of it are entirely different matters. That is a basic reason for obtaining as much practice as possible in learning how to induce a trance. Once that is learned, the student can then be confronted with a major problem of what he is going to do with a trance state.

Confidence

Another important factor is the matter of confidence. Recently a doctor was asked to hypnotize a subject. Everything went well until the operator asked the subject to review a book on chemistry. The operator did not believe that it would be possible for the subject, who was in a very deep trance, to review a book on chemistry. The operator manifested that lack of confidence immediately and the subject, awakened from the deep trance, asked, "What's wrong with you?"

The importance of cooperation in hypnosis

The importance of cooperation in hypnosis has been mentioned earlier. The subject must cooperate with the hypnotist and, more than that, he must in turn cooperate with the subject very completely and thoroughly. Anesthesia cannot be induced in a subject if, at the time the anesthesia is suggested, the hypnotist is thinking, "But it won't work; I know it will not work." He will inevitably convey through the intonations of his voice and his inflections, his belief that it will not work. The hypnotic subject is going to be convinced by this. He is not going to pay attention merely to the words. He will pay more attention to the inflection. Everyone knows that a woman can say, "What a beautiful hat!" and the woman wearing it looks at the speaker as though she wants to murder her. The words are all right; the inflection happens to be all wrong.

In the matter of cooperation, one tries to deal with the subject as thoroughly and completely as possible. Remember that the subject is the important person.

Orientation should focus on the subject

One's orientation should concern the subject, not himself. It is generally recognized that early in the practice of hypnosis, when the operator tries to hypnotize someone, he is likely to think, "What shall I say now; what shall I say next; how can *I* get him to do something?" Actually, the hypnotist should be thinking about his subject, wondering what next the subject can do. Would the subject like to levitate his hand? Would he like to close his eyes? Would he like to nod his head? In other words, the hypnotist's thinking should always be oriented around the subject, not around the complete unimportance of what he himself can do in the process of hypnotizing the subject.

RECOGNITION OF THE TRANCE

The question will come up over and over again: "How does one recognize the hypnotic trance?" The best way of learning this is to observe experienced hypnotists as closely as possible. In addition, during practice sessions, it is essential to watch the subject carefully, because the hypnotic subject is in contact with the hypnotist, in rapport with the operator. He is not necessarily in rapport with a wealth of other ideas; he is responding to the ideas within his head, rather than to externals. The result is that all his physical movements are altered. His face is immobile, ironed out in expression. There is a delay in his responses to external things. A subject may be told to look at the wall of the room to his left. In ordinary everyday life he would simply turn his head to face the wall, but in a trance he will turn his head and his eyes independently until both eyes and head are facing the wall. Moreover, there will be a time lag in his responses.

Here is an important thing that should help in the recognition of states of hypnosis. Catalepsy is not necessarily manifested in the way just described. Look at the eyeballs and see what type of eyeball movements the subject is making. Look at his face and see what sort of facial rigidity there is— the frozen face of the hypnotic subject, the loss of mobility.

Look at the way the hypnotic subject walks and the economy of effort he expends.

Special motor phenomena

Margaret Mead made a motion picture study of the Balinese, who employ hypnosis extensively in their daily life. When the Balinese walk across a field, they may be consciously aware at the start but they lapse into the consciousness of the hypnotic state halfway across the field. Watching these movies, an observer can realize that there has been a sudden change in the motor activity of the walking. It is possible to recognize the exact point when the walker drifted into an autohypnotic state.

Economy of movement

Watching a subject do automatic writing in the trance state, one can note the economy of movement, the frozen face, the loss of mobility, the loss of reflexes, and the loss of swallowing. There is a failure to make involuntary reflex responses. For example: if someone were to turn and suddenly speak your name, there would be a tendency for the head to jerk, the shoulders to move, or the eyeballs to move. There would be a momentary hesitation of the lips, because of the response. The hypnotic subject would not do that. There is a certain tonicity throughout the body that prevents the subject's doing that immediately.

Time lag

Another manifestation of hypnosis is that of time lag. One can suggest to the subject that his hand is going to lift, that sooner or later it is going to lift higher and higher and higher, that soon it will give a little jerk. It is a few seconds later that the jerk occurs. There is a time lag during which the hypnotic subject mentally digests and understands and puts into action the idea presented. It takes a little time for the response to be made.

Giving the subject time to respond

Too many persons work with a hypnotic subject and say, "Now I want you to do so and so," and expect the subject to do it immediately. A subject needs time. If one is working with a subject in a group or audience situation and one wishes the subject to become negatively hallucinated, one can tell him, "The audience has left the room and there's nobody here but you and me. There really isn't. We are all alone." The subject can look out over the audience and see everybody. But when one is willing to wait and there is no urgency that the subject develop negative hallucinations immediately, when one waits a little—perhaps five or ten minutes—the subject can look around and say, "Where did they go? I think it's rather rude that they all left like that, but at least you and I can go ahead and have a good time discussing hypnosis." He has had time for the psychoneurophysiologic processes necessary to blot out his perception of the visual stimuli afforded by the audience.

Literalness

There is also a tendency for subjects to be literal in their behavior. If a subject is asked to raise his hand, he will lift it at the wrist and then perhaps lift the arm as well. Yet, in everyday life all of us have learned that raising our hands means lifting the arms as well. If a subject is asked, "Will you tell me your name?" he will respond with either "yes" or "no," and that is actually the correct response. This literalness in the hypnotic subject's behavior is especially important. When it is not recognized and observed, the hypnotist may very well not know what the suggestions were that he actually gave his subject and will therefore be at a loss to understand the behavior which develops.

Special techniques

WORDS AS THE TOOLS FOR HYPNOSIS

One of the most important aspects of hypnosis is concerned with communication or words. Any surgeon ought to know what instruments, sutures, and sponges he has. Similarly, anyone interested in hypnosis should have some ideas of what words are, and how one communicates understandings and ideas to another person. A very brief illustration of this is the simple statement, "The teacher says the principal is a fool." This is an easily understood statement. It communicates a certain idea. But how can exactly the same words be said to mean something that is entirely different? "The teacher," says the principal, "is a fool." There, another meaning, completely different, is expressed. The use of words has not been altered; the same words have been used, in the same order, but the pause gives an entirely different meaning.

When learning hypnosis, it is essential to listen carefully to what is being said to the subject, to understand why it is being said, and to make note of the inflections, the pauses, the words, and the sequence of ideas that are presented. As work progresses with subjects, their tremendous tendency to be literal will become apparent. An effort must be made to understand what hypnotic subjects understand by what is said. Primarily, the hypnotist must be constantly aware of just what he is saying to the subject.

INDIRECT SUGGESTION

Too many persons think that the best way of dealing with a subject is to give him direct suggestions, to order him, to command him, in order to induce or to bring about hypnotic phenomena. It is most important to recognize that the communication of ideas, thoughts, or feelings to hypnotic subjects can be accomplished not only by direct authority methods. It can also be suggested indirectly. For the most effective use of hypnosis, it is essential to study the hypnotic suggestions given, to appreciate the importance of indirect suggestions.

One does not tell the contrary little baby, "Go outdoors and play," for the baby then knows it is a good time to stay in the house and irritate his mother. One wonders, instead, if there is a bird out in the back yard and the contrary little baby goes out there to see the bird and everybody is pleased. Good hypnotic suggestions are not always necessarily direct. Indirect suggestions may be even more effective for indirect suggestions enlist the participation of the subject.

MAINTAINING THE TRANCE

Spontaneous arousing of the patient

A number of points should be stressed. One of them is the matter of hypnotizing a patient, working with him, and having him suddenly and spontaneously rouse from the trance state. Many operators are very much at a loss when this happens. It may represent an error in their own understanding or an error in their technique, or it may represent a need on the part of the patient. The hypnotist must be aware of the fact that a subject can arouse at any time that he pleases, even if this does not happen to please the operator. In all work with a patient, it is necessary to bear in mind that each new procedure is a new experience for the patient. Since this is so, the question arises in his mind, "Should I remain in a trance for this procedure?" Therefore, in inducing a trance, it is essential to point out what procedures are going to be used and to instruct the patient that, as long as he remains in the special situation, the trance is to be maintained unless given instructions otherwise. As part of his interpersonal contact with the patient, the dentist in particular should make brief comment from time to time about the importance of remaining relaxed, should compliment the patient upon the relaxation of his arms or of his face or of his neck. The trance must be reinforced continually.

Allowing patient to arouse and go back into trance

If the patient has the need to arouse, the operator will soon find that out and can give a posthypnotic suggestion to the effect that the patient can arouse at any moment, take a look around, and go right back into the trance. Some patients need to have that particular assurance before they can continue in a deep trance. Thus, a dentist may extract a half dozen teeth and want to proceed to something else. The patient, however, wants to rouse to see how things are progressing. He arouses and looks around. It is a very natural inclination. If the dentist has given him the posthypnotic suggestion that he can look around and drift right back into the trance state, that is what he usually does.

Lapse of patient into sleep when neglected

Another question that has been raised is about the reverse sequence. A doctor will have the experience of putting his patient into a trance, doing some work, then stepping out of the office, coming back and, to his surprise, finding the patient in physiologic night-time sleep. This can happen, especially with children, but now and then it happens with adult patients. By stepping out of the office, by discontinuing his contact with the patient, the doctor terminates the trance, but the patient feels so comfortable, so relaxed, and drowsy that he immediately shifts into physiologic sleep. With this type of patient, it is sufficient to point out that he can enjoy all the satisfactions of night-time sleep and remain in the trance, even though the hypnotist has discontinued his contact with him very briefly to answer the phone or to step out to see another patient. It ought not to be a problem, but it should be something of which to be aware as a possibility.

Refusal to arouse

With patients who object to certain suggestions, the hypnotist is entitled to bring about other phenomena in order to achieve his purposes. Now and then he will encounter a refractory patient who flatly, absolutely refuses to arouse; probably the psychiatrist encounters these patients more often than they are seen in the other professions. In such a case, all the hypnotist needs to do is to recognize one fact: It was he who induced the trance, it was a cooperative venture, and now the patient is insisting upon continuing it. The hypnotist may have induced the trance by the suggestions that the patient get tired, sleepy, that his eyes close, that he relax more and more, go deeper and deeper into trance. All he needs to do now is to reverse the record. "You're deep in trance now and you do not want to arouse.

You're really in deep trance." The patient has to agree with this. "But you're beginning to arouse just a little bit, your relaxation is disappearing just a little. Hang onto it just as long as you can, but it's disappearing just a little bit at a time and, even though you're trying hard to stay in trance, you are arousing a bit more and just a little bit more, rousing more and more and more." All of this is the exact reversal of the procedure that was used to put the patient into the deep trance. He can also tell the refractory patient, "I want you to be sure to continue in trance. I want you to be sure to remain deeply in trance until you get the signal to arouse. Shall I give you the signal now or five minutes from now?"

When a child refuses to go to bed on time, the parent can ask, "Do you want to go to bed at eight or five after eight?" They certainly are going to choose the five minutes after 8:00. It is the patient's commitment of himself to arouse at a signal rather than now. Yet the operator has really pleased the patient by letting him have his way, instead of forcibly compelling him to follow the operator's will. That is the important thing.

Hypnotic phenomena

Before discussing hypnotic phenomena as such, it is important to add something to the concepts of general orientation and to some of the basic theories of hypnosis. All human nature is characterized by the ability to respond to ideas and the capacity for accepting them, elaborating them, and developing them. In hypnosis the subject is particularly responsive to ideas. The capacity to respond to ideas is of special value. Every physician and every dentist knows the experience of wishing that he could talk sense to his patients. With the utilization of hypnotic techniques, the practitioner has the opportunity of getting a patient into a psychologic state of awareness in which he can actually listen to the ideas offered.

The capacity to respond, to be hypnotized, merely means that there has been manifested and developed, rather adequately, our ability to listen to, to receive, and to respond to various ideas and thoughts: to a mental concept, in other words. One of the striking phenomena of hypnosis is the ability of the hypnotic subject to substitute mental ideas, visual, auditory, and tactile images for actual, concrete reality. A waking person can look at a glass of water and he thinks about the glass of water in terms of a particular silicate structure with H_2O in it. But the hypnotic subject has an idea of what a glass of water looks like, of what it should be, and he can see the glass of water because he can substitute his mental image for the real one. He can actually see a glass of water that is not really there. He is using his mental images, his memories and understandings of how a glass of water appears. Thus, in hypnosis the subject is taught to respond to ideas and thoughts, to feelings and concepts, as well as to reality objects.

The phenomena of hypnosis are rather extensive. Brief definitions or discussions will be given of a number of phenomena. Every professional user of hypnosis needs to be aware of the variety of experiences that he will encounter when he uses hypnosis in his own practice.

First of all, the difference between the conscious mind and the unconscious mind. It is common experience to talk about things being in the back of one's mind, in the depths of the mind, or in the forgotten part of the mind; one can also readily think about the conscious mind. Those minds—the conscious mind and the unconscious mind—exist within the same person. The unconscious mind is constantly feeding the conscious mind.

It is possible to emphasize this distinction by mentioning something entirely unrelated. Take the word "house." Just to hear the word or to see it unexpectedly brings forth a flood of memories. Yet, where were they just the moment before? Another example: most individuals would declare emphatically that they are well aware of themselves and that they know what is going on, but, as mentioned before, until the individual's attention is specifically directed to the feeling of shoes on his feet, he is not likely to be particularly aware of them. Thus one's attention can be directed to this or to that particular phenomenon that has been going on without conscious awareness.

When using hypnosis, the particular phenomenon that should be employed is this direction of attention to things within the subjects or patients, so that they can attend to these and be directed to utilize their own capacities to respond to ideas. The hypnotist wants his patient capable of responding to any idea, any concept, whether it be anesthesia, memory, or otherwise.

RAPPORT

One of the first conditions of the trance state to be noticed is that of rapport. Exactly what is meant by rapport? It is that peculiar relationship, existing between subject and operator, wherein, since it is a cooperative endeavor, the subject's attention is directed to the operator, and the operator's attention is directed to the subject. Hence, the subject tends to pay no attention to externals or the environmental situation, to respond only to the person doing the hypnotizing.

Subject's choice of persons with whom to be in rapport

CASE OF MRS. DOROTHY P.

A medical student brought his wife in with the request that she be taught to go into a trance for hypnotic delivery. She demanded that her husband be present. She wanted to be in rapport with him. She also brought in a former classmate of hers, a female medical student with whom she also wished to be in rapport. When she was put into a trance, she found herself in rapport with her classmate, out of rapport with her husband, and in rapport with the hypnotist. It was only consciously that she thought she wanted to be in rapport with her husband.

The subject always has the privilege of including in the hypnotic situation anything that he wants. He also has the right to exclude from the hypnotic situation anything that he wishes.

Transfer of rapport

Rapport can be transferred from one person to another. Thus, one could hypnotize a subject and be in complete rapport with that person, and that subject in complete rapport with the hypnotist alone. But the hypnotist could ask the subject to be in rapport with someone else who, in turn, could transfer the rapport to still another individual, who could suggest a termination of the trance with the original hypnotist.

The matter of rapport is a very important consideration because it is based upon trust and confidence in the persons who are involved.

CATALEPSY

By catalepsy is meant that peculiar state of balanced muscle tonicity where a subject in the deep hypnotic trance is enabled to remain in a set position for an indefinite period of time. Thus, the subject's arm can be raised and it remains elevated. Catalepsy is a phenomenon that may appear in the light, medium, deep, or stuporous trance.

It should be re-emphasized here that all hypnotic phenomena, in the main, do not necessarily belong to any one particular stage of hypnosis. Catalepsy can be present in the light stage and absent in the deep stage, or present in the deep stage, not present in the medium stage, but present in the light stage. Each subject is a law unto himself; he manifests the various types of hypnotic phenomena in accord with his own experiential life.

IDEOMOTOR ACTIVITY

Another significant phenomenon is ideomotor activity. What is meant by ideomotor activity? A person can be sitting in the back seat of a car, mentally braking the car with the pressure of his foot on the floor until he notices that his leg is getting tired. Then he takes his foot off the floor but, before he knows it, he may have his foot on the "brake" again. He may go to a football game, eager for his team to forge ahead. As he watches the game, he bends forward until he is touching his neighbor and has to apologize. A few minutes later, he may be leaning over and touching that person again. A number of hypnotic techniques are based upon ideomotor activity. Some of them will be illustrated in the text in the descriptions of hand levitation or related procedures.

Another form of ideomotor activity is automatic writing. Here, one offers to the subject the idea that his hand will pick up a pencil and will write a sentence, a phrase, or a whole story, giving an account of some long-forgotten experience. As the subject gets the idea of picking up a pencil and actually writing, his arm becomes dissociated and proceeds to write freely and easily. Automatic writing can be used to advantage by the psychiatrist, physician, dentist, or clinical psychologist.

IDEOSENSORY ACTIVITY

Just as there can be ideomotor activity, so can there be ideosensory activity. Take, for example, the lover, who gazes intently into the fireplace and lets the flames outline his sweetheart's face, or the girl who lies on the beach, looking at the filmy clouds above and seeing a beautiful dress. Consider the patient sitting in the dental chair, who recalls that once before a dentist used procaine and made his jaw numb. He sits there with all the sensations of numbness imaginable, just from hypnotic suggestions. That is the development of ideosensory activity.

INTERRELATIONS OF SENSORY EXPERIENCE

The visual life of the person is connected with his auditory, gustatory, and tactile life. When one induces a visual alteration in the person's experience, one is also likely to induce some auditory alterations, unknowingly. The various aspects of the experiential life of a person are interrelated. It is helpful to bear this in mind. When difficulty is experienced in producing, for example, visual hallucinations, these can often be accelerated and promoted by bringing about an alteration of the subject's auditory experience, or an alteration of his sensory experience.

The dentist reports that he can have a child look at an imaginary television screen or a window with a patterned curtain on it and see things there. Because the child hallucinates things there, the child develops an anesthesia all the better. In working with hypnosis, it is important to remember that there are relationships of all the modalities of experience.

MULTIPLICITY OF POSSIBLE PHENOMENA: SENSORY ALTERATIONS

There can be any number and variety of sensory alterations. One can produce hallucinations in the visual, olfactory, gustatory, auditory, or kinesthetic field, in any way that is desired, if the subjects are given an opportunity to vary their psychoneurophysiologic processes. Hallucinations of all sorts, positive and negative, can be elicited. In positive hallucinations something is seen that is not there; in negative hallucinations, there is failure to see something that is actually present.

CASE OF FRANK J.

A subject recently reported, "I'm not really in a trance, and what I cannot understand is that I hear everything that is going on in this room. I know my eyes are shut. I know I am fully conscious. I am certain that I am not hypnotized, but why do I have the feeling that I am in the living room of my childhood home? Because I can see the walls and I can see the pictures and I can feel the floor with my feet, but I *know* I'm not hypnotized and I really am wide awake."

Frank J was actually experiencing a positive hallucination, the revivification of a past memory that was part of his mental history, his experiential history. He was actually experiencing it, while at the same time he had a conscious awareness of his surroundings. This is one example of a particular type of dissociation, with a duality of conscious and unconscious functioning.

AMNESIA

What is amnesia? In everyday living it is possible to forget, literally and instantly, things that seem impossible to forget. It is a frequent and embarrassing experience to be introduced to someone, to repeat his name, utter a few polite remarks, then wonder what his name is. A man stops for directions, listens very carefully, but as he turns his attention to staring off down the road, he asks himself, "Now just what did he tell me?"

It should be borne in mind that the hypnotic subject has had plenty of experience in forgetting any number of things. The hypnotist helping him to develop an amnesia for a certain thing is merely utilizing that capacity of the individual to forget, directing it to some one given thing.

The best way to produce an amnesia is by distracting the subject's attention and then proceeding to utilize the knowledge of hypnotic techniques. In the hypnotic state, the subject can direct his attention to the forgetting of things. Often in a light trance there is a tendency for the subject to forget a few of the things that occurred. He may have the feeling that he has actually remembered them all, however, because he cannot remember that he has forgotten some of the things.

Amnesia is a common phenomenon in the trance state. In the deep trance, the subject can go into a profound hypnotic state and awaken from it an hour later, after a wealth of activity, and still think he has just entered the office. Amnesia is one of the phenomena that tends to develop spontaneously. It may vary from time to time, according either to the purposes of the operator or the purposes that the subject wants served.

SELECTIVE AMNESIA

Selective amnesia is still another phenomenon. Here the word "selective" is the important thing. Since there can be selective hallucinations of all sorts, it is possible to have selective amnesias: it is possible to forget the names of all friends whose first names begin with the letter "J," for example. A subject can single out all those persons whose first names begin with the letter "J," and develop an amnesia for these names. Or he can develop a negative hallucination or selective blindness for everybody in the audience who has white hair.

Thus the subject can be asked to develop an amnesia for certain experiences or certain classes of experiences, for certain attitudes or for certain learnings. Since the subject is capable of responding to ideas in the hypnotic trance, one needs merely to direct the ideas to which the subject is to respond.

HYPERMNESIA

Just as there can be amnesia, so can there be hypermnesia: the increased ability to remember. It is astonishing how detailed and extensive the memories can be. Memories that belong in the remote past seem to be elicited with exceedingly accurate detail. The law of parsimony or Morgan's Canon must be kept in mind in dealing with this area of psychologic functioning, however. All phenomena must be explained on the simplest possible basis.

One can induce a subject to remember a number of things long forgotten, but one must also beware of trying to have him remember impossible things. It is doubtful, for example, that anyone can remember things that happened *in utero*. To remember things, there must be some kind of conceptual foundation. *In utero* sensory experiences are limited to those of mechanical pressure. They are certainly not visual, not auditory, except as transmitted in fluid waves. Therefore, the hypnotist should not try to carry on a conversation with a hypnotic subject on the level of his intrauterine life.

If someone were asked what he had eaten for dinner on his fourth or even his fourteenth birthday, he might gaze at the questioner in bewilderment. He might spend hours and days and weeks and months analyzing and trying to remember. In the hypnotic trance, he could be regressed so that he might recall completely and accurately what he had for dinner and under what circumstances on that particular birthday. Memories long considered forgotten can be secured in this way, for in the hypnotic state there is no feeling about too many things having happened since. The hypnotic subject can direct his attention, utilize his attention, and take advantage of all the associations that are recorded in his mind to help him select specific past memories.

CASE OF PATRICIA M.

A dentist recently reported the following about a patient of his: Patricia, a girl in her twenties, came to his office. She hadn't had any dental work for many years because of an upsetting childhood experience. A dentist had then slapped her face for crying until he stopped her. She subsequently developed a fear of all dentists. Because of recent dental difficulties, she was compelled now to come in for treatment. As soon as she sat down in the dental chair, she started shaking and shuddering, said, "I can't stand it in here," and started to go into a hysterical panic. The dentist took her back to the reception room. When the girl explained what had happened, he tried to reassure her. Nevertheless, when she returned to the dental chair, she had another hysterical episode.

The dentist decided to put her in a trance. He spent the time of the first appointment inducing a trance, and suggested an amnesia for what had happened in her childhood. He was able to lead her back to the dental chair and to do two extractions. She came out of the trance prematurely, however, developing another hysterical episode. Again, he took her out of the operating room and into his office, induced another trance, and, this time, explained to her the importance of remaining in the trance. He took her back, did some more work, then aroused her sitting in the dental chair, and explained everything to her. Now she is a willing patient.

SUPPRESSION AND REPRESSION

It is a common tendency to try not to think about unpleasant things and to keep them, if possible, altogether out of the mind. Eventually, the thing that has been suppressed and kept out of the mind becomes a forgotten thing, a matter of repression, involuntary and beyond the conscious control of the person. It governs behavior at an unconscious level. Hypnosis can bring forgotten material, repressions, to the foreground. It can be done by visualization or by having the patient develop auditory hallucinations, tactile hallucinations, or whatever seems appropriate.

DISSOCIATION

What is meant by dissociation? Several examples will serve to explain. The subject, Frank J, who was in his living room, telling of the scene as a child, yet stating at the same time that he saw himself in front of a group of doctors, was showing a type of dissociation. In the hypnotic trance, one can ask a subject to dissociate and to see the self sitting on the other side of the room.

CASE OF MISS BURT

Miss Burt, who had had a radical mastectomy, knew from experience that she always fainted whenever sutures were removed. She decided to use autohypnosis to let the surgeon take out the stitches. When he came into her room for this purpose, she asked him, "Doctor, do you mind if I take my head and my feet and go out into the solarium?" As far as she was concerned, her head and feet were out in the solarium; she was looking at the pleasant scenery there. She merely left her body behind. All her mental experiences, all her skin sensations, were those associated with the solarium. Her body was left behind in the room and, of course, she had no feeling of the sutures being removed. When she deemed a sufficient time had elapsed, she picked up her head and feet, and returned to join her body on the bed.

CASE OF SUZANNE

In a hypnotic study on color blindness, Suzanne, an excellent subject, did not want to spend the time necessary in the laboratory. She asked very simply, "Why don't you send me to my room, where I can read a book, and just work with my body while I go there?"

In other words, Suzanne wanted a certain type of dissociation. She was permitted, psychologically, to go to her room and reread that book in which she was interested, while the hypnotist worked with her body in the hypnotic state in the laboratory. Then later she was aroused and it was necessary to call her back from her room. It was discovered that she had reread several of the most interesting chapters. Of course, she could not read the chapters she had never seen, but she could be interested in rereading. In her dissociated state, the conscious part of her mind was greatly absorbed with reviewing a previous bit of reading, while her unconscious mind cooperated with the hypnotist in the matter of developing color blindness.

DEPERSONALIZATION

A person is generally acutely aware of his identity, but he can forget about himself in certain situations. When some persons go to suspense movies, they become experiencing creatures absorbed in the movie and all question of personal identity is lost. In the hypnotic state, a subject can be induced to forget his personal identification. He can actually be persuaded to assume the identity of others, as he understands those other persons.

Many individuals have had the experience of awakening spontaneously in the morning and of wondering briefly just where they were, who they were, or where their feet were. All this may develop simply from a loss of contact with the various parts of the body in that half-awake state. It is an example of pure depersonalization.

SOMNAMBULISM

By somnambulism is meant that type of hypnosis in which the subject goes into a very deep state and presents to the observer the appearance of being wide awake, but when one watches him, listens to him, and observes him closely, it becomes evident that he is really in a deep hypnotic trance. The behavior of somnambulists will be presented in later demonstrations to illustrate deep hypnotic phenomena, so that the same manifestations will be recognized in subjects who are put into light or medium trances. Reading alone is not sufficient for gaining concrete understanding of this or most other phenomena. The greater one's practice with patients or subjects and the more opportunity one has to observe experienced operators, the better he will recognize, understand, and be able to utilize hypnotic phenomena.

SUBJECTIVITY AND OBJECTIVITY

One can either be highly subjective or highly objective in the trance state. Thus, a psychiatric patient can be hypnotized and told, "I want your assistance in dealing with a very difficult problem. I want you to see over there a man named John Jones. He has a name that is the same as yours, but there are a lot of John Joneses in this world. While you yourself are John Jones, there is also this other John Jones over there, who has a certain kind of problem. I want you, as a thinking creature, but not necessarily as a remembering creature, to assist me in helping that John Jones over there." One simply has the patient objectify in that hallucinated John Jones all his own problems, having him describe that John Jones as a worried, anxious, fearful, phobic sort of personality, or whatever may be applicable to the particular situation. Then this John Jones, who is a thinking creature, is asked to discuss objectively that John Jones's problem. His personality is objectified without any conscious awareness that he is looking at and examining his own personality.

Or, one can have him look at a hallucination that he does not recognize and with which he feels no kinship, and he can be told, "That person there, whose name you don't know, whom you cannot recognize, is going to suffer acute emotional distress. I want you to feel what it is, so that you can tell me what kind of distress that person is suffering." Thus he is asked to subjectify his own experiences for objective evaluation.

TIME DISTORTION

Many individuals have had experiences centering around time distortion. One can be sound asleep in bed, dreaming that he is climbing a mountain and that he slipped and fell, for miles and miles, for hours and hours, until finally he crashed at the bottom of a bottomless canyon. Actually, he fell out of bed. It did not take very long to reach the floor, but in that process, at night when the dreamer was asleep, that little fall from the bed to the floor seemed an endlessly long experience. There are many records of similar instances in the scientific literature.

In other words, time can be a clock experience or a subjective experience. On a cold, wet, rainy day, the bus is two minutes late and the waiting passenger feels that he has waited hours for the bus to show up. Then on a nice, bright day he sees his girl. He hasn't seen her for some time, because he has been out of town, and he now has a wonderful chance to chat with her while he is waiting for the bus. Then, of course, it seems as though the bus appears before he has even had a chance to say hello. In actuality, the bus may be ten minutes late. Subjectively, it is much too early. Subjective time can be long or it can be short.

Another item that should be stressed is that thought is exceedingly fast and, consciously, one can be aware of only a small portion of the actual thinking one does. For example, a reader may see the word "dog," and a wealth of memories of dogs of all sorts, belonging to the past or present, come unbidden and with great rapidity into the mind.

In hypnosis, the feeling of subjective time can be utilized and shortened or prolonged. The person can be made aware of the wealth of his thinking when one gives him a sense of short or prolonged subjective time. It is a common experience. The work that Linn Cooper did in this regard was an original contribution to psychologic thinking.[1]

[1] Linn M. Cooper, M.D., and Milton H. Erickson, M.D. *Time Distortion in Hypnosis*. Baltimore: Williams and Wilkins Company, 1954.

CASE OF MISS ANITA A.

Erickson's Miss Anita A is an excellent example. He worked with her for about three months, using every hypnotic technique that he could, but found himself unable to break down her amnesia for the first twenty-two years of her life and for most of the eight subsequent years. Every hypnotic device he knew proved of no avail. But when he used time distortion, in just twenty seconds of distorted time he was able to get Miss Anita A to recover, for later narration, her entire history.[2]

Special considerations

DANGERS OF HYPNOSIS

Let us consider the dangers of hypnosis. Aside from all the harm that a stage hypnotist can do in making patients resent hypnosis, there are other possible dangers. They do not derive from the fact that hypnosis was used; they are rather due to oversight. There is no harm from surgery, but the sponge left in the abdomen can be a very harmful thing. The sponge does not signify that the surgery was necessarily the wrong procedure, but it represents an error. A posthypnotic suggestion given the patient to govern his behavior in the dental office is a parallel example. It should not be

[2] Cooper and Erickson, *op. cit.*, pp. 167-73.

given in such fashion that it governs his behavior outside, except within those limited circumstances where the dentist wants it for that particular purpose.

CASE OF DR. RUDOLPH F.

An accidental experimental situation will serve to illustrate this point. A physician and a dentist, both well experienced in hypnosis, were experimenting one day. Doctor F, the physician, gave the dentist a loss of the sense of smell, so that he could smell household ammonia and have no reaction to it. About a year later the dentist happened to mention that he was having some trouble in the office. All the spirits of ammonia that he had purchased seemed to be absolutely flat and dead. He had also noticed that there had been a change in the taste of his food, that he could not smell his wife's perfume, and that flowers were scentless, etc. As the dentist discussed this, Doctor F recalled that a year previously he had given the dentist a hypnotic loss of the sense of smell. He immediately corrected his posthypnotic suggestion. The dentist's reason for having permitted this to continue was his own experimental-mindedness. After a year, his intellectual curiosity was thoroughly satisfied and he thought that he might as well go back to smelling things again. Had a physician done that with a patient, the patient might have resented it very bitterly at an unconscious level and might have kept away from the doctor thereafter; he would have been justified in doing so.

When giving posthypnotic suggestions or suggestions intended to govern a patient's behavior, the practitioner must be sure to give them in such manner that the suggestions are limited to the purposes serving medical or dental reasons. The suggestions must not intrude into the extrapatient life of the subject or the extraprofessional life of the operator.

CONTROL OF ANESTHESIA

Adequate control of hypnotically induced anesthesia cannot be too strongly stressed.

CASE OF MRS. FANNY D.

Mrs. Fanny D, a hypnotic subject, telephoned her physician, stating that she had sprained her ankle. She said that she had a particularly busy day planned. She requested that she be given an anesthesia over the telephone, so that she could do her necessary house and yard work. She was told that there was a possibility that she had fractured the ankle and that she would be given an anesthesia to last until she got to the doctor's office. She could reach that in half an hour. As soon as she arrived at the doctor's, or at the expiration of the half-hour period, the anesthesia would disappear. She reported as instructed. The doctor diagnosed a sprain that could tolerate a reasonable amount of exercise.

When Mrs. D called with this information, her anesthesia was re-established. She was advised, however, that it governed only the pain developed from the ankle. If she did more than the average amount of housework, the anesthesia would weaken. If she attempted yard work, it would surely disappear. To keep her anesthesia and do her moderate amount of housework, she had to abide by the suggestions given.

Mrs. D. telephoned again that night to request hypnotic anesthesia for menstrual cramps. She was asked whether her period was early, late, or on time. She stated that it was early. She was asked if she was sure it was menstrual cramps and how long it had been since she had had menstrual cramps. She hadn't had any for over a year. She was asked the location of the pain. She replied, "It's on the right side, but it's a typical menstrual cramp." Mrs. D was advised that she could go to sleep and be free of all menstrual cramp pains, but any other pains would not be covered by the suggestion. She went to sleep, slept for about two hours, then called back to state she had persistent, severe pain. She was given some relief for her pain but only with the definite promise from her that she would see a surgeon early the following morning. She got some sleep for the rest of the night, went to see the surgeon the next morning, and remained in the hospital for an emergency appendectomy.

Suggestions must be given only for the purpose that is being served, never for any other purpose. The suggestions that are given must be explicit.

CASE OF MISS AMELIA L.

Miss L walked into her psychiatrist's office with a badly swollen jaw. Her statement was, "I have just come from the dentist's. He shot my jaw full of stuff; then he let me drive home. By the time I got this far, I found I was pretty wobbly, so I decided to stop in and see you and have you put me in a trance, because I've got to get home. I have a five-mile trip to make in the car and I must get home soon. I want to go into a trance and I want the anesthesia to continue a few days, a week, or a month, whatever I need." The patient was demanding, but obviously the psychiatrist's task was not simply to accede to her wishes.

She was given instructions to have a posthypnotic anesthesia only if she drove home carefully. Then a further limit was placed upon the anesthesia. It was to be maintained only for a reasonable length of time, so far as body healing, tissue healing, etc., were concerned. She could not keep the anesthesia for her own amusement later. Knowing this patient as he did, the psychiatrist realized that she was quite capable of entertaining a posthypnotic anesthesia for her jaw for a month, just for the fun of it, as an experiment. Miss L was also given a further restriction upon the anesthesia, so that if any new or different sensation developed in her jaw, it would not be governed by the anesthesia. She was told that this might imply the presence of a new condition, and in such event she should consult her dentist. Miss L was a hysterical person who could quite conceivably do harm to herself because of her own personality patterns. Thus the limitations placed upon the anesthesia were designed to protect her. One always tries to protect the patient from the self.

Use of hypnotic aids

USE OF RECORDINGS

For developing a hypnotic technique

Records are used by some hypnotists to induce trances in their patients. In developing a hypnotic technique, it is often worthwhile for the student to make a tape recording of his own voice, to listen to it, and find out exactly what he says to a patient. He needs to listen to his own voice to hear how convincing it is and to discover how he can improve it. One physician has stated that in developing a hypnotic technique, he wrote out thirty typewritten pages, single spaced, of all the ideas he thought he should employ in working out a verbal technique. He then reduced the thirty pages to twenty-five, to fifteen, to ten, then to five, cutting out the unnecessary verbiage, recognizing the progression of ideas and their emphasis. The student who has an appreciation of his own voice and of how he says things can understand his own inflections better. He can learn a great deal about hypnotic techniques with the use of the tape recorder.

Adapting someone else's language

The question is often raised as to whether one should get a ready-made script that someone else has developed, use the same language in one's own voice, or develop an individual script. If he uses someone else's script, the student should read it through, then rewrite it in sentences and paragraphs adapted to his own literary style. It would also be advisable to make a tape recording of it. It is perfectly all right to follow an outline if the student can adapt it to his own voice, literary style, and manner of talking, to incorporate it into his own way of giving suggestions. Tape recordings can be very valuable in this way as a teaching method.

PRACTICING HYPNOSIS WITH AN IMAGINARY
    SUBJECT

Another question may arise: Where will the student get a patient to work on, just to practice on? At a seminar recently, one doctor carried out an interesting test. She was instructed to get up on the platform in front of an empty armchair and told to imagine that she had a patient sitting there. She was advised to go ahead and hypnotize the patient. The instructor would sit beside her, watch her, listen to her, and be ready to criticize her. The doctor did an excellent job, hypnotizing her imaginary patient and giving him some posthypnotic suggestions. In doing this, she went into a trance, which was a good way of learning autohypnosis. The student of hypnosis can have a tape recorder in operation. He will observe the time he spends hunting for something to say. The thing that he has just finished saying is usually the cue to what should be said next. In making the tape recording and listening to it, he can actually lull himself into an autohypnotic trance and analyze the recording in the trance. In this way, he can get his ideas of how to talk to patients and how to bring about desired results.

Demonstration 3: **THE DEEP HYPNOTIC
    TRANCE**

Anybody can learn to go into a deep hypnotic trance. Some people learn to do it very rapidly, some very slowly. It required three hundred hours to teach one good hypnotic subject how to go into a deep hypnotic trance. The capacity of the subject to go into a deep trance is an ability of the mind to respond to ideas, to accept them, and to understand very quickly how to carry them out. Every hypnotic trance demonstrates the responsiveness of the mind to ideas, thoughts, and concepts of various sorts, as well as the operation of varying psychological mechanisms and behavior.

The following is an illustration of the type of pyschological behavior that can be employed, even in the light or medium trance. It is a demonstration conducted before an audience of students:

ERICKSON *(to subject)*

Do you want to come up on the stage here? I understand that you're a somnambulistic subject. Tell me, are you wide awake or not? *(Subject nods.)* You're sure of that? Whom do you know in the audience? Your husband and the Jennings. Anyone else? *(Subject shakes her head.)* May I call you by your first name, Jane?

Trance induction

ERICKSON *(to audience)*

I am going to ask Jane a number of questions and I am going to find out, when I'm talking to her, how rapidly she goes into a trance.

ERICKSON *(to subject)*

Do you still think you're wide awake? You're positive of that? Really positive? Now, tell me. You say you're sure that you're wide awake and I wonder if, when you nod your head "yes," if your head will shake this way when I ask the next question. Are you wide awake? (*Long pause.*) Do you know? Do you really know if you're wide awake, or whether you're in a trance? You can think you're wide awake, can't you? You can also think you're in a trance, but you really don't know. Isn't that right? Now, can you shake your head this way? Can you nod your head "yes"? All right, now when I ask you, "Is your name Jane?" you're going to shake your head, even though you know it is Jane. Is your name Jane? Do you think it is? What is your name? You don't know.

ERICKSON (*to audience*)

One can see there a very, very rapid development of the somnambulistic state.

ERICKSON (*to subject*)

By the way, your name *is* Jane. That's all right. Do you want to keep your eyes open and talk to me?

Rapport: pattern of unconscious thinking

ERICKSON (*to subject*)

So your name is Jane and you're deep asleep. Is that all right? Now, do you know where you are? You are where I am. That's right. Where are we? Do you know where in Shreveport? In the hotel? Where in the hotel are we? On the second floor. And where on the second floor? In a big room? On the stage.

ERICKSON (*to audience*)

What has just been demonstrated is an example of spontaneity in the association of ideas. The subject started in Shreveport, in the hotel, on the second floor, in the big room, on the stage. Had I asked a person in the waking state his whereabouts, he would have started his associations with where he was, of course. The subject started with "you," defining the state of rapport. And when asked, "Where are we?" "Shreveport. Captain Shreveport. The second floor. In the big room. On the stage." An excellent, systematic association of ideas was shown.

When one wants to use hypnosis therapeutically, one must bear in mind how clearly hypnotic subjects think. They start with general understandings, then they come closer and closer to an exact understanding. Too often, the physician, the dentist, the psychologist tries to define a situation for his subject by pinpointing it in a very direct way. He should instead be laying the general fundamental, psychologic background. For this subject, it was sufficient to define the fact that she was with me. That defined a state of rapport, the relationship in the hypnotic state to me.

Spontaneous negative hallucination

ERICKSON (*to subject*)

By the way, Jane, was I talking to aynbody? Is there anyone here but you and me?

JANE

Just with you.

ERICKSON (*to audience*)

The subject has just stated that she was here only with me. In other words, she has defined the rapport, demonstrated that she has dropped all interpersonal relations with any group present. Her response was, "Just with you," the hypnotic situation itself. The group does not belong in the hypnotic situation and that is a very clear and beautiful definition of the two situations. When she is in rapport with me alone, she does not hear me talking to others. The tone of my voice is not such that it arouses her attention. As far as she is concerned, I cannot be talking to anybody else because she cannot conceive that there is anybody else here to talk to. She developed her spontaneous negative hallucination very quickly as a function of the state of rapport.

ERICKSON (*to subject*)

Now, Jane, is your husband here? He's not here. I'm going to ask you to look straight ahead of you. Look over in the general direction in which I raise my hand. Now what do you see? You see a room. What's in the room—anything? There are a lot of chairs? Are they vacant chairs? Just vacant chairs.

ERICKSON (*to audience*)

I cannot very well be talking to people when there are just empty chairs. She looked around. What did she see? She looked all around and she saw a room. I had her look again: Was there anything in the room? Well, what do you find in a room? You have the general concept of furniture and she saw chairs. Now, if I had wanted to, I could have had her see the audience, but since she had developed a negative hallucination for the audience, that was expressive of her wish. She is desirous of working with me, rather than with the audience.

Transfer of information from the conscious to the unconscious mind

ERICKSON

Are you resting comfortably, Jane? You're feeling rested, at ease? Do you remember speaking to me earlier today?

JANE

Yes.

ERICKSON

Do you know who I am?

JANE

Yes.

ERICKSON

Who am I? Yes, I'm Dr. Erickson.

ERICKSON (*to audience*)

Now, there is another indication. She went into a trance, a very deep trance. She obviously did not seem to know who I was, especially when I raised that gently searching question. Had I spoken to her earlier today? She really didn't know, but actually, of course, did her unconscious speak to me earlier today? She spoke to me consciously. Therefore she had not talked to me with her unconscious. Naturally the unconscious had not been sufficiently curious about me to discover my identity. The knowledge did exist within her conscious mind; she went through the process of abstracting information from her conscious mind and getting it down into her unconscious mind. This is the reverse of the more usual procedure, when the unconscious mind puts information into the conscious mind.

ERICKSON (*to subject*)

Well, Jane, you are in a trance, a deep trance. Is that agreeable to you? Is there any particular thing that you would like to have me do? Any particular experience that you would like to have? May I do some of the things that are instructive? For whom would they be instructive? They might be instructive for you, isn't that right? Therefore, I would like to have you think over some of the things that you'd like to have me say to you, some of the things you'd like to do for the experience of it, for the understanding that you can get. Is that agreeable? Would you like to have me surprise you with some of the things that you can really do?

Positive hallucination

ERICKSON (*to subject*)

All right. What is your husband's profession? He's a physician, a general surgeon. Would you like to have an experience that can be of value to him? There's something I'm going to ask you to do, Jane. Do you see that chair right there? I want you to watch that chair. Shortly you're going to see, down in front of that chair, some red open-toed shoes, with a white cross over the top. They're open-toed, they're high heeled, there's a strap that fits around the heel. I want you to see those shoes. Then you'll see the feet in those shoes and then you'll see the legs extending up, but still that chair will be empty. It's an odd-looking sight, isn't it? Then you'll begin to see at knee level and there'll be a dress covering the knees, but you won't be able to see further than halfway up the thighs.

Catalepsy

ERICKSON (*to subject*)

Just be comfortable. This arm can be moved any way you want it to be. Really enjoy watching that figure grow. Now you can see up to the waistline of that dress. I suppose you'd call it a print dress, sort of a gray with white figures on it. How does that person look? It seems to be that the legs are stretched out comfortably at rest. Any questions come to your mind? It looks like your dress. That's right. If you'll look over to the side, you'll see a little pearl button with a small pearl knob on it. That's your dress. That's right. Now, you'll look a little higher and you'll reach the shoulder level. Higher. Are you sure that's you? (Arms and legs in cataleptic position.)

Dissociation

ERICKSON (*to subject*)

Now, if you'll look, you'll not only see yourself there, but you'll feel yourself sitting there. How does it feel to sit over there? It's not as comfortable over there as it is here. Are there really two of you? There must be two of you. You don't understand that?

Recall

ERICKSON (*to subject*)

All right, Jane. There's Jane over there and here's Jane over here. I want some help from you sitting here, Jane. I want you to look at that Jane over there, because the one who sits over there is going to think about something, something that you've forgotten, something that you don't even remember. It's something that happened when she was about seven or eight years of age, something that amused her or pleased her very much. Or it might be something that displeased her very much, but it is something that she would, or you would, be glad to tell me about that Jane, something that that Jane would be willing for me or for any stranger to know. I want you to watch her face as she begins to remember something that happened when she was seven or eight years old. She's going to get a very illuminative expression on her face, either of pleasure or displeasure. You tell me how her face looks. Watch it now. Don't miss a single phase of that expression. Tell it to me ⁻apidly. There was a trestle that she had been wanting to walk, except her mother wouldn't let her. So she did anyway. And how does she look now?

JANE

It was fun on that trestle, but she got a spanking when she got home.

ERICKSON

What does her face look like now? I can't see it.

JANE

You can't see it?

ERICKSON
> No, I can't.

JANE
> A little sad, you know, but it was fun and worth it.

ERICKSON
> Sad? How do you feel toward that Jane?

JANE
> She's a pretty good Joe.

ERICKSON
> Does she still look sad?

JANE
> No.

ERICKSON
> How does she look?

JANE
> She just looks.

ERICKSON (*to audience*)

This matter of getting a detached and dissociated view of oneself, this matter of being objective, is well illustrated here. She can look at herself and see sadness and gladness all at the same time without really feeling that she is participating.

ERICKSON (*to subject*)
> How do you feel, sitting here, about Jane over there?

JANE
> A little peculiar.

ERICKSON
> In what way do you feel peculiar?

JANE
> Just sort of like there were two of me.

Age regression

ERICKSON (*to subject*)

Now, suppose you watch that Jane over there. What do you think is going to happen to her? You don't know. Well, I want you to look over there and watch Jane, because things are going to change. She's going to get faint and hazy and then all of a sudden you'll see her sitting there, a seven-year-old child. Do you like her? You really do? How is she dressed?

JANE

Oh, she has a cotton dress on, you know, with ruffles.

ERICKSON

Anything else, Jane?

JANE

Shoes. Mary Jane shoes.

ERICKSON

Look at her. Tell me what she is thinking. Look at her! What is she really thinking about? She's thinking about the rash on her arm? I don't see that rash. Where is it on her arm?

JANE

Both arms, from eating too many strawberries. Ma told her not to. The strawberries were good.

Depersonalization

ERICKSON (*to subject*)

That girl is changing. If you don't want any of this, you won't understand. You don't know who the girl is, but that little girl is the same little girl, only you don't know her. Tell me about her.

JANE

I don't even know her.

ERICKSON

Well, what does she look like?

JANE

A little girl.

ERICKSON

A little girl? She's about to cry and you'll be able to guess why she's crying.

JANE

I don't know her.

ERICKSON

You don't know her. That's right. You just know what's in her mind. That gives you an odd feeling, doesn't it, to know what's in her mind?

JANE

No.

ERICKSON

Well, just look in. You'll see what's in her mind. What is she crying about? You don't know. Oh, she must have got a spanking? What made you think she got a spanking?

JANE

Because she's crying and there isn't anything else to cry about.

ERICKSON

Well, look into that girl's mind a little bit more, just sort of feel the way a little girl does. Now what thoughts come into your mind? Look at her again and tell me why she's crying. Maybe she fell down and hurt herself? Well, why don't you ask her?

JANE

I did.

ERICKSON

And what did she answer?

JANE

She won't answer.

Literal thinking

ERICKSON (*to subject*)

Oh yes, she will. Listen carefully, because she's answering. Hear it now. She fell down on her skates? That's what she said? Her knee isn't skinned up. How did she fall?

JANE

Did you fall down and skin your knees? She didn't. Her feet went out from underneath her. (*Laughs*)

ERICKSON (*to audience*)

It came as a surprise to Jane that there is another way to fall. She discovered that. The subject's behavior illustrates the limitations, the restrictions, and the absolute accuracy with which human thinking can adhere to a single line of thought and be separate from all other lines of thought. Jane was actually recalling her own memory, but even though it was her own memory, she could limit her thinking about her memory very, very nicely.

ERICKSON (*to subject*)

Would you like to look at that girl again? What is she doing now? She feels better. Why?

JANE

Because it doesn't hurt so bad. (*Regression of vocabulary.*)

ERICKSON

Who is that little girl?

JANE

I don't know her.

ERICKSON

Well, suppose you ask her what her name is. Her name will surprise you when she tells you.

JANE

What's your name? She says Betty.

ERICKSON

She said it is Betty? You don't know anyone named Betty? Have you ever been called Betty? Now you look at that girl. Look at her carefully. She says her name is Betty. Now keep your eyes open and watch her. Does she still say her name is Betty?

JANE

She changed.

ERICKSON

Changed? In what way did she change?

JANE

I don't know.

ERICKSON

Well, she looks like you. About how old is she?

JANE

About eight.

ERICKSON

Well, why did she say her name is Betty?

JANE

I don't know.

ERICKSON

Would you like to find out why she said her name is Betty? Would you? We'll do that later.

JANE

She looks kind of like me.

ERICKSON

Of course! That's you when you were a little girl!

JANE

She's pretty snaggle-toothed.

ERICKSON

Were you given any nicknames when you were seven or eight? What were the nicknames? Can you tell me? You let a boy friend call you Betty? I think that is a very pretty name, don't you? You did then. Jane is a better name, isn't it? It still is, isn't it?

Age regression

ERICKSON (*to subject*)

All right, now. I'm going to let that girl grow. Watch her. Watch her. She's growing up. Ten years old; then all of a sudden she's fourteen; then sixteen. Look at her. Watch her—Eighteen—

JANE (*laughs*)

ERICKSON

Did you enjoy watching her? Have you ever watched yourself grow like that before? All right, now close your eyes. I'm going to arouse you and I want you to remember afterward everything that happened in the trance state. Will you do that? I want you to discuss it for the audience and you'll do that with comfort, will you now? Now take it easily, comfortably, and wake up, ready and willing to tell the audience everything that happened in this trance state. Awakening, wide awake. Now what do you think you're going to do?

(Indirect reference to posthypnotic suggestion, so that subject may elect to have amnesia for the suggestion itself.)

JANE

Oh dear, I never talked with one of these. (*Indicates microphone.*) I get mike fright. Do you just talk into it? (*To Doctor Erickson*) You see, I don't need to tell them; they already know. (*Laughter*) They weren't here, were they? Yes, they were. That's a most peculiar feeling, when you know somebody isn't there and all of a sudden you know they were and they've been here all the time. Makes you feel sort of odd. It really does. I've had that done to me before. It's a strange feeling, but I was sitting over there in that chair. Hmm . . . I went all the way back (*regression*) when I was seven years old and walked the railroad trestle and my mother spanked me. It was fun though. Then I grew up. Oh, you know I had forgotten that little boy that lived next door to me and called me Betty. I really was pretty snaggle-toothed.

ERICKSON

You actually had forgotten that little boy?

Return of subject to trance by recall of regression material

JANE

What was his name? Maybe it was George. (*Laughs*) And I grew up. (*Voice changes back into trance*) When I was first over there, I had on this dress, but then I went back and was a little girl and then I grew up to eighteen and you must have awakened me, because I don't remember. I stopped there. Did I stop there? (*Amnesia for waking state.*) Hmm . . . you know, I can still see her.

ERICKSON

I think that the audience thinks that you're wide awake.

JANE

Maybe I am.

Recall of subject to reality situation

ERICKSON (*to subject*)

I think you've got a better understanding than they have. You're talking to the audience; you're aware of the audience, but you're still seeing yourself over there, isn't that right?

JANE

That's strange, yes . . .

ERICKSON (*to audience*)

And you'll agree she's wide awake, won't you? (*Laughter*)

JANE

Where did they all come from? Oh my, I'm confused! There wasn't anybody here. What did we do with that little girl? So that's in my mind? I can still see her.

Manipulation of trance

ERICKSON (*to subject*)

You can still see it in your mind?

JANE

Yes, it must be.

ERICKSON

Well, who is that little girl?

JANE

It was me.

ERICKSON

And where are you?

JANE

I'm at the Hotel Captain Shreve.

ERICKSON

Where?

JANE

I'm in Shreveport. Do you mean what street?

ERICKSON

Where are you right now?

JANE

On the second floor, in the . . . I've forgotten the name of the room.

ERICKSON

Lakewood?

JANE

Lakewood. All those people. But they weren't here before, were they?

ERICKSON

Were they?

JANE

Yes.

Indirect suggestion

ERICKSON (*to subject*)

Look.

JANE

Where did they go? (*Whispered.*)

ERICKSON

Where *did* they go?

ERICKSON (*to audience*)

Where did they go? I said "look" and all I needed to say was that one word, in a questioning way, in a doubting way. And she picked it up immediately. The importance of the use of intonation, inflection, the interpersonal communication has been discussed previously. The ability of patients to pick up a lack of confidence in the voice must constantly be kept in mind.

Ability of subject to steer own thoughts

ERICKSON (*to subject*)

What are you looking at, Jane?

JANE

Why does that little girl stay there?

ERICKSON

Why does that little girl stay there? Maybe she's enjoying herself. Maybe you'd like to find out some other forgotten memories that she has. She's the one that's got the boy friend who calls her Betty. What's his name?

JANE

George.

ERICKSON

What is George's last name?

JANE

Uh . . . Gates.

ERICKSON

George Gates.

ERICKSON (*to audience*)

Now she'd completely forgotten his first name. She'd forgotten the incident of being called Betty, so she asked the little girl over there what the little boy's last name was. Think of what a circuitous route her memory took of projecting outward, then verbalizing, then getting the answer back, and all that is happening within her.

Automatic writing

ERICKSON (*to subject*)

Have you ever done any automatic writing, Jane? Yes? Do you know what automatic writing is? All right. After you're awake, I want you to be very puzzled about George's last name, but your hand will write it automatically. Now go to sleep, Jane, deeply asleep, and I want you to rouse up, just as you were before you came up on the stage. (*Implied amnesia for all preceding demonstration.*) I'm going to talk to you about automatic writing. You will write what I've told you to write (*Avoidance of restimulating memory.*), but it'll seem to you as if you've just gotten up on the stage. Wide awake. Wake up, Jane. Wake up, Jane, wide awake, completely awake. Is it very hard to face the audience? Are you stage struck?

JANE

A little.

ERICKSON

Just a little. Where'd the notebook come from? Did you bring it up with you?

JANE

I don't know.

ERICKSON

It isn't yours? Does sitting in front of an audience distress you at all? Make you shed tears? . . . What's that?

JANE

Makes me shed tears, I think.

ERICKSON

Where'd you get the notebook? Maybe there's a name on it. It is? I think it's pretty, too. Were you shedding tears? No, I don't really think you were. By the way, have you ever remembered something that you've completely forgotten?

JANE

What do you mean?

ERICKSON

Something you had completely, absolutely forgotten. Did you ever reach back and get it? By the way, do you know what automatic writing is? You don't know what it is? You really don't. Well, I wonder if the audience knows what it is. Don't you think they'd like to see some automatic writing?

JANE

If they're here. (*Borderline* state implied.)

ERICKSON

Well, that's another question. (*Issue evaded.*) Do you think they'd like to see some automatic writing? There's a pencil. You know, very shortly somebody is going to pick up that pencil and write the name. This sounds like nonsense, but it really isn't. That someone will write the name of Betty's boy friend. You just watch that pencil. Just watch it. Look at that pencil. A hand is going to reach out and pick it up and write the name of Betty's boy friend. (*Subject has opportunity to depersonalize her hand completely, if she chooses.*) Who is Betty? Somebody in the audience? Do you know Betty's boy friend's name? What is it?

JANE

George.

ERICKSON

Can't remember the last name. Those people lived next door, but you can't remember it, can you? Your hand is going to pick up that pencil and write it. Watch your hand. The hand is going to pick it up. It's going to write a name and you won't know what the name is until the last letter is written.

JANE (*writes*)

That's it, too!

ERICKSON

That was it. The mind is an amazing thing. Funny how the pencil turned out to be one of those that writes with ink that fades out. Now you'll have to write the name all over again.

ERICKSON (*to audience*)

Not only has the name faded out on the paper, but the name has also faded out of her mind.

ERICKSON (*to subject*)

Would you like to know that name?

JANE

All right.

ERICKSON

Well, you could write it on that blank piece of cardboard. What's that? Oh yes, you can write it. Do you see it there? It's hard for me to read it, mixed up with that other writing. Is your husband in the audience? Hold it up and ask him if there's writing on that card, other than yours. Is everybody gone, too?

JANE

How come the people are coming and going? Why don't they stay put?

ERICKSON

Well, shall I order them to stay put? What's that? They're back now and they'll stay put.

JANE

That's funny.

Subject's defense of suggested idea (negative hallucination)

ERICKSON

What's funny?

JANE

Do you see some writing on there?

ERICKSON

Yes, I see some writing there.

JANE

There's no writing there.

HUSBAND

Yes, there is.

JANE

Well, what are those things?

HUSBAND

There's some other, too.

ERICKSON

He's wrong? Husbands often are. (*Laughter.*) But you might ask this gentleman here if there's additional writing on that.

He's probably somebody else's husband? Find out if there's a bachelor in the crowd. Let's see, there's a lady over there. She's nobody's husband. Ask her.

JANE

Can you see anything?

WOMAN

Yes.

ERICKSON

Where did you write it? Show me.

JANE

Right there.

ERICKSON

Now look. (*Laughter at subject's look of surprise.*)

JANE

That's turned the wrong way.

ERICKSON

And the other side is blank?

ERICKSON (*to audience*)

Many doctors want to talk sense to a patient when they have no real understanding of why the patient makes false or contradictory remarks. They will try to talk sense when they should be trying to understand the peculiar situation that makes the patient tell them something that isn't so. Here's a perfectly normal person in a trance state, demonstrating the extent to which knowledge can be kept out of the mind. To her, all people are wrong when they say that isn't a blank card. Everybody's wrong. There is no doubt at all in her mind. Somehow or other, she cannot see that writing.

ERICKSON (*to subject*)

I think your husband was right for once! Oh, I shouldn't let him hear this.

JANE

Oh, all men do it.

ERICKSON

Well, this is the one and only time he's ever been right, except that one other occasion when he said, "I do."

Time distortion to see movies

ERICKSON (*to subject*)

What was the last movie you attended?

JANE

The Trouble with Harry.

ERICKSON

Did you enjoy it? Is it worthwhile seeing again? Would you like to see it again? Well, just go to sleep, go deeply asleep. Now I want to tell you something. While you're asleep time can change and become very, very slow, or it can become very, very rapid. You know, when you wait for someone, even if it's only two minutes, if you're anxious for them to come, that two minutes seems so-o-o-o long. Isn't that right? It seems as if you could have done a whole day's work in that two minutes. All right. We all have that experience at one time or another and now I'm going to let you have the experience in a pleasant way. I'm going to have you see a movie, a movie that you'd like to see again, *The Trouble with Harry*. Over to my right there's going to be a movie screen. I'm going to give you more time than you need to see the entire movie, more time than you need to see it from beginning to end. It won't start until I say START and, when I say STOP, the movie will be ended, more than ended. Do you understand? It will be just as you saw it before, no faster and no slower. You'll really enjoy seeing that movie.

Now I'm going to give you ten seconds in which to do it and that's sufficient in your mind to see the entire movie. You know that, don't you? Now when you think about the speed of thought, you know that ten seconds is enough to see the complete movie and more and you're going to do that, aren't you? While you are asleep turn your head slightly, open your eyes and see the movie screen over there. Get your eyes accustomed to the darkness and keep them open, because the movie's about to start. Did it start? All right. Now it's just about ready to start and I'm going to give the signal. Now it's ready, ready, START! . . . STOP!

No, I didn't see it. I should have? Did you see it all?

JANE

Yes.

ERICKSON

You saw it all. Anything more?

JANE

No.

ERICKSON (*to audience*)

I had her do that to emphasize the point of time distortion. It is a very real subjective phenomenon. They do see the movie from beginning to end. In a recent demonstration, I gave a subject fifteen extra seconds. And she saw four or five extra cartoons. The speed of thought is extremely rapid and there is no motor behavior to slow up the subjective experience.

Now she has done automatic writing; she's shown time distortion; she's uncovered memories, and she's demonstrated the capacity of the retina to become anesthetic to stimuli. She was unable to see the writing on a card. She saw the card with her own writing on it as a blank. She readily accepted the suggestion that her words had been written with a pen that had disappearing ink.

Limits to age regression

Here are the questions, answers, and discussion which followed the demonstration.

QUESTION

I don't want to go into the Bridey Murphy situation, but how far can one be regressed?

CASE OF LEONARD A.

ERICKSON

I think the best answer that I can give you from personal experience is to tell you about an excellent subject. I spent an entire day, from about eight o'clock in the morning until four o'clock in the afternoon, without any interruption, regressing Leonard A from the age of 19 down to infancy. I had him sitting in a chair, very carefully fixed up with pillows. It was a nice armchair, on a platform that was especially rigged for the chair. Those seven hours were spent regressing him, with my suggestions being built up very carefully. At about one o'clock he was given his last really verbal suggestion, to the effect that as he continued to sleep he would keep on going back and back and back into his infancy; just my breathing and just my touching of him would constitute a suggestion that he would get younger and younger, until he was as young as he could possibly be.

Of course, some time in the afternoon, Leonard had regressed beyond the stage at which I could talk to him, but he could feel and he could hear me breathing. Then, when I felt he had regressed as far as possible, while he was sitting there acting and looking infantile, I reached over with my foot, which was out of his range of vision, and touched the trigger on the chair. The chair looked as though it were a stable thing to bounce around in, but the trigger released the chair and the chair fell back.

The normal reaction of a man who suddenly found himself in a chair that was falling back would be to throw out the feet and the hands in a righting reflex. But this nineteen-year-old subject did not kick out his feet, nor did he throw up his hands from where they were hanging beside him. Instead, he let out a frightened, inarticulate squawk and wet his pants, the correct behavior for an age under one year. In his studies on infants, Watson has described the reflex behavior for a baby of six or eight months as a squawk and urination. But there was not only the loss of the righting reflex here. A worker came in and tested Leonard for a Babinski. He showed what the neurologist thought was a positive Babinski.

When Leonard wet his pants, showed the loss of the righting reflex, and the apparent Babinski, there was nothing I could accomplish with him for he could no longer understand me. All I could do was to have him cleaned up and put to bed, and let him slowly come out of the hypnotic sleep and go into physiological sleep, then wake up next day; he was out of contact with me. Much of the night the subject was still apparently in the infantile state for he continued to wet his bed. I had a lot of apologizing to do because he blamed the hypnosis for his bed-wetting. This was an experimental subject where we can try that kind of work. With a nonexperimental subject, one never attempts regressions of that sort.

CASE OF JANINE M.

Regression was also employed with another subject, Janine M, a twenty-year-old nurse, who had never seen her father. All she knew about her father was that her mother had secured a divorce, moved to another state, and severed all connections with friends and relatives. The mother had refused to give the daughter any information whatsoever about her father. The girl was about five feet three inches tall; the mother was approximately the same height; both were brown-eyed and dark-haired. The mother had changed her name. Janine M didn't even know what her name had been originally.

When the girl was hypnotized, she was regressed and told to visualize herself as an infant. She was then told to pick out some incident and, on the screen where she visualized herself as an infant, she saw herself high up above the ground. She described a man with reddish-gold hair and an upper gold front tooth. She estimated his height at six feet. She scrutinized him, observed what the man and the baby were looking at. There was a lot of noise and it looked like a parade. After she'd done that and I had obtained all the information, she said to her mother, "Mother, I have just come from seeing the psychiatrist. I know what my father looked like. He was over six feet tall. He was blue-eyed. He had a moustache and reddish-gold hair. He had a gold upper front tooth." The mother replied, "No psychiatrist ever told you that. Has your father been in town? Has he looked you up? How did he find you?"

Janine was actually ten months of age at the time her father held her in his arms to watch the parade. The mother answered all the girl's questions, when she found her daughter really knew how her father looked. That was a ten-months'-old memory. The father had disappeared shortly after that parade.*

Revivification of memories

That gives you some idea of how far back you can go, but it is a different matter to get the patient really to regress to that degree. No ten-months'-old baby could talk to me, but my patient could look at a screen and see these things. They're merely projections of memories, just as Jane projected herself in a certain cotton dress with ruffles, a little girl who was thinking happily that her name was Betty, when she was entertaining that child fantasy. Jane was still Jane, sitting here in the chair, yet still Jane over there, but in a different sort of way, a way that Jane could talk about.

* Milton H. Erickson, M.D., "Pseudo-Orientation in Time as an Hypnotherapeutic Procedure," *Journal of Clinical and Experimental Hypnosis*, II, 4, October 1954, pp. 269-272.

Trance persistence and rapport

QUESTION

From all appearance, when you brought her out of that trance, she appeared normal, but she was still in a trance. What did you suggest for that state?

ERICKSON

Well, the situation is this. Jane came up to the platform to assist me in instructing the group. She will therefore remain in rapport with me and be very acutely aware of and alert to anything that I say to her. As soon as the demonstrating situation is broken up, she will be in the ordinary waking state. But as long as she is on the stage before the audience, assisting me, she will remain in a trance, no matter how wide awake she seems to be. The same would be true of any member of an audience who is a good somnambulistic subject.

Suggested alteration of sense of taste

QUESTION

Can you demonstrate a change in the sense of taste?

ERICKSON

I will demonstrate it with Jane. (*To subject.*) All right, Jane. Look at me. You're still asleep, aren't you? Now the audience is here; you're aware of it. You just saw me drink a glass of water, didn't you? I would like to have you drink a glass of water, too. Would you like to? It's nice and cold and refreshing, but after the first three swallows you're going to find that it is very bitter. I want you to describe that bitterness. Will you? All right.

JANE

You gave me some water. It was bitter.

ERICKSON

What did I put in it? What did it taste like?

JANE

Strange.

ERICKSON

Go ahead. If I gave you green persimmons to drink—go ahead and use the handkerchief. It was awful? How would you like to try this glass?

JANE

Is this one all right?

ERICKSON

Well, you find out. You had only two sips. Take another. That was nasty, too? Well, I'll give you a glass to take the bad taste away. It'll be very delicious and you'll enjoy it. What did that taste like?

JANE

Better. It was decent water.

Preparation of somnambules

QUESTION

Had you prepared her for this beforehand?

ERICKSON

I was introduced to her last night. This morning I walked in and recognized her. I sat down at her table, but spent most of my time talking to another doctor there. That's the preparation she has had. She is a remarkably good subject.

Refusal to demonstrate panic reaction for subject protection

QUESTION

Could you demonstrate a panic reaction, or would that take too long?

ERICKSON

Well, to demonstrate a panic reaction is a rather painful thing. I never like to induce a panic unless there is an immediate gain. For example, I recently induced a panic state in an expectant mother. I did it for a very definite reason. Often, when the head hits the perineum, the patient reacts with a panic response. Knowing this patient as I did, and knowing her capacity to develop shock responses, I let her develop a panic and then let her discover that a panic could be handled, dealt with and resolved, so that when she does have her baby, she will not get a shock response when the head reaches the perineum.

I don't think there would be any object in producing a panic in Jane. It's a rather shaking experience and would not be instructive in any way.

Posthypnotic hallucination

QUESTION

How about posthypnotic hallucinations, like a photograph or a picture on the wall when you wake her up?

ERICKSON (*to subject*)

Jane, after you're awake and down in the audience, do you

mind being a bit embarrassed by that powerful orange-colored tie that your husband is wearing? He really ought to have better taste.

JANE

I'm going to throw that one away.

ERICKSON

You are, are you? I wonder why he put that one on today. To irritate you? I wouldn't be surprised. Husbands are that way. He knew you didn't like it.

JANE

He wasn't going to be bossed around by me.

ERICKSON

You know, some people won't ever learn to take advice about their clothes.

JANE

He does pretty well most of the time.

ERICKSON

There's nothing like coming to his defense, but that orange tie—you just don't like it. Shall we let him wear it very long, for the rest of today?

JANE

I let him do those things once in a while, so he won't feel henpecked.

Indirect induction

ERICKSON (*to subject*)

You know, that's the best way to henpeck a man. Let him think he isn't being. It's a good hypnotic technique, too, to hypnotize, but not to let them know they're really being hypnotized. Are you going to start looking at me with a sidelong glance after that comment? Any other—what's that?

JANE

You did it to me.

ERICKSON

That's right. I did it to you.

Now I think we can give Jane a rest. Thank you very much for helping us, Jane. You were a wonderful subject.

Handling of conflicts

QUESTION

When you discover a conflict, what steps do you take to remove it? Do you suggest amnesia, or do you have some other solution?

ERICKSON

When I discover a conflict by hypnosis, I usually leave it untouched and walk around it until I find out what it is and something about its nature and character. I might try to deal with it, later, but first I try to outline it without getting the patient at all disturbed by that conflict.

Loss of contact with patient

QUESTION

Regarding loss of contact with a patient at a certain depth, would you care to comment on that?

ERICKSON

Yes, I lost contact with a patient not long ago. I asked this patient to recall a memory. It was a very general memory about the time she was approximately sixteen years old. She started thinking about it. Then, since she was quite a good subject, she slipped into a very deep trance while she was trying to recall it. She regressed to the age of sixteen and found herself at a camp in Maine. (This occurred in Phoenix.) She hadn't met me at the age of sixteen. She'd never heard of Phoenix at that age. There she was at the camp, looking around to find out what had happened to the other campers. She looked around for quite a while. Of course, she couldn't hear me, because I wasn't there. I was completely out of contact with her. Fortunately, at the time we were making a tape recording for some research and I started to talk, gradually making references to the things I already knew about her and very shortly I had re-established contact with her. Had I established a physical contact, it would have been much easier, but she had taken me by surprise. Another way I might have gotten in contact with her would have been to violate her rights and privileges as an individual. She happened to be sitting with her hand raised and I could have jerked her hand down rudely. Or I could have pushed her, which would have made her look around and come out of the trance, but she certainly would have resented these things had I done them.

Duration of posthypnotic suggestions

QUESTION

How long can posthypnotic suggestions remain effective?

ERICKSON

I gave a posthypnotic suggestion to one of my subjects and she carried out the suggestion fifteen years later. That suggestion was, "I don't know when we'll meet again, but sooner or later, somewhere, some time, we'll meet again. When we do, if the time, the situation and occasion are appropriate, after we greet each other, you will go into a deep trance." Fifteen years later, I was in a restaurant with an anthropologist. He looked around to find a place for us to eat and said, "There's a booth over there and only one girl in it. I'll go over and see if she'll let us join her." When he inquired, she said "yes." He came back to get me and my tray. We walked over. I stepped into the booth and there was the subject. She greeted me and I greeted her. I introduced the anthropologist. She knew of him and, since he was in my company, she felt that the situation was appropriate. After greeting us, her head went down and much to the anthropologist's surprise, she went into a deep trance.

Handedness and automatic writing

QUESTION

Suppose the subject had been left-handed and you had not known it. If you told her that her right hand was going to write that name, what would she have done?

ERICKSON

She might have corrected me, or she might have discovered that she had an unusual facility with her right hand and written it with her right hand.

Reactions to attacks on personal standards

QUESTION

Someone has mentioned the opposition some individuals may have to being approached on their religious tenets or moral persuasions. What are the manifestations of this?

ERICKSON

They tend to tighten up; they tend to show anxiety or a willingness to argue with you, or to explain to you that this is a topic that does not enter into the hypnotic situation.

Handling of posttraumatic experiences

QUESTION

Can you, with posthypnotic suggestion, blot out the memory of some previous unpleasant experience?

ERICKSON

You can blot it out, but there's a better way of doing it. Let the patients examine their previous unpleasant experience, understand it in full, and reduce the value and importance of it. For example, the high school girl who slips on the dance floor and sprawls out, just "simply dies." Then for the rest of her life she's afraid to dance. Yet, you can put her in a trance and have her examine the experience and recall it in full. Then you raise the question with her of just how terrible it actually was. Let her appreciate the feeling she had then, but also ask her how she should view that little episode now that she is an adult? In this way she sees it in its proper perspective and then it's very easily blotted out as an unimportant thing.

Readiness for hypnosis

QUESTION

In the demonstration you started out by saying, "Do you think that you're really awake?" and you seemed very, very sure that she wasn't awake. However, I wasn't sure!

ERICKSON

I raised the question if she were really awake and that aroused a doubt in her mind that allowed her either to awaken or to go into a trance. Since the situation was one that required a trance, she went on into a trance.

QUESTION

There was no induction?

ERICKSON

She was already in a trance, a light one. Coming up on the stage, she came for a definite purpose. She was going to assist. Therefore, she was in the proper mental set, the physical set, the psychological frame of reference.

QUESTION

Would that be more or less the stage that the dental patient would be in on returning for future visits after having been in a trance once? He would induce himself even before he got to the office.

ERICKSON

That's right.

4
Induction Techniques

The material that follows is presented largely as it was taken from seminar tape recordings, since the purpose is to show how individual hypnotic techniques vary. The important thing for the student of hypnosis to bear in mind is that each individual approach should be studied and evaluated carefully, in an effort to determine which aspects of the techniques presented may best be utilized or adapted to fit the student's own personality requirements.

Progressive relaxation

Demonstration 4: ENTIRE GROUP

DOCTOR S

If you would like to relax and have the sensations of what complete relaxation can be, make yourselves as comfortable as you can. Usually it is nice to sit loosely, limply in a chair, with your feet flat on the floor or in any other position that may be comfortable, with your hands on your laps or hanging down. Find a fixation point on the ceiling. Pick any point, but stick to it.

Pay attention only to that point on the ceiling and to my words. Just pay attention effortlessly. Now, your eyelids should be getting quite tired from looking up at that point. Let your arms hang loosely and your legs hang loosely. Take a slow, deep breath and let it out very slowly, becoming aware of the comfortable feeling as you begin to breathe deeply. Then take another slow, deep breath and hold it while I count to five and then let it out slowly. Hold it now. One—two—three—four—five. Really enjoy that nice, pleasant, comfortable sensation in your abdomen. Now, with relaxation comes a feeling of heaviness. That's one of the signs of relaxation.

And while your eyes are occupied with that point you've selected, pay attention to your feet, to the soles of your feet and, as you become more relaxed, let your feet become heavier and heavier. Think to yourself, "My feet *are* becoming heavier," and, as you think that they are becoming heavier, they *do* become heavier, moment by moment, heavier and heavier. Then this heaviness creeps up into the ankles, the feet and ankles, heavier and heavier—up the legs, into the thighs, the whole body from the waist down now, heavy with relaxation. Moment by moment your body feels heavier and heavier and it's so pleasant, so comfortable. And that heaviness creeps up into the chest, up the hands and arms into the neck. Now, the whole body from the neck down feels heavy, the feet, the ankles, the legs, the thighs, the abdomen, the chest, heavy, heavy, heavier. Pay attention to your jaws as your lower jaw relaxes and notice that your mouth opens slightly. That's the proper position of the jaw at rest, with the teeth and lips apart. If it helps you to keep them apart by wetting your lips, it is perfectly all right to do so. The jaws are limp and loose, lips apart, teeth apart. Many of you have been blinking your eyelids to protect your eyes against fatigue. Blinking is the way the body prevents eye fatigue. Let them blink. It takes tension to keep your eyes open and we're fighting tension. Let's not fight to keep the eyes open. Let them do what they want to do, let them c-l-o-s-e. Once they're closed, keep them closed. Don't fight to keep your eyes open, relax completely, close them now. Just close them and keep them closed.

With your eyes closed, visualize a darkness, the color gray or black. Empty your mind of thoughts, think of nothing, do nothing. That's the secret of relaxation. Relax all over now, in mind and body. Just relax and enjoy the nice comfortable feeling. Now breathe slowly and deeply, exactly as if you were asleep, and with each breath that you take, go deeper, deeper and deeper relaxed, deeper and deeper relaxed. Soon you'll be as close to sleep as it's possible for you to get and yet remain conscious and cooperative. So comfortable, breathing slowly and deeply and enjoying every moment.

Now I would like you to use your imagination, your ability to visualize. You can visualize yourself standing in front of your easy chair and, as you think about it, the image of it becomes more clear and you can see yourself more clearly in front of that easy chair. Just think about it. As the picture gets more and more clear, let your right hand extend straight in front of you, just as a signal to me that you are visualizing the picture. That's fine, let your arm stand right out in front of you. Keep it out there; that's fine. It will be easy for you to maintain it there pleasantly and comfortably. As you visualize the chair, just think about that chair. Now visualize yourself with your back to the chair and think about yourself with your back to the chair s-l-o-w-ly descending into that chair. And, as you descend into that chair, you go deeper and deeper and deeper relaxed. Your arms are dropping, heavy with relaxation, as you sit down deeply, deeply into the chair. You can feel yourself in the chair, becoming warm, with your seat becoming firmly attached to the seat of the chair, your back and the back of the chair becoming as one, so that you cannot move yourself from the chair without changing the way you feel. And you feel so comfortable, so pleasant, that you wouldn't do anything at all to change the way you feel.

In just a moment I am going to ask you to do something, and you're going to try to please me by doing it. I'm going to ask you to lift yourself up from that chair and you're going to try to do it because you want to please me. Yet on the other hand, you're not going to want to change the way you feel. To lift yourself up from the chair will require tensions and you're really not going to want to exercise tensions, because you really want to be completely relaxed. When I count to three, you will deliberately try to move from your chair, but you won't be able to move because you really don't want to. You want to please me, but you won't be able to and it's going to be difficult. So, at the count of three, try to move yourself from the chair, but you can't.

One—two—three—try. Stop trying now. It's too much like work. Just relax a-l-l o-v-e-r now.

Continuing in this manner could result in hypnosis. It's a pleasant sensation but, even in the deepest stages of hypnosis, you are no more unconscious than you are now. There is always an awareness. It's a kind of detached feeling. You can ignore what you wish to ignore and pay attention only to what you need and want to pay attention to. You can pay attention to me, or you could pay attention to any of the panel members. During this period you will hear our voices, sometimes separately, sometimes together, but you will find it worthwhile to learn how to relax and how to be able to teach others to relax.

ERICKSON

You can keep right on relaxing, going deeper and deeper into the trance, and all the time you do, you are learning to understand with your unconscious mind and you're learning to understand also with your conscious mind. You can all learn from this experience and carry it into the practice sessions. You can also do this in your own offices, where you can learn by yourselves through your own efforts. Now I want time to seem infinitely long, infinitely l-o-n-g, and then slowly and gradually I want you to arouse, slowly and gradually arouse. Arousing, arousing, knowing that you can go back again some other time, arousing, arousing—and all of you can now waken, wide awake. You might all like to twist around in your chairs and reorient yourselves.

Now I'm going to call on Doctor A to demonstrate a technique. Pay attention to exactly what Doctor A says, what he does, and what the subject does. After Doctor A has finished, I will offer my critique.

Trance induction in previously unhypnotized subject

Demonstration 5

DOCTOR A

For the best demonstration of trance induction techniques we require a different subject than we would if we were demonstrating deep hypnosis and the phenomena that occur in deep hypnosis. When deep hypnosis is presented, obviously we need to have a subject who is capable of going into the deepest stages of hypnosis and this usually is best accomplished with a well-conditioned subject. On the other hand, were I to work with a well-conditioned subject now, he would go into hypnosis so quickly that little would be learned about trance induction. For this reason I am going to ask for a volunteer to work with me in this demonstration who has never used hypnosis, who has never been hypnotized, upon whom no attempt has ever been made to induce hypnosis. Now with that limitation or qualification, may I have a volunteer, please?

DOCTOR A (*to subject*)

Now, first of all, Doctor R, you have some idea of what a patient does in regard to the way he adjusts his body, so that he is comfortable. We got that from Doctor S's demonstration, so suppose you do just as his subjects did. Make yourself as comfortable as you can. Also, I'm going to ask that you select a spot somewhere on the ceiling. It doesn't make any difference, just select a spot that will be convenient for you to focus on. I'm going to ask that you keep your eyes focused on that spot until I ask you later to do otherwise. As you keep your eyes focused on that spot, Doctor R, you will notice that your legs begin to get very heavy, very pleasantly heavy. Now, as you keep your eyes on the spot, your arms begin to get very pleasantly heavy. And, as you keep your eyes on the spot, your body itself begins to get very pleasantly heavy. And now, Doctor R, your legs are heavy, your arms are heavy, your whole body is pleasantly heavy, and soon your eyelids, too, will begin to get heavy. When they do, you will let them close. Your eyelids are heavier and heavier and heavier.

If I may, I'm going to touch your forehead with your eyes closed and you will go deeper and deeper asleep as your eyes stay closed. Sleep deeply. And it seems, Dr. R, that with each breath that you take, you are feeling yourself slipping more deeply into this lovely, delightful, heavy, sleepy state, and you sleep deeply, sleep deeply. You sleep deeply, yet you are completely aware of everything that happens. You will listen only for the sound of my voice; everything else you want to shut out from your awareness, as you slip more deeply into hypnosis.

As you sleep deeply, Doctor, I should like to have you think about your hands and, with your eyes closed, I should like you to get a picture in your mind's eye of what those hands of yours look like. As you think of your hands, you will notice that something begins to happen to the fingers of one of them or to one finger of one hand, or possibly the thumb. It doesn't make any difference really, just so that you feel that something is happening. It seems that a great deal is happening to the little finger of your left hand. As the finger begins to twitch a little more, you will probably notice that it begins to feel a little lighter than the other fingers, with a very pleasant sensation of lightness of that finger which soon will spread to the other fingers of that hand. Soon all your fingers will be so pleasantly light that they will start to lift in the air and get lighter and lighter. That feeling of lightness seems to spread through your hand, just as a tiny grass fire will spread through a dry field. Spreading, spreading, your hand is getting lighter and lighter. Soon your hand will be so light that your wrist will bend and your hand will begin to come up floating into the air.

Your arm gets light, your forearm, your hand, and your fingertips. Your forearm gets lighter and lighter and it feels as if something were actually tugging on that arm, lifting, lifting, lifting so that soon your arm will be floating, lifting and floating. You're going to be tremendously interested in this feeling of lightness in that one hand and arm. You're looking forward now to that arm really coming up. Soon, you'll feel a decrease in the pressure of your arm on the arm rest of the chair. You will be aware of the arm starting to lift more and more, lighter and lighter. That's fine.

Now, Doctor, as I touch your arm and your hand, they both become completely normal. That's right, that's right—completely normal, while your whole body remains completely relaxed. It's been very nice working with you, Doctor, and I want to thank you for your great willingness to cooperate for the benefit of the entire group as well as yourself.

In a moment I'm going to ask you to arouse yourself. Just take your time and, when I reach the count of three, you'll be wide awake, alert, tremendously interested in learning still more and, when you are awakened at the count of three, your body will be completely normal in every respect. One—two—three—almost awake—wide awake. That's right. Well, thank you very much, Doctor. Now while Doctor Erickson comments, suppose you just rest. Doctor Erickson suggests that maybe you would like to comment. Maybe you would like to tell the gentlemen here just what you experienced.

SUBJECT

Well, it wasn't hard to relax after driving in from New Orleans! You feel very easy and a certain numbness gets to the soles of your feet and you get very drowsy. I could listen to every word. I heard him give a command to raise my hand, but the best I could do was just to raise my wrist. I couldn't, I didn't feel the lightness that he suggested in my arm, but I did feel it up to about the level of the wrist. And I definitely had some influence from the suggestive direction which he gave.

DOCTOR A (*demonstrating*)

Doctor, have you used hypnosis yourself ?

SUBJECT

Well, I think that more or less in your practice and mine, we all use it to some degree. But I haven't used it directly.

DOCTOR A (*demonstrating*)

Have you seen stage hypnosis?

SUBJECT

Yes, I've seen stage hypnosis.

DOCTOR A (*demonstrating*)

I think that some of you will understand why I asked that question. The subject used the word "command." He said that I had commanded his arm to rise. That's one thing that we, in this work, should not think of: commands. Certainly, there was no command. But the subject revealed some connection with stage hypnosis when he used the word "command."

ERICKSON

Now for a comment on what Doctor A did. The first thing that he did was to talk casually to the subject, giving general explanations. Then, the next thing he did was to suggest that the patient choose a spot to look at—not one that Doctor A commanded or chose for him. By suggesting that the patient select the spot, he gave him the freedom to participate. One always wants to give a patient the freedom of participation.

Then Doctor A went on, "I'm going to suggest that you keep your eyes on that spot." After a pause he said, "As you keep your eyes on that spot, you will notice that your legs are getting heavier and heavier." In other words, Doctor A introduced himself in the first person pronoun, emphasizing his role, then he shifted to the second person pronoun, placing the responsibility on the patient's own activity.

Then he showed repetition. From the legs he went on to the arms: "As you continue to keep your eyes on that spot, you will notice that your arms are very, very pleasantly heavy." He paused between these words. There is no sense, unless you want to be a stage hypnotist, in rushing your suggestions to the patient. You want the patient to cooperate slowly and comfortably and actually; at the same time, you expedite matters very much. Also, Doctor A paused between his suggestions to give the subject time to digest their meaning, their significance, and to initiate within himself some activity: "Now, as you keep your eyes on the spot, your body will get heavy, your legs, your arms, and your body. Now your eyelids will get heavy." You are emphasizing the positiveness of the legs, the arms, and the body as a whole.

At this point Doctor A speeded up by touching the patient on the head and closing his eyes. He did that as a courtesy—not as a means of forcing him, but as a means of demonstrating one way of expediting things. Then he quickly shifted into, "With each breath that you take, you will relax deeper and deeper," making it contingent upon the patient to respond to his own behavior. Certainly every patient does breathe and he does so repetitiously. Why not utilize the patient's own repetitious behavior to induce more and more the deep trance phenomena? I think all of you noticed that the patient began breathing a little bit more slowly, a little bit more deeply, and he was responding to something that was happening within himself.

Finally, Doctor A started with the subject of finger movement, hand movement, and arm levitation. There was a little twitching of the finger. Then Doctor A introduced the hand, the wrist, and of course, time passed too quickly to permit the further levitation, but there was a slow progressive spread of movement. Also, while the patient was still in the light trance state, Doctor A expressed thanks to him. One really ought to respect the unconscious and give thanks to it, just as you give thanks to the ordinary conscious mind. Then, when the patient was aroused, I think all of you saw him trying to open his eyes and not succeeding, and I think all of you saw him reorienting himself in relationship to his hands and his hand movements. It was necessary for him to get back in touch with himself, because early dissociation had begun.

Hand levitation (indirect permissive technique)

Demonstration 6

DOCTOR H (*demonstrating*)

I wonder if there is somebody who would like to volunteer to assist me in demonstrating hand levitation to the group as an original induction technique? We can try this first with the eyes open, perhaps.

Come forward, Doctor. Thank you for coming forward to help.

If you'll sit very, very comfortably in the chair and allow the palms of your hands to rest comfortably on your thighs you might find it very interesting to watch those hands and perceive exactly what's going to happen, or you might like to experience now the feeling of all the sensations in your hands, really feel them. You can feel, for example, the texture of the cloth as your hands rest on your thighs. You can feel the warmth of your thighs coming through the cloth and touching those fingers and those hands. You can feel that ring on the left fourth finger which perhaps you didn't even notice until I just mentioned it. All these sensations I'd like you really to feel intensely to enjoy the feelings of those sensations and to wonder what other sensations you might feel in your hands as you watch them and feel them. You may find that possibly one of those fingers has a very, very strong desire to move.

Now, just sit there and wonder what will happen to those hands next. Keep feeling every sensation in those fingers, wondering which finger will first have the desire to move. Will it be on the right hand; will it be on the left hand? Will it be the right middle finger; will it be the left middle finger? Or perhaps the left index finger—one of those fingers can very, very easily get the sensations of wanting to move. There, the left index moved ever so slightly. You can watch it move. You can watch it more, ever more, as the sensation gets stronger and stronger. Then perhaps you can see the finger next to it begin to move now. There, the index finger moved again, just a little fraction. The left index finger slid down and you can feel every little bit of texture of the cloth of the suit that you're wearing. You can feel those fingers beginning to feel an even stronger desire to spread apart more, or perhaps to move closer together, or perhaps press down or even lift up.

You can feel those things and enjoy them and I'd like you to feel them more strongly and ever more strongly, to feel them getting stronger with every sensation. The left index finger, perhaps, begins to feel lighter, and the one next to it, and the fourth finger, and the middle finger. You can allow the sensations of lightness to get stronger and stronger until those fingers actually begin to lift off your thigh. You can watch them and really see it occur. You enjoy the feeling of the fingers on your left hand wanting to move, or possibly the fingers on your right hand. Perhaps, as one hand is moving upward, the other may have an intense desire to press down, or perhaps they will both want to press, or both of them may want to lift. Just keep watching them, keep wondering what is going to happen to that finger that has moved ever so slightly before. Wonder if it is really getting lighter, if you can feel that next finger getting lighter and still lighter. If you think about it and wonder about it, perhaps you can feel the fact that the thumb just moved a little bit. You can feel your breathing getting more and more relaxed, and you can feel your whole body getting more relaxed. You can feel more comfortable as you sit and allow these sensations to get stronger and you can enjoy all the feelings. Just wait and see how long it will be before those fingers lift up, because the lightness that is getting stronger and stronger in those fingers can spread, can radiate throughout all the fingers, the entire hand, the elbow, the arm and shoulder. You can feel yourself relaxing more and more.

Perhaps you might even begin to feel a heaviness in your eyes. The index finger keeps lifting and looks as if it is about ready to lift off the trousers. There's no hurry. There's plenty of time. Or perhaps you might really like to experience the comfort of going into hypnosis more rapidly. The experience is yours. You may utilize it as you please. You can feel your eyes getting more and more tired, you can feel those fingers increasing in their sensitivity. If you keep on wondering when that finger will lift, which one will be the first to leave your trousers, your hands will continue to get lighter and lighter, and you will feel the sensations getting stronger. Perhaps you will feel that ring you are wearing.

Possibly your ring finger feels as though it were attached to a string with a gas-filled balloon at the end of it and you can feel the gas balloon pulling away at the ring, tugging it upward. You might even get the idea of six or eight or ten balloons having been attached to that string. Then, perhaps that string now has twenty or thirty or forty gas balloons attached to it. The hand gets light as the sensation of lightness increases. The hand gets lighter and still lighter and still lighter. You can feel it getting stronger now. You can watch it. Feel your eyes getting more and more relaxed. They are beginning to close; you are breathing more deeply. With every breath you take, that hand continues to get lighter and lighter.

Now, notice how the right hand is pressing down harder, while the left hand continues its lightness and feel yourself getting drowsy and sleepy. Perhaps you might enjoy closing your eyes and you can feel those sensations even more strongly. You can keep your eyes closed and you can continue to sleep deeply and soundly and begin to visualize the lifting of that left hand as it continues to get lighter and lighter. Really begin to feel it lifting, lifting higher, as it gets lighter and still lighter. Enjoy the sensation there. Notice that the middle finger moved a little bit; really see that hand move, even though your eyes are closed, beginning to lift higher as you go deeper and sounder into a very comfortable state of relaxation, into a type of sensation that we describe as sleep, despite the fact that it is really not physiologic sleep. It differs from sleep in that you are not unconscious, as you are in sleep. You are conscious of every sensation that you feel as the hand gets lighter and lighter. You can hear everything I say and you can make yourself aware of anything that you think is important to the situation, or you can make yourself unaware of anything that you feel is unimportant. The important thing is for you to be comfortable, to be relaxed, and to feel that hand getting lighter, still lighter, still lighter. In your mind's eye, really begin to see that hand lifting, lifting, lifting higher and higher. As you continue to think about that and wonder about when that hand will want to lift, wonder whether it might occur as you go back to your seat, or whether you need to wait until tonight or tomorrow. Notice that as I count to three, that you begin to feel more alert, more awake and at the count of three, find that your eyes are open. I want to have you feel very free and comfortable. One—two—three.

SUBJECT

It was nice. I was just beginning to relax when you brought me out.

DOCTOR H (*demonstrating*)

We're sorry we can't spend all the time we'd like to Doctor. You'll have to forgive us. Thank you very much.

ERICKSON

Doctor H thanked the subject for coming forward to assist in the demonstration. Your patient, when he sits down in your dental chair or medical office, is there voluntarily. Appreciation is tremendously important to him—and to you. "You might like to feel all the sensations in your hand." . . . "You might like to . . ." Thus you give the patient adequate opportunity to participate and to participate in his own way. "You might enjoy all those feelings." Certainly you do want the patient to enjoy his own feelings. In fact, that is why he is coming to you. Then, as Doctor H talked, he gave his suggestions, urgently some of the time, then more slowly at other times.

That matter of rhythm is important. At times you want to rush a patient along, then you want to give him time. Doctor A likes to make long pauses—he pauses between words. Doctor H has shown you another way of making pauses, i.e., by urgency and then slowing down, and then again urgency—by a certain rhythm. Doctor H gave the subject a wealth of opportunities. His hand could lift, the fingers could spread, they could move forward or backward. He could press down or could lift up. In other words, he gave the subject an opportunity to respond in any way, and any response would be the one that had been suggested to him. "The feeling will get stronger in your hand, until you can feel it actually lifting." This creates urgency, but postponing the actual lifting as the feeling gets stronger makes it a waiting situation, a very impressive waiting situation.

Then Doctor H introduced the matter of breathing and of going into a trance. Having made that general introduction, he went back to the movement of the hands again, but he had laid the foundation for a general trance state. After suggesting further hand levitation, he went on to the matter of the eyes, introducing another type of behavior. Then he introduced still another type of behavior by the alternation of the hands—one pressing down and one lifting up. You never know whether your patient wants to resist you or cooperate with you. They often have both feelings, so you can have them resist by pressing down with one hand and lifting up with the other. You are meeting their needs in a very comprehensive fashion. Doctor H also said, "You can keep your eyes closed." It was not a command; it was an observation, something that could be accepted by the subject. He then showed how to utilize the slow progress into the trance by explaining the entire trance situation here in terms that the doctor could understand, but in the dental office or the medical office, you would explain in terms that the patient could understand.

Dr. K, I think I'll let you go ahead now.

Direct authoritative hypnosis

Demonstration 7

DOCTOR K (*demonstrating*)

Since we've had several subjects among the males here, how about one of the ladies coming up and offering to be a subject?

Now for teaching purposes I'd like to run briefly over some of the usual questions that the patient is likely to ask about hypnosis. It's always a good idea, before you attempt an induction, to correct some of the popular misconceptions and ideas, so that the patient knows what he is supposed to do, what he is supposed to feel, and how he's supposed to react.

(*to subject*)

Thank you for coming up, Sandra. Now you've been here all morning. Did you know very much about hypnosis, Sandra, before you came here?

SANDRA

No.

DOCTOR K (*demonstrating*)

Well, try to put yourself in the place of one of your patients and see what questions you would ask if you were coming in to see me for the first time.

SANDRA

You mean I'm to . . . ?

DOCTOR K (*demonstrating*)

You're a patient. What questions would you be apt to ask?

SANDRA

Am I going to sleep?

DOCTOR K (*demonstrating*)

Well, you will hear everything that I say and you will also hear extraneous noises, or extraneous sounds, unless I tell you that you won't, or unless you yourself don't want to hear them.

SANDRA

If I don't want to be hypnotized, can you hypnotize me?

DOCTOR K (*demonstrating*)

No, it's difficult to hypnotize an individual against his will.

SANDRA

I can't think of anything else.

DOCTOR K (*demonstrating*)

Well, for a few more, first of all, it's always a good idea to tell the patient that hypnosis is a learning process, that we will start with simple, elementary suggestions. Some of these suggestions are: Close your eyes; start counting to yourself; your legs are getting heavy. I have no way of knowing that you are going to count to yourself, but if you're willing to cooperate on these simple, elementary suggestions, then of course you will be willing to accept the more complicated suggestions that you so ardently desire, assuming that you are a patient coming in for, say, pain relief or for the relief of illness. The sequence is important, doing exactly what you are told to do, or what I suggest that you feel. If you do these, then you are going to be in a complete state of relaxation, which we will call hypnosis. Would you like to ask any questions?

SANDRA

No.

DOCTOR K (*demonstrating*)

All right. Would you mind getting yourself into a nice comfortable position? It's always a good idea to have the patient's neck in a relaxed position. Thus, while we are talking and she is trying to follow suggestions, she need not be bothered by the tension in the neck muscles as a result of sitting upright, because this may be a very distracting influence.

What I'm going to demonstrate is a direct, authoritative technique, which we have found to be especially efficacious with obstetrical patients and in group therapy. The latter is a treatment not ordinarily associated with hypnosis, in which you train your patients as a group. For psychotherapy, it is more advantageous to use the direct, permissive approach which has been demonstrated previously.

(to subject)

Now, Sandra, would you mind looking up at any spot that you'd like to on the ceiling and just concentrate on that spot? Think and feel, if you would like to, that your eyes are going to get very, very heavy; that your lids are going to get very tired as you gaze intently at that one spot on the ceiling. If you'd really like to experience what it's like to go into a nice, deep state of relaxation, you are going to say to yourself, "I really think that my eyes are going to get very, very heavy, very, very tired, getting heavier and heavier all the time." As you look at that spot, you notice that your lids are getting heavier and heavier. They are beginning to droop. Keep your lids open. They are beginning to water. Your eyes are beginning to water, which is a good sign. At the count of three, if you would really like to experience relaxation, it's very easy to go into this deep state of relaxation. All you have to do is just let your eyes close. After you close your eyes, then you will notice that

your state of relaxation—that's good, take a deep breath—
is going to get more profound. One—they are closing still
more, then opening slightly; two—so heavy, but it feels
good; three—shut your eyes tight and with each breath now,
you are going to go deeper relaxed, and deeper relaxed and
(*whispering*) deeper relaxed. That's right.

If you would like to go still deeper, Sandra, all you have
to do is think that your legs are getting heavy, beginning
with your toes. You will feel a sense of numbness or heaviness in your toes, which is going to go up, up your legs.
Your legs are going to be so heavy that you can't uncross
them. As your legs get heavier and heavier, you'll feel yourself going deeper and deeper (*whispered*) relaxed, so pleasant, deeper and deeper relaxed with each breath that you
take. And, if you want to go deeper, then start counting
backward from 100 to 0, and with each count backward, you
will find yourself slipping deeper and deeper into relaxation. It's so soothing, so pleasant. If you want to go very,
very deep, if you would really like the experience of what
it's like to go into a deep and profound state of relaxation,
all you have to do is raise your arm straight toward the ceiling. If you want to go into a deep state of relaxation, spread
your fingers apart.

Now, if you want to go still deeper and even deeper, you
can just raise your hand slowly toward the ceiling. But if
you don't want to go deeper, you don't have to. But if you
want to go deeper, just raise your right arm straight up
toward the ceiling at the count of three. Your head is getting so heavy and you feel so drowsy, deeper and deeper
relaxed. At the count of three, you will raise your right arm
straight toward the ceiling. One—two—breathing deeply,
soundly, deeply relaxed—three—that's right, straighten out

the fingers now. Now your right arm is getting stiff and rigid. Just straighten your fingers out if you want to. If you want to let your arm drop, it will drop like a lump of lead right into your lap, completely relaxed. (*Sandra drops her arm.*) I lift the arm. It falls limply, right into your lap, completely relaxed. That's fine. You're a very good subject. Let this arm, every muscle, every fiber of your body, be completely relaxed, in sound, deep, relaxed sleep. Very good.

When I count to three, you will open your eyes and you will have no headache. You're going to feel wonderful. You'll feel as if you've had a few minutes of actual sleep, but of course you know you weren't asleep, because you've heard every word that I said. At the count of three, you will open your eyes and you will feel fine. I'd like to tell you one more thing, that no one will be able to put you into this deep state of relaxation unless you wish to be put into it and this includes myself or anyone else. You will open your eyes slowly at the count of three. You'll feel wonderful, completely relaxed, full of energy. You never felt better in your entire life. One—two—three.

SANDRA

Very pleasant!

ERICKSON

Comment on Doctor K's technique is rather difficult. First of all, he tried to answer the patient's questions and I think all of us should bear in mind the real importance of answering a patient's questions, trying to answer them so that the patient really feels that you've tried hard to give him an adequate understanding. Then Doctor K stated that he was going to use an authoritative technique. Everybody objects to crass authority asserting itself, so he followed that by the simple statement that the direct authoritative technique works best on obstetrical cases and in group situations. That is correct. In the obstetrical situation, patients can't dispute reality; there *is* something that's going to happen and they're really faced by an authoritative situation. You are merely utilizing a part of their reality situation. In the group situation, everybody knows that the leader spoke to the other fellow, not to him! Thank goodness, he spoke to the other fellow authoritatively. Thus, we can accept authoritative instructions in the group, because we do not need to take them personally and we can make more adequate response. Then, as Doctor K gave his instructions to Sandra, he also talked to the audience. It is hard to distinguish what he was saying to the audience and what he was saying to the subject, but he talked in a casual tone of voice, as if he were really interested in what he said to her. For example, "Your lids'll get *very tired,*" not, "Your lids'll get very tired." And you could really feel that suggestion of "v-e-r-y t-i-r-e-d," which would make the subject look within herself to find out how tired that "v-e-r-y t-i-r-e-d" was.

While very authoritative, Doctor K always introduced his authority by a reasonable question: "If you *really* would like to go into a deeper state of relaxation—if you would *really* like to —just take a deep breath and relax still more." Doctor K gave his suggestion, but he prefaced it with a question and the question in itself was actually a suggestion. "And if you'd *really* like to go *still* deeper, it's *so* easy. Just shut your eyes at the count of three. . . . And if you'd like to go *still* deeper. . . ." All through Doctor K's remarks there was that constant repetition. "If you feel you'd like to go a bit deeper; if you'd like to go *still* deeper; if you'd *really* like to go *still* more deeply; if you would *really* like to go into a very, very, very deep trance. . . ."

Of course, Doctor K offered his suggestions in his own individual way, as we have already discussed. There are many different ways of verbal communication. One can certainly communicate by intonation and Doctor K demonstrated that technique very nicely. "You're going deeper, and deeper, and deeper (whispered) and deeper," giving his suggestions by that type of communication, just as Doctor H showed urgency by a slowing down and a sort of rhythm. Doctor K did it by inflection and intonation. Then there was his method of raising the hand. I don't know whether Doctor K did it intentionally, but if you paid attention to what he was saying, "You could raise your hand," was what he said, instead of "raise your arm," and each time, very correctly, there was that lifting of the hand, but an apparent inability to lift the arm. As you looked at the arm, you could also appreciate another fact and that was that the subject's arm was tremendously heavy. It therefore became necessary for Doctor K to say, "And now your arm will lift *straight* up." There was a definite emphasis upon that word, "straight," even though it was said in a perfectly casual way.

It is important to note the posthypnotic suggestions that he gave in awakening the subject. One gives posthypnotic suggestions simply, unaffectedly, and without any elaborate way of stating them. Doctor K told his subject that she would feel better, wouldn't have any headache, and would have enjoyed her experience. These are simple, straightforward comments. Yet they carry a tremendous amount of weight with the subject.

Coin technique

Demonstration 8

DOCTOR S (*demonstrating*)

> I am not going to talk about hypnotizing people, because I realize how people prefer to hypnotize themselves and it works out a lot better that way. If there is someone who would like to go into the hypnotic state, especially someone who has never experienced it before, I'd like to have such a person first. Later, perhaps, we can get someone who has tried and failed. But for the first subject, we would like one on whom we can demonstrate an ordinary psychophysical technique and show the patient what it is that he needs to do to go into the hypnotic state.
>
> I'm very glad to meet you. Have you experienced hypnosis before, Doctor?

SUBJECT

> No.

DOCTOR S (*demonstrating*)

> Is there any question that you would like to ask me about going into the hypnotic state?

SUBJECT

> There are no psychological after-effects, are there?

DOCTOR S (*demonstrating*)

> No, except in this respect, that you may feel much more comfortable than you do now. That is one psychologic after-effect that you might probably enjoy.

SUBJECT

> Could it relieve this slight pain in the back of my neck?

DOCTOR S (*demonstrating*)

Very likely. As a matter of fact, we could even look forward to accomplishing that and it would probably give you an excellent reason for following my instructions exactly as I give them to you, would it not?

SUBJECT

Yes.

DOCTOR S (*demonstrating*)

All right. Now, all you really have to do is follow instructions and it's quite simple. I'm not going to ask you to do anything that you wouldn't want to do. The only instructions that I am going to give you are ones designed to show you what it is necessary for you to do to enter the hypnotic state. This business about people hypnotizing others is a fallacy. Even here this afternoon, where people were helped into the hypnotic state, I think you were able to see that it was the individual himself who accomplished the fact. Right?

SUBJECT

Yes, but I doubt my ability to do it.

DOCTOR S (*demonstrating*)

Well, let me tell you this. It merely consists of the need to follow a definite program. Are you a dentist or a physician?

SUBJECT

A dentist.

DOCTOR S (*demonstrating*)

You're a dentist. O.K. Now there are many laboratory procedures, which, if followed exactly as the manufacturer specifies, will bring results just as advertised. Right?

SUBJECT

Yes.

DOCTOR S (*demonstrating*)

When you vary this procedure, according to your own ideas, you may get a variation in the result. Right?

SUBJECT

Yes.

DOCTOR S (*demonstrating*)

Later on you may be able to vary this procedure according to your own experience, but right now let me be the manufacturer providing the material with a rigid specification: so much water to so much powder; bake at such-and-such a temperature. O.K.? You follow me exactly as I tell you and that's all there is to it. We'll get the results.

Now this is called a coin technique. Here is the way it works. I place this coin in the palm of your hand. Then I ask you to close your fingers gently over it and turn your hand over. Hold it only tightly enough so that the coin doesn't fall. All right? Now we stretch your hand straight in front of you and you keep it there. You'll find it's rather easy to do that. We let your thumb come right out here. (*Away from the hand.*)

Now here is instruction number one. You keep your eyes fixed on that thumbnail. From now on, until this exercise is over, you keep your eyes glued on that thumbnail until I suggest otherwise. O.K. That's the first instruction.

I'm going to start counting now and, with each count, you will feel changes in the fingers of your hand. While your eyes are visually occupied with this thumb, your mental processes, your mind can pay attention to the feelings in your fingers, to the relation of the fingers to the coin, how the fingers feel against the coin, and the feeling of relaxation and looseness that follows. Now, as I count, allow your fingers to relax and straighten out with each count just a little more, so that eventually the fingers straighten out to a point where the coin drops. When the coin drops, that is a signal for two things to happen: first, for your eyes to close; second, for your whole body to go limp and melt right into the chair, just as if you were going to sleep, into a deep, deep sleep. Sometimes, though, the eyes get so heavy from fixating on that thumbnail, so tired, that they close long before the coin drops. That's fine, if it happens. If your eyes close before the coin drops, let them stay closed. Then you can pay all your attention to the way your fingers feel.

I'm going to repeat these instructions so that you can follow them exactly. You keep your eyes glued on the thumbnail. I count and, as I count, you pay attention to your fingers and feel them straightening out and relaxing. They relax to a point where the coin drops. Then, unless your eyes are already closed, the eyes close and you go deeply relaxed. The thud of the coin on the floor takes you into a deeper relaxed state. If you were in the dental chair right now, I would say, "I will hold my hands over here so that, when you drop your arm, you will not bang it and hurt yourself, so that you don't have to fear to relax." I think that you really understand these instructions quite thoroughly. I'm going to go ahead with the procedures, and you can follow through and do your part.

All right. Pay attention now. One—pay attention to your fingers and feel the nice relaxation that's going to come into them. With each count just a little bit more. Your fingers are relaxing and straightening out. Your eyes are getting heavy and wanting to close. They're starting to blink. Soon they will be closed and that will be perfectly all right. Two —eyes getting heavier, fingers straightening out fine, doing very well. Three—eyes beginning to tear a little bit, eyes beginning to tear, eyelids blinking, fingers straightening out, doing very, very well. You're making an excellent subject. Four—eyes can h-a-r-d-l-y keep open now, fingers straightening out more and more. Five—eyelids closing, fingers opening. It's perfectly all right for you to close your eyes any time you want to. Six—fingers straightening, eyes closing and eyeballs rolling up. You're doing fine. Let them close, if they want to, but keep your mind deeply relaxed. (*Coin falls.*) Breathe slowly and deeply. With each breath that you take, go deeper and deeper relaxed. (*Catches subject's arm as it drops.*)

When I let go of your hand, you'll feel the heaviness of it pulling it down toward your lap and taking you deeper and deeper relaxed as you go, deep, deep asleep. Each time you do this, you do it quicker, you do it better, and you go deeper. Now, for your convenience, so that you may have something to remind you of what it is that is necessary for you to do to re-enter the trance state quickly any time you want to and it is advisable, this will be the signal. Pay attention. A pressure on the right shoulder by anyone with whom you want to work—and only when you want this— can be a sleep signal or a relax signal. A pressure on the left shoulder can be a waking signal. Is that agreeable with you? Only when and if you desire. If you like, we will practice those signals so that you can see that you can do it quicker and deeper every time.

At the appropriate signal you will respond appropriately. This is the sleep signal. This is the waking signal. The only difference in response is this. To this (right shoulder) you respond quickly. When you feel it, you can respond quickly and go deeply to sleep. It isn't the signal that makes you go to sleep, you know. It merely reminds you of what it is that you have to do to re-enter the trance state. To this (left shoulder) you respond slowly, so that you always awaken feeling refreshed, alert, sharp, wonderful, and without a headache. Is that agreeable to you?

Let's practice these signals. Now wasn't it really easy to relax? Wasn't it now? So-o-o nice, so-o-o comfortable, and so-o-o easy to relax, deep, deep relaxed. It's easy to wake up any time you want. (*Presses subject's left shoulder to awaken him.*) I appreciate your being such a good subject, Doctor. Thank you very much.

Doctor, you have been an excellent subject and you will find that you can do this any time you wish. It's such a wonderful thing to be able to relax.

SUBJECT

I do feel very relaxed. Now I'm trying to test my neck.

DOCTOR S (*demonstrating*)

How does your neck feel?

SUBJECT

Now, it's all right.

DOCTOR S (*demonstrating*)

It *is* all right, isn't it?

SUBJECT

Yes.

DOCTOR S (*demonstrating*)

Yes, it's easy to relax and so very comfortable. You can hardly hold your head up; that's how relaxed your neck muscles are. The tensions that produce pain are leaving your neck. You can feel it gradually becoming more and more comfortable. As you become completely comfortable in every respect, just open your eyes and feel wide awake and alert. (*Thirteen-second pause.*)

SUBJECT

> I guess my pain is better. Thank you for taking so long to make me feel well.

DOCTOR S (*demonstrating*)

> You've made an excellent subject, Doctor.

ERICKSON

> You might even relax as you sit down in the chair, Doctor. For just a few minutes, sit down in the chair and let the pain get looser. Now I'm going to discuss Dr. S's technique. While I'm discussing it, having experienced it, Doctor, you will remember infinitely better than the others, because you experienced it. They merely saw.

ERICKSON

Very little discussion is needed for this technique since it was described in such detail in the demonstration. There was evident a freedom and willingness almost to argue with the patient, almost to put him on one side of the fence in the argument and then, making the point of the argument not as an argument, but merely as a matter of understanding what the situation was. The understanding was that certain things could be done by the subject, that the subject could go into a state of relaxation. I think all of you saw the trembling of the thumb and had some realization of the amount of tension that was there. Yet, in spite of all that tension, he did experience the relaxation. Then, the other thing is this: While I signaled for you not to laugh, not to create a disturbance, actually those of us sitting up here were much, much more aware of the disturbance than the patient was. I made a point of signaling you to stop your laughing, to impress on you that there was noise, then to call your attention to the fact that the subject did a most thoroughly competent job of ignoring you. He was much more interested in his own feelings within himself, in his own experience, than he was in what was occurring outside him.

This is a technique that dentists seem to prefer, but which is applicable in all medical areas. It is wiser not to rely on any one technique, however. You should learn a variety of techniques to use in working with your patients.

Group "experiment" with previously unsuccessful subjects

Demonstration 9

DOCTOR S (*demonstrating*)

Many people have tried to go into a trance with someone else and have failed. Many resist hypnosis because they have a subconscious fear that their privacy may be invaded. Some worry about being required to tell something they do not want to tell. Others cannot accept the idea of someone having a "power" over them. I have stopped trying to hypnotize these people, and because I know that they would probably very much like to go into the hypnotic state, if they could be sure that they were doing it by themselves, I arrange for them to direct their own hypnosis.

In exploring that thought, we conducted an experiment with a dental psychosomatic group. We asked six dentists to come up. We made the qualifications that they all be dentists, who use hypnosis successfully in their practices, and that they all be dentists on whom an unsuccessful attempt at hypnosis had been made. Each member of this group went into deep trance, with all developing anesthesia, transferring it to the jaw and maintaining it posthypnotically. We have carried out this experiment in the seminars several times since and I would like to demonstrate that experiment at this time.

I would like six volunteers to come up to the platform now. These are the conditions: That you all use hypnosis successfully on your patients, but that attempts made to hypnotize you have failed; that you come up now with the idea of having me show you what to do, rather than showing me that I can't hypnotize you. I admit that I cannot accomplish that, *but* I can show you what it is that you have to do.

Good morning, gentlemen. Which of you are dentists and which are physicians? Three of each. Now it will be interesting to watch the comparative responses of the physicians and the dentists as this experiment takes place.

All of you use hypnosis? Then you really know what it is that you have to do. You ask your patients to do certain things and actually you can do those very same things yourselves. But each of you has failed to go into hypnosis when someone has tried to lead you into the hypnotic state. Is that correct? Now, I suggest to you that the reason was probably on a subconscious level and you can go into hypnosis, but you just didn't like the idea of someone pushing you there. If you will follow my instructions, I will give you a different routine to follow. You need not analyze it consciously. It is better if you just pay attention effortlessly without trying to analyze the technique. If you follow my instructions and go into hypnosis, you will remember the technique better by not trying to remember it. Now, if you just go along with what I say, I will try to guide you.

So that you need not be distracted by what the others are doing and by what the audience is doing, let's start with an eye-closed technique. Most techniques start with the eyes open. Now, close your eyes. Make yourselves comfortable, as comfortable as you can, feet flat on the floor and hands on your lap, the palms of your hands right on your legs above the knees.

I want you to pay attention and follow instructions, just as I give them to you. You'll find yourself slipping into a trance, as you move from one series of ideomotor activity and ideosensory activity to another.

I want you to press down on your right knee, very firmly, so hard that you will eventually be able to push your foot through the floor. Now you know and I know that you are not going to push your foot through the floor, but when I come and try to lift your hand up from your leg, I should be unable to do so. If I can do so, you're not pushing hard enough.

I'm going to try here, Doctor. That's fine. You keep that rigidity and push and maintain it. Do it right along until I ask you not to. . . . That's fine. Now a little harder, Doctor. That's it. Now keep that up. Pay no attention to anyone but yourself. That's it. A little harder, Doctor. Fine.

Now pay attention. You keep that pressure up until I count to three. At the count of three, suddenly let go of that pressure and, as you let go, you'll have a feeling of lightness in your hand and the hand will start to slide forward on your leg. As it slides forward, it straightens at the elbow. As it straightens at the elbow, it leaves your leg altogether, then starts to rise higher and higher, higher and higher, until it reaches a point parallel to the floor at shoulder height, then it stops. So, at the count of three, you just let go, the hand slides forward, and so on. One—two—three. Let go that tension. The hand is sliding forward on your leg. As it slides, it bends at the elbow. That's fine. As it bends at the elbow it goes up, up, up, lifting and lifting and the elbow straightens. It is as if there were a rope tied around the wrist pulling it up, up, up, lifting, lifting, lifting until it reaches a point parallel to the floor at shoulder height. At that point it neither moves up nor down nor sideways. There, there, very, very fine. Just keep that up. Doing fine. Very, very good. Lifting, lifting, as though there were a rope tied around the wrist.

Now let that arm get stiff and rigid from the shoulder, through the elbow, through the wrist and through your finger tips, as if I had inserted a bar right through the long bones into the fingers, so that you can't bend your arm, or your wrist, or your elbow, or any joint at any time. . . . That's it. Stiff and rigid. Maintain that stiffness and rigidity. Very good.

Now pay attention to the back of your arm as you keep it stiff and rigid. Just imagine that I placed a couple of shopping bags there. Each bag has about twenty pounds of groceries. You realize and feel the weight of it and that weight keeps pushing your stiff and rigid arm back to where it was before, pushing your leg through the floor. You try to keep it there, but soon the weight becomes too much for you; the weight pushes your arm downward, downward, getting heavier and heavier all the time. That forty pounds seems like fifty now, and that fifty like sixty. You try to hold it up, but soon give up the idea of trying and let your stiff and rigid arm be pushed down to your knee where it stays stiff and rigid. Now, in addition to the pressure that you put on your knee, you will also have the weight of the shopping bags, heavy, heavy, heavy. That's fine. Keep it up. That's good. Push hard there, harder and harder. Push, push, back where it was before. Then, if I try to take your hand off again, I will be unable to do so. Pushing, pushing down against your leg, down, down, down.

This time pay attention and, at the count of three, let go quickly and melt into the chair, as quickly as you would pull the trigger on a gun, as quickly as a stretched-out rubber band collapses when it's let go. So, melt into your chair and go deeply relaxed, as if you were going deep asleep. At the count of three, let go and go deeply relaxed. One—two—three. Deep, deep, deep relaxed. Breathe slowly and deeply. With each breath that you take, you go deeper, deeper, d-e-e-p-e-r relaxed. Now you are breathing comfortably, enjoying yourselves and, with every breath that you take, you go deeper relaxed. Your eyes are closed and you can keep them closed until I ask you to open them. When I ask you to open them, you will have no difficulty doing so. You will open them, feeling wide awake, refreshed, relaxed, alert, having enjoyed the entire situation, but until I ask you to open them, you will please keep them closed. Now I'd like an acknowledgment from you that you will keep them closed until I ask you to open them. You may nod your heads. That's fine, that's fine. Also, in order that you may learn more about this situation, you are to follow my instructions as I give them immediately, exactly, precisely as I give them. I will not ask you to do anything that you wouldn't want to do.

All right now, pay attention. Just pay atention now to your right hand, if you will. Imagine that I have given you an injection of procaine all around the wrist, one of these newer materials like Xyclocaine which acts rapidly, thoroughly, deeply, and profoundly. You will begin to feel the effects, the onset of anesthetic as if it were a real chemical anesthetic and you know how those things react in regard to displacement of tissues and pressures, etc. As soon as you begin to feel the slightest change between your right hand and your left hand, indicate that by raising the right index finger as a signal to me that you are noticing the change. That's fine. Keep that finger up there, if you will. Fine. Good. It continues to get deeper and more profound and, when I get to the count of five, there will be a deep and profound anesthesia in that right hand, as deep as it needs to be. At the same time, the left hand will become hypersensitive. One —right hand becoming more and more numb. Two—still more and more profoundly anesthetic; at the count of five, deeply numb and anesthetic. Three—four—five—that right hand is completely numb and anesthetic, but that left hand is hypersensitive now.

I have an instrument here with which I'm going to test these hands. When I test the left hand, it will seem to you that I'm jabbing it with an ice pick and you will withdraw and show that it is a painful stimulus, but with the right hand, the harder I push, the more numb it gets. The sensation will be as that of pressure from the eraser part of a lead pencil.

DOCTOR S (*to subject 1*)

Now here, Doctor, pay attention. Here comes that ice pick in that left hand and you just don't like it. But the right hand, the harder I push, the more numb it can get. You feel pressure but no discomfort. The harder I push, the number it can get; go deeper and deeper relaxed. Obviously there is a difference in the response, because that left one is sensitive, but with the right hand, the harder I push, the more numb it gets. You made a very, very good patient, Doctor. You can keep that numbness there, even after you are wide awake. Allow nothing to let it go, except a certain cue word. Is that O.K.? Would it be O.K. with you if that cue word were Shreveport? Allow nothing to let the anesthesia go out of that right hand except my enunciation of the word Shreveport.

(*To subject 2*)

Now I'm coming to you, the next subject, and I'm going to

test that left hand with the ice pick and you will withdraw it. You don't like it at all, do you? But the right hand, the harder I push, the more numb it can get. Are you willing to keep those feelings posthypnotically, Doctor T, until I say the key word Shreveport? Fine.

(To subject 3)

And next, the doctor here—Let's see how you react. First, I'm going to jab that ice pick into your left hand. You didn't like that either, did you? But the right hand is different. The harder I push, the more numb it can get. You heard the suggestion I gave the other two doctors. Would you like to have that, too, Doctor? O.K. Keep that posthypnotic feeling until the release with the same cue word.

(To subject 4)

I'm coming to you next, Doctor. Pay attention to that ice pick in your left hand. So far, everybody's responded perfectly. Here's that ice pick coming into your left hand, but in the right hand you don't care. The harder I push, the more numb it can get. Is there anybody doubting that I am pushing very hard? Very, very good. Would you be willing to keep that in your hand posthypnotically and allow the same suggestion to apply to you? Fine. The word Shreveport, when I utter it, can allow the anesthesia to leave.

(To subject 5)

And you, Doctor, I want to test your left hand with this ice pick. Pay attention. You don't like it, do you? You just don't care for it at all, but in your right hand, the harder I push, the more numb it gets. You, too, can retain a posthypnotic anesthesia, with the same key word releasing it.

(To subject 6)

Doctor, pay attention in the left hand to the jab with the ice pick. But see, in the right hand, you get more numb as I push harder. Is it O.K. with you to retain the same anesthesia until I utter the same key word?

(*to audience*)

All these people have previously failed to go into hypnosis because people wanted to hypnotize them. It is much easier to go into hypnosis if you know what to do and you do it yourself.

Now, gentlemen, in a few minutes I am going to count to three. When I count to three, you will be wide awake, sharp and alert, normal in every respect, able to maintain that anesthesia in your right hand, allowing nothing to let it go except the word Shreveport, when I enunciate it or when another member of the panel does so. Is that agreeable with you, gentlemen? Fine. One —two—three.

(*to subject 1*)

Doctor, I'd like to test this hand over here to see the response. Is there a difference between one hand and the other?

SUBJECT 1

It's hard to tell.

DOCTOR S (*demonstrating*)

Well, look what's happening to your hand over there. Is that normal? You think about that for a while.

(*to subject 2*)

Doctor, do you feel a difference?

SUBJECT 2

I sure do.

DOCTOR S (*demonstrating*)

You certainly do. (*To subject 3.*) Do you feel a difference, Doctor? You don't believe you do. (*To subject 4.*) Do you feel a difference, Doctor? In the unanesthetized hand?

SUBJECT 4

Very much.

DOCTOR S (*demonstrating*)

Would you say I'm applying equal amounts of pressure? Probably even harder on the right hand than on the left? Isn't that right? (*To subject 5.*) Do you feel any difference? You think you do? Fine.

SUBJECT 5

I didn't feel it as much before as I do now.

DOCTOR S (*demonstrating*)

Yes, that's quite possible.

(*To subject 6*)

Doctor, will you pay attention? Is there a difference between one hand and the other?

SUBJECT 6

Now the right is worse.

DOCTOR S (*demonstrating*)

I would like you gentlemen to consider something that might at first seem silly. Do you think the geographical location of this area has anything to do with what happens? Do you think that if you were in Chicago, this same experiment could have been repeated? Do you think that if I were to come to Shreveport one year from now this thing would happen again? It's possible. Now let's see what happened over here. They feel identical now? O.K.

SUBJECT 6

It may be wishful thinking.

DOCTOR S (*demonstrating*)

It's still more numb on the right? Even though it's in Shreveport, it's still numb? O.K., you can have the privilege of keeping it. How about you, Doctor? Do you want to come to Chicago or do you want to let it go to Shreveport again? It's already gone, isn't it? It tickles now.

ERICKSON

I think it was possible for each of you to follow the entire procedure. You saw the use of an authoritative technique, but it was presented as a participation on the part of the subject with the operator and it merely called for the willingness of the person to participate fully. I think all of you realize that the subjects accomplished a great deal, possibly more than they themselves realize. You noticed some of the arm movements and the catalepsy that was actually demonstrated.

Now I'll call on Doctor C.

"Expectancy" technique

Demonstration 10

DOCTOR C (*demonstrating*)

May I have a volunteer? Have you tried hypnosis yourself, Doctor?

SUBJECT

Very limited.

DOCTOR C (*demonstrating*)

What sort of effects do you feel that you have had? That is, how easily do you think you could go into a deep state of hypnosis without knowing it? In fact, do you think you *could* go into a deep state of hypnosis without knowing it?

SUBJECT

Possibly.

DOCTOR C (*demonstrating*)

Actually, you have probably been in a deep state of hypnosis many times in your life. . . . I have in mind trying a variety of testing techniques here. I would like to have you watch my thumb and index finger and, as they go together, you may or may not find yourself drifting off into a very deep, relaxed state. . . . It may turn out that you are feeling very relaxed; you feel extremely contented. . . . (*Reversal of technique when patient displays resistance.*) Or you may find that things become much clearer . . . your perception is heightened . . . your awareness is much, much greater than usual . . . you may have awareness of various things, but possibly not of others. Now, without looking, I would like to have you imagine something about your right hand, something that may or may not happen. At the same time, your perception of the audience noise can become very, very complete. How does that feel?

SUBJECT

It feels very light.

DOCTOR C (*demonstrating*)

Now if you feel that you can go deeper into a state of hypnosis, you will find that your right arm lifts. If you feel that you are as deep as you can conveniently go, the arm will drop. This may happen very suddenly or very slowly. While we are waiting for it to happen, what are your own subjective impressions?

SUBJECT

I am waiting for something to happen, too. . . . I feel my left hand starting to get light now. (*Right hand has already lifted.*)

DOCTOR C (*demonstrating*)

And I might add, too, beginning to lift. Now, why, why do you suppose that your left hand decided to lift?

SUBJECT

I don't know.

DOCTOR C (*demonstrating*).

Now, at whatever time you are basically convinced of the reality of the phenomena—that you are hypnotized—one or the other of your hands will drop. It might happen right off, or there may be a delay. . . . The right hand is jerking up and down noticeably now, showing a sense of struggle at the moment. The right arm is trying to go higher. Doctor, since your eyes are shut, can you tell me just about where the hands are?

SUBJECT

I think the right is just about level with my nose and the left is possibly six or eight inches below that. (*This was about correct.*)

DOCTOR C (*demonstrating*)

Deep, deep . . . just relax completely now, completely, completely . . . deeper and deeper . . . and, as you go deeper, the arms will drop and you can relax . . . relax and not have to notice. Gradually go deeper, still deeper, much deeper than you have ever thought you could go. In the future, you can go much deeper than this. The depth, the mark of going deeper, the conviction of depth, are all within your own control and are evidenced to you and to us by the movements of your arms and your hands . . . just relax, deeper and deeper . . . relax. Now, I wonder if you would open your eyes and look around and see how the room looks. Is there anything strange?

SUBJECT

There *is* something strange. It is hard for me to determine what it is. My hands are still not relaxed. They don't seem to want to drop.

DOCTOR C (*demonstrating*)

I think they can relax now. Is that better?

SUBJECT

Yes, I would like to go to sleep.

DOCTOR C (*demonstrating*)

Do you feel you have been asleep? Were you on the verge of it when your head started to nod? What happened?

SUBJECT

I just felt that my head was going down on my chest and I was about to go to sleep.

DOCTOR C (*demonstrating*)

Did I interrupt, or what?

SUBJECT

No, I don't believe that you did, but I noticed my arms were coming down again and I think you told me I would awaken when my hands touched my legs. (*Actual instruction was: "If you feel that you are as deep as you can conveniently go, the arm will drop." Instructions applied to the right hand only; no instructions were given about the left hand.*)

DOCTOR C (*demonstrating*)

I don't know if I told you that, but I know I had that thought earlier. Do you feel wide awake now?

SUBJECT

No.

DOCTOR C (*demonstrating*)

Do you want to feel wide awake?

SUBJECT

Not particularly.

DOCTOR C (*demonstrating*)

Shall we leave it that way? Thank you very much.

ERICKSON

It's a nice feeling, isn't it, Doctor? You can keep it as long as you wish. Now one of the purposes of the technique that you have just observed was to rid your minds of a lot of misconceptions. Are you really sure that you need to have a technique in which you tell a patient, "Now I want you to get tired and sleepy, and more and more tired, and more and more sleepy"? Or can you sit down with a minimum of words, a minimum of ideas, actually look at your patient, and really expect him to experience a hypnotic trance?

Your manner and your attitude, the simplicity of the thoughts you offer to your patient are highly essential. You saw how the demonstrating doctor, with a very few ideas, a very few thoughts, just thought-provoking questions and an attitude of willingness, led his subject into a trance. He was thoughtful; he was considerate; he was interested; and he really addressed his remarks to the patient. He didn't have a tremendous wealth of ideas about saying this and that. He expected catalepsy. He expected every phenomenon that the patient was interested in experiencing. That is one of the important attitudes to remember in using hypnosis. A good hypnotist proceeds with simple expression. He does not sit down and wonder, "Is the subject really going to get tired? Is he really going to close his eyes? Is his arm actually going to lift?" The demonstration doctor did not entertain these negative ideas. He was willing to wait. And the subject felt the induced state, liked it so much that he wanted it to continue.

Hypnosis with previously unsuccessful subject

Demonstration 11

DOCTOR S (*demonstrating*)

Those of you who have attended seminars on hypnosis before are familiar with many ideas on the interreaction between the doctor and his patient in hypnosis, but for the benefit of those who have not, I would like to preface my demonstration with just a few remarks.

Many persons fail to enter into hypnosis during their initial attempt for a variety of reasons: They may not be ready to be hypnotized, or they may have doubts about the situation. These same persons would readily go into hypnosis, however, if they could resolve their fears or doubts and if they knew that they could terminate the situation any time they wished. I would like, at this point, to demonstrate a technique.

If there is someone here who has previously failed to enter hypnosis, I will undertake to show that individual what he has to do to go into hypnosis quickly, readily, with an economy of time and motion. If such a person will seat himself at my side here, we will demonstrate a technique that is calculated to be effective, even with resistant people.

(*to subject*)

Thank you, Doctor. You have used hypnosis quite a bit?

SUBJECT

Yes.

DOCTOR S (*demonstrating*)

Have you ever been in a trance state?

SUBJECT

No.

DOCTOR S (*demonstrating*)

Have you ever attempted going into it?

SUBJECT

Yes.

DOCTOR S (*demonstrating*)

With what results? Not very successful? Now, one of the things that is necessary, you know from your own experience, is really getting the patient ready to be hypnotized. A readiness to be hypnotized is most important. Fears or doubts are factors that deter a patient's readiness. Of course, you know that it is not you who produce the hypnosis in the patient. You are only taking advantage of your knowledge of what it is that the patient can do and is willing to do to help him go into hypnosis. Now, all you have to do here is to relax and follow my instructions.

For a professional person—a physician, a dentist—it is often difficult to go into hypnosis because he is trying to do two things that are mutually incompatible: he is trying to learn responses that will enable him to go into the hypnotic state and, at the same time, be active mentally to the point where he can recall those responses, so that he can use them as a hypnotist. Now those two aims are mutually exclusive. You have to narrow your sensory input to go into hypnosis, to widen your cerebral activity when you try to recall. You will be more efficient in recall and learning, if you just go into it without trying. If you try to recall while you're learning to be a hypnotic subject, you fail in both. Well, do you think you are now ready to follow instructions, with a form of procedure such as you have successfully tried on others? Will you readily do so?

SUBJECT

I think so.

DOCTOR S (*demonstrating*)

Now, just to demonstrate this procedure, we will refer to it as the Coin Technique. Have you seen it demonstrated?

SUBJECT

Yes.

DOCTOR S (*demonstrating*)

So you know that it works with even resistant patients. Have you ever tried it?

SUBJECT

Yes.

DOCTOR S (*demonstrating*)

Successfully?

SUBJECT

Yes.

DOCTOR S (*demonstrating*)

All right. Now don't anticipate. Just try to be passive and wait for my instructions. Let the results come about without any apparent effort and you will find that it will be relatively easy. I am going to pretend that you are a naïve patient who has never heard of hypnosis, doesn't know what hypnosis is all about. All you have to do is to follow my instructions and, as you follow them, you will find it easy to go into a sleeplike state, but you will not be asleep. You will be conscious of a large variety of things, just as you are in sleep. You know, and you are aware, and you can hear. So, let us use a coin. (*There then followed the statement as it appears on page 155.*)

That is the procedure, Doctor, by which you can help

others and, by repetition, help yourself. Slowly now, at your own discretion and in the way that you find most convenient and comfortable, arouse, feeling wide awake, alert, and with a knowledge that you have really gone deeper than you have before and that you enjoyed the situation. You have been most cooperative, a good subject. Thank you. What do you think about it?

SUBJECT

I was very comfortable.

DOCTOR S (*demonstrating*)

If your patients would tell you that their subjective feelings were the same that you felt, would you have estimated that they were hypnotized?

SUBJECT

I think so.

DOCTOR S (*demonstrating*)

At what stage?

SUBJECT

A little deeper than light.

DOCTOR S (*demonstrating*)

I think that is about right. Thank you.

ERICKSON

I want to point out the contrast between the technique we have just observed and that of the previous demonstration. Doctor C's approach was one of quiet and relatively infrequent suggestions of ideas. Doctor S used a great many more words. We want to demonstrate techniques that illustrate every possible variety, from the much elaborated technique to the exceedingly indirect and nonverbal technique, for all of you must learn the technique that best suits your own personality and the techniques that best fit the individual patients you will encounter.

Doctor S offered ideas to the patient, ideas that the patient could sense, ideas in which he could participate and to which he could respond on a motor level. Doctor C wanted motor response, too, but also simultaneous intellectual and internal response on the subjective level. Doctor S had had his subject realizing his behavior externally.

Indirect hypnosis

Frequently, in the practice of medicine, a situation may arise wherein the doctor, in the therapeutic situation, realizes the need to produce hypnosis in an individual who is not knowingly the patient. One method through which this can be accomplished is to use that individual as an aide in producing a trance state in the person he believes is the patient.

To demonstrate this, two doctors have consented to cooperate. For the sake of clarity, I shall refer to them as Friend and Patient.

This is the situation. Friend, sitting in the chair, has come to my office with Patient. Patient may be a child with enuresis, with a behavior problem, a nail-biter, a thumb-sucker, etc. In the opinion of the doctor, this child—or adult—requires therapy, but the friend or relative involved also needs help. Therefore, while my conversation with Patient is taking place, my purpose will be to induce a trance in Friend, or in both.

Now, Patient, your friend here has brought you to see me. We have to discuss many things and what I would like you to do is to be willing to go into a trance state to try to alleviate or remove the condition of which you complain. Friend has shown much interest in you. He has brought you here. He has recommended that you come here for treatment. He has done this because he is intensely interested in you. Therefore, perhaps Friend would be willing to help me teach you how to go into the trance state. If he would like to help me, he can, of course, do so by having you watch him. He knows you very, very well; he probably understands certain things about you and can help you go into this trance state. You might get some hints or some help from just watching Friend. Despite the fact that I shall be talking to him, you can hear me perfectly plainly and you can watch him. As you watch him very, very carefully, see if perhaps you can receive from him some little hints of things that could be done.

Friend, you'd be willing to help by doing anything that you think may be helpful to Patient. Patient, you can stare very intently into Friend's eyes, if you like; you may find there a means of concentration. You may find that you can start to see yourself relaxing. Really relax yourself more and more and Friend can help you in any way he thinks may be advisable or helpful to you. You can watch him very, very carefully. You can seat yourself comfortably in the chair. You can move the chair around. You can allow your hands to rest on your thighs and Friend can cooperate in any way he thinks would be of help to you.

As you sit there looking at Friend, you will begin to have a feeling of drowsiness, a feeling of relaxation coming over your body. Watch Friend very, very carefully for little hints. Perhaps he can demonstrate some of these things to you, to give you a clear idea of what it is I am speaking of, because he knows you very, very well and he knows in what manner you will best be able to respond. You can allow your hands to rest on your thighs just exactly as you are doing. It might be interesting as you are doing that, Patient, to get all the help you can from Friend, to feel the sensations in your fingers and in your hands, feel every sensation regardless of what it might be, feel the texture of your trousers as your fingers rest against them, feel the warmth of your skin coming through, feel the wrinkles in the trousers, feel the sensation of every finger of your hand, feel the tingling sensations as they occur. Feel the motion of the left thumb as it just moved, feel it getting lighter perhaps, or maybe heavier; feel the right hand, feel every little sensation, and let those hands move as they please. Perhaps one of them may get light, or it may get heavy. It may get light and start to raise up slowly. You may feel very relaxed and drowsy if this occurs. You may even feel a heaviness in your eyelids. Your eyes may feel like blinking and closing. If they do, you may allow them to close. You may close them very tightly and relax and be very soundly and profoundly in a deep trance state.

Friend can cooperate by showing exactly how these things are done. You can allow yourself, Patient, to go deeper and sounder asleep. You can notice and feel, even though your eyes are closed, the fact that Friend can cooperate with you. You can feel that lightness getting more and more intense in your left hand, or in your right hand, or in both your hands. You can feel the sensation of one of those hands beginning to rise in the air. It looks as if it may be the right hand. That right hand begins to get lighter now, still lighter, Patient, and still lighter. It begins to rise slowly up in the air, higher and higher. The fingers will start curling, the index finger, then the rest of the fingers, then the hand will leave your thigh, continuing to go still higher, and still higher, as you go deeper and sounder and more profoundly into this deep state of relaxation.

The hand continues to rise up higher and still higher. That feeling of lightness and the pleasantness of relaxation can be felt. You can feel the intensely interesting sensation of hand levitation. Feel those hands (*inclusion of Friend without using names, which would interfere by causing recognition that he, too, is going into a trance*) beginning to rise up higher, still higher, constantly going up higher and higher into the air without your perhaps even having a knowledge of the fact. But they will continue to go because you can now begin to concentrate on relaxing deeper and sounder, letting those hands continue to go up still higher, still higher, constantly going upward, upward, getting lighter and lighter, as they continue to rise up higher into the air, continuing to rise up, in your own time, in your own fashion.

You can take as much time as you like with this; you can allow yourself to go into a very, very deep trance, timing it in accordance with the rate of speed of those hands. You can let those hands go up very, very slowly, or you can let those hands go up very, very rapidly. The time you take is actually unimportant. Take your time, there's plenty of time. Let those hands continue to go up higher, higher, as your trance deepens and gets still more deep. The hands continue to rise up. They keep on going higher, still higher, as your trance state develops deeply and more profoundly. You can begin to sense the feeling of relaxation becoming more and more profound. You can feel very, very comfortable.

It might be interesting as those hands go up to think about the possibility of a very nice trip. It could perhaps be a boat cruise. You can feel yourself sitting in the boat, watching the gentle waves as they splash against the sides of the boat. You can feel yourself getting more relaxed as the hands go up. I would like to suggest to you that you do not allow your hand to touch your face until you are ready to go into a deep trance state. At that point, you may allow the hands or one hand or finger to touch your face and think about that boat trip again. Think about how serene the situation appears, how nice it is to sit out there in the sunshine, watching the water and the waves bounce up against the boat. You can continue to sleep deeply and soundly all the while, allowing those hands to continue to go up higher and higher, until finally they will touch your face and you will go into a very deep state of relaxation.

Patient, you're going along very well. It was kind of Friend to come here with you and help demonstrate this technique, both to this group and to you, so that you could use his willingness to help you to allow yourself to go deeper and sounder into this trance state as you are doing. The hands may continue to keep on rising. They will go higher and higher, not touching your face until you are ready to go into a very, very deep state of relaxation. They get still lighter, then the forearms and the arms and the shoulders relax. That's right, higher and higher until they rest on your face. You can enjoy this experience.

(*Directed to both.*) You can use the ability you have learned here to further your aims, to allow you to understand the learning process, to allow it to be absorbed and retained and to be useful to you when the situation arises. When those hands touch your face, you can feel a tremendous satisfaction and know that you've done an excellent job, then allow yourself to awaken, feeling refreshed and relaxed in every way.

Thank you very much, both of you, for coming up.

Now, for an application of this demonstration: In your office, you need merely do the following: Include the friend or relative in whom you want to induce the trance state indirectly without his awareness of that fact. Include him in your conversation so that he becomes a part of the situation. Encourage in him a feeling of willingness to cooperate for the interest or benefit of his son, daughter, father, mother, friend—the patient. When you start to talk about "you" to the patient, that "you" includes both subjects. You'll get a reaction in both of them, because the "you" now becomes the entire therapeutic situation and you have developed the therapeutic situation surrounding the two subjects. Actually, with this type of indirect technique, with the indirect suggestions that you are apparently giving to the child, but which will also be accepted by the parents, you can do a tremendous amount of re-education in the area of child training.

QUESTION

After you have got them both hypnotized and want to do therapy on one, would you dismiss the other?

ANSWER

You mean at subsequent sessions, or at the same session?

QUESTION

At the same time. You are going to do therapy on one of them, aren't you?

ANSWER

Yes. Actually, the suggested situation was: A mother or father brings the child in for therapy, but both require therapy; you really treat them both.

QUESTION

Suppose you want to talk to only one?

ANSWER

In that case you say, "Sonny, I would like you just to continue to sit there. I would like to speak to your mother for a few moments." Then, you've excluded him, and you speak to the mother. "Thank you, mother, for listening to me. Now I'd like to speak to your son for a few moments." Merely by mentioning that, she will then be excluded. Or, "Mother, you can listen to me while I tell your son some of these things, and perhaps as the days and the weeks go by, you will be able to help him to understand them. Perhaps in some way, you will be able to contribute to his education." You are then including her in the situation again and extending your suggestions to the two of them.

QUESTION

Which subject do you choose, child or mother, for the most concentrated induction effort?

ANSWER

It makes no difference which one you select. By including the other, you can produce a trance state in both. This is an indirect method that I was trying to demonstrate. You hypnotize the mother without her knowing that you're going to induce a trance state in her. It would be very difficult for a psychiatrist or a general practitioner to tell the mother, "Now look, I understand that you have a problem with this child, but it's not his fault. It's your fault. You're the one who needs the treatment." By inducing the trance state in her while she's sitting there believing that what you are doing is treating the child, you are indirectly making the suggestion to her.

QUESTION

Would you condition a mother to therapy while hypnotized?

ANSWER

Oh, yes, you can stimulate a great deal of motivation for further therapy on the part of the mother.

QUESTION

Do you continue to use the indirect technique of trance induction at subsequent sessions?

ANSWER

It would again depend on the situation. If the mother decides at the end of the session, "You know, Doctor, I felt kind of relaxed there, and I—I think that maybe you ought to talk to me that way again," then you agree. Actually, once you've induced hypnosis, it is no longer necessary to go through the same induction procedure. You can merely have them sit down and go to sleep without more than a moment's time.

Trance deepening

Demonstration 12

ERICKSON

I want now to demonstrate a technique that can be used in deepening trances. Is Doctor L here? Do you mind assisting me, Doctor, while I'm talking.

Will you step up here, please? Just face the audience.

Now, you're well aware of the fact that Doctor L is alert and that he certainly does not know what is going to come next. Isn't that right, Doctor?

SUBJECT

It certainly is.

ERICKSON

This is a rather simple technique. It is also a technique that you can use with many subjects.

Now listen to me, Doctor. You can look at me. You've been in a trance before and you know it. You're an excellent subject. I'm going to suggest something to you. You can go to sleep very easily, go into the trance just by fixing your attention. I think the best way for you to learn to do it and to demonstrate it for the audience is this: As you stand there, I am going to count from one to twenty. I can count from one to twenty by ones or twos, fours, fives, or tens. By the time I count to twenty, you will be asleep. When I've reached five, you'll be a quarter of the way asleep. When I reach ten, you'll be halfway asleep. When I reach fifteen, you will be three quarters of the way asleep. And when I reach twenty, you will be fully asleep. You'll take a deep breath and go way, sound asleep. Will you sit down, please?

Now look at the audience and be aware of them, because I'm going to start counting. 1, 2, 3, 4, 5, 6, 7, 8, 9, 10—half asleep—11, 12, 13, 14, 15,—and three-quarters asleep—16, 17, 18, 19, 20. Take a deep breath and go deep, sound asleep, way deep, sound asleep, deep and sound asleep. Keep on sleeping and really enjoying it.

I want you to sleep what seems to be a very, very long time, and you'll feel rested and comfortable, as if you had slept for eight hours, then I'm going to awaken you. I can count backward, from 20 to 1, and then you'll be awake. At 15 you'll be one-quarter awake; at 10, you'll be one-half awake; at 5 you'll be three-quarters awake, and at 1 you'll be fully awake. All right now, I'm going to count backward. 20, 19, 18, 17, 16, 15—one-quarter awake—13, 12, 11, 10, and 9, 8, 7, 6, 5, 6, 7, 8, 9, 10—and half asleep—11, 12, 13, 14, 15, 16, 17, 18, 19, 20. Take a deep breath and go way deep asleep. You are, are you not? You can nod your head. You are, are you not? (*Subject nods.*)

Now I'm going to awaken you. And at ten, you'll be half awake, and at five, almost awake. I'm going to have you stand up to do that. Just stand up, Doctor, just stand up while you're still asleep. 20, 19, 18, 17, 16, 15—one-quarter of the way awake—14, 13, 12, 11, 10—and half awake. You're beginning to get more and more awake. 9, 8, 7, 6, 5, 4, 3, 2, 1. Wide awake! How are you?

I can count by fours. That's one of the things children

like to learn. They start out 4, 8, 12, 16, 20—and deep asleep. Then you can count backward by fives—15, 10, 5, 1 —wide awake. Tell me, how did you feel, Doctor?

SUBJECT

Very relaxed, very good.

ERICKSON

What happened when I started counting backward, then started suddenly forward?

SUBJECT

You get more and more conscious of what's going on around you, of people and sounds. Then all of a sudden, bam, everything goes back and you start sagging all over again.

ERICKSON

All right, thanks very much. (*Subject starts back to his seat.*) 1, 2, 3, 4, 5, 6, 7, 8, 9, 10, 11, 12, 13, 14, 15, 16, 17, 18, 19, 20. Take a deep breath and deep asleep.

You may think all of this a bit dramatic. But sometimes you have to do this in order to get people to understand that you can attract a person's attention, even when he is doing something, such as walking across the floor. You can secure his attention and get his response very readily, no matter what other activity is going on. It ought to give you a confidence in your own office. Regardless of the disturbance created by patients in the waiting room, your nurse rattling things, or whatever does happen, you can expect your patient to do his particular task. It is not an utterly impossible thing, and 20, 19, 18, 17, 16, 15, 14, 13, 12, 11, 10, 9, 8, 7, 6, 5, 4, 3, 2, 1. Wide awake!

Thank you very much Doctor. This sort of up-and-down technique will often enable you to deepen the patient because it is such an easy way of repetition.

QUESTION

Doctor, how would the patient know what you're doing when you start back from 20?

ERICKSON

Ask him.

QUESTION

Will you answer that question, Doctor L? At what point, when you were walking back to your chair, were you aware that you were being spoken to by Doctor Erickson for a specific reason? At what number?

ANSWER

Around 13, I think. At about that point I couldn't move as fast and I was a fit subject for a chair!

QUESTION

Could he have resisted at any point?

ERICKSON

He could have resisted, but the situation was a good one. He was participating and it took him completely by surprise, because he thought he was just going back to the chair.

ANSWER

It was more pleasant not to resist.

QUESTION

Could you get a patient to go still deeper by telling him that you will count above 20?

ERICKSON

That can be done, but it may slow the rate of induction. If I tell a subject that at the count of 20, he will be deeply asleep, he can respond in the same way that Doctor L did. Then I can say, "Now I'm going to continue to count, and you'll go still deeper." He will then actually go deeper, but if you tell a patient that you will continue to count beyond

20 before you count to that number, he is going to hold back in reserve enough deepening to allow you to finish your count. On the other hand, if you let him give all his deepening possibilities up to 20, then count higher, his only answer is to find still further deepening possibilities.

QUESTION

If you deepen the patient by bringing him in and out, how do you know how deep he went?

ERICKSON

You really have to question the patient to know, unless you have had enough experience, but they have the feeling they are awakening very nicely, when all of a sudden there is a definite change as they start back into the trance. Is that a fair statement, Doctor?

ANSWER

Yes, I think it's in line with what was said about beginning to hold back. I found myself getting ahead of you and holding back. The first time I went to 20, I didn't get nearly so deep as I did when you backed me up. Then I couldn't hold back at all.

ERICKSON

I think that is a very important statement. He couldn't hold back when I stopped and started counting up to 20 again.

QUESTION

Was that because he might be willing and, when he realized he might awaken, he knew subconsciously that it's a nice feeling and just automatically wanted to go back?

ERICKSON

There it is, the psychologic expectation that you'll continue to count backward. The subject is all set for it and, when you suddenly reverse the count and go forward again, there's a terrific pause in his thinking and in his feeling. He has got to get hold of something and here you are counting forward again, so he grabs onto that and goes deeper asleep.

Indirect induction (confusion technique)

Confusion techniques may be employed for the induction of hypnosis when the subject is not even aware that hypnosis is contemplated. This sort of procedure requires great skill and extensive experience on the part of the operator. More often, the problem is one of circumventing unconscious resistance on the part of an individual who consciously wants to be hypnotized. In such cases, it is a question of setting up the situation in such manner that the subject or patient cannot be sure when he is cooperating and when he is not. His defenses then become ineffective.

DOCTOR H (*demonstrating*)

The methods of going into any hypnotic trance vary with each individual. The common concept is that one needs to be unconscious or asleep. This is not true. Actually, in a deep trance, you should be able to hear, to see, to feel and experience anything that may belong to the situation. For example, it might be extremely necessary for you in a deep trance to hear traffic noises because you do not know how your unconscious mind works or what it needs. The baby who gets tired and wants to sleep can very easily teach you a great deal. It hunts up its favorite doll, then discards it. It finds its favorite toy, then discards that. It gets big sister's reader, examines it and discards it. Then, seemingly in discouragement, it picks up an old block, takes it to bed, and falls asleep immediately. Our assumption would be that the child would prefer the favorite doll or favorite toy, not just a block picked up, seemingly at random. Of course, it was not a block picked up at random. It was hunted for, because in that particular state, the child wanted something special. It doesn't make sense to the adult, but it makes absolute sense to the child, although the child cannot recognize or understand that fact. Any subject going into a trance, going very deeply into hypnosis, may hang on to what seems to be a full, conscious contact with his surroundings. That full conscious contact with the surroundings serves a purpose for the unconscious. Perhaps this is the only way that the unconscious knows of distracting the conscious mind, so that it can do its own thinking, its own feeling, its own organizing.

In the matter of going into a trance, there is a need to recognize that it is the experience of the unconscious mind that is the important thing. Now the question may come to your mind: When am I going to hypnotize you? The answer to that question is that the time is not at all important. You are here and I am here. The time should really be chosen by your unconscious mind. For all that you know, you may be already in a light trance. What difference does it make whether you think you are wide awake? Perhaps it is a very useful thing for you to think that you are wide awake. Perhaps you may think that you are beginning to go into a trance. Perhaps that is useful, but let's rely upon what your unconscious mind is actually doing.

Practically every patient with a problem has the feeling that he should be helped in this or that way. Actually, the help should be given in a way that the patient's unconscious mind can best use. It may be very interesting for you as you sit here to recall that the time is now just past 4:30, and as you sit and think about the time, it is interesting to remember that today is Wednesday. Yesterday, also at 4:30, you may have been sitting around the house, or going for a ride, or having cocktails at your relatives', or thinking about what you were going to do at 5:30, or maybe at 6:30, or maybe at 7:30. You know, too, that on the day before, you were also doing something at 4:30 that may have been interesting. Or maybe at 4:30 on Friday or Thursday or Wednesday of the week before, or some Wednesday in November, you may have been thinking at 4:30 in the afternoon of what might be interesting to do at that time. As those thoughts occurred, you were reminded of the fact that last June in the afternoon on a Saturday, you were doing something that seemed interesting. Thinking about last June in the afternoon brings back the fact that yesterday afternoon you were also engaged in some activity. What was it that you were thinking yesterday? What was it you were thinking last June? What was on your mind in June of 1959 and 1958, because also in June on a Saturday afternoon, some thoughts were going through your mind. You were engaged in some activity, whether you were interested or not. You were thinking of something else to do. It reminded you that in 1955, in 1954, and in 1950—many years and days—there were Saturdays at 4:30 and at 5:30 and at 3:30 and at 2:30 in the afternoon, times when you had just gotten up or were just going to sleep, when you were rested and when you were tired. Many summer days, nice spring and fall days back in 1949 and 1948, you had many pleasant days in June. Sometimes it was on a Saturday. Sometimes on a Sunday. Then there were Mondays and Tuesdays. And in 1952 and in 1953 and in 1951, you had some very pleasant Saturday afternoons.

All the time, as you think of these things and the wonderful things that you were doing and the things that were not as interesting, wondering what you would like to do that evening, whether it should be done in June, July, or August, whether the year should be 1959, or 1956, or even 1952, you were reminded some evenings of the fact that you wanted dinner and what did you have for dinner on that Saturday in 1956? What did you have for dinner on a Saturday in 1952? What did you have for dinner on Friday and on Thursday and on Wednesday and on Tuesday?

All these things are returning to you and you think about them and, as you do, you notice a drowsiness and a sensation of relaxation that creeps over your body. You remember that it was very pleasant that June Saturday in 1951 at 4:30 and you wondered what you might be doing at 6:30 that evening. What you might be wanting to eat that Saturday in June 1951, or was it in 1952? The June and July and August nights on Saturdays—and you relax and revel in the fact that you had some pleasant experiences. Some of those times you were sleepy, as you may be becoming now, and you allowed that sleepiness, when it overtook you, to allow you to relax completely and let your eyes close and, if you desired, go deeper and sounder asleep. You were very comfortable on those afternoons when you lay down to sleep. You were comfortable and you enjoyed relaxing and allowing your head to relax and your eyes to close, allowing yourself to sleep deeper and sounder and think about a day in June or July or August, possibly September, in 1954, or 1953, or even in 1952. You might even think about what might happen this year, in December two weeks before Christmas, or three weeks before Christmas, or even a month before Christmas, about Thanksgiving time, or even in November, October, or the very pleasant things that might happen to you at that time. And the nights when you might be very relaxed, very restful, very sleepy, and you might just want to sleep soundly and deeply, remembering that in 1957 you were sleeping very soundly, very deeply, very comfortably, very relaxed. As you speculate on those things, the thought comes to you that it is a summer day, and even now you feel sleepy, relaxed, restful, and drowsy. You allow the sensation to grow stronger and stronger because it is a nice pleasant sensation. It grows stronger and stronger as you think about the fact that it is very relaxing and very restful. As the relaxing, restful, sleepy sensation creeps over you and grows stronger and stronger, it allows you really to relax and to rest and to sleep comfortably and to think about many pleasant things.

As you awaken in the next few minutes, feeling very refreshed and very relaxed, you will undoubtedly realize that you have been completely relaxed, completely hypnotized—a very comfortable, relaxing sensation—knowing that the next time will be much easier, much more simple. You will find that by merely thinking of the fact that you are back again to the present, you can easily allow your eyes to open and awaken feeling very relaxed and comfortable.

Autohypnosis

DOCTOR H (*demonstrating*)

Another hypnotic technique is that of autohypnosis. This form of hypnosis can actually be divided into two different types. It may be produced either as an originally self-induced state. Or it can be more readily and easily induced as a posthypnotic suggestion following heterohypnosis.

In the self-induced state, one must be willing to allow the unconscious to rule. One cannot decide in advance that a certain task is to be performed within a designated period. This makes the situation a conscious one. For autohypnosis to be accomplished, the conscious element needs to be completely removed. One can compromise, however, by allowing thirty, or forty, or sixty minutes for just sitting or lying in a comfortable position with no predetermined task, but willing for a trance to develop and speculating on just what might be accomplished. Actually, our subconscious is always aware that there are many unfulfilled ideas or tasks. Some may be initiated or partially completed; some may be totally completed. Such an accomplishment will certainly prove of value, because it was unconsciously selected. It is not always necessary for the conscious awareness of the accomplishment to be immediately manifested. For unconscious reasons, the awareness of completion of a task may be kept repressed for hours, for days, or even for weeks. Delayed or postponed satisfaction may result in a greater feeling of personal accomplishment.

There is no set way of selecting a particular method. Each individual needs to go about accomplishing autohypnosis in his own individual manner. Trying to think of a conscious method cannot succeed. One needs to sit quietly and allow some technique to develop that best suits one's personality. Here are some ways one might begin: One could sit in a comfortable chair and stare into blank space or at a spot on the wall. One could sit in a chair and stare into a mirror. One could lie down on a sofa or a bed and gaze at the ceiling, or one could be lying down comfortably with the eyes closed, just waiting and wondering and speculating as to what could happen. The busy doctor, with a few minutes to spare, could just sit at his desk, just sit there and wonder, perhaps to discover that thirty or sixty minutes had passed, that he had dictated some letters or some notes or some case histories, and find that the time was very pleasantly spent.

Autohypnosis can be accomplished in this manner. It is important to note, however, that it might not be accomplished the first time one tried, or the second time, although it occurs more readily with some individuals. One just needs to allow the time to wonder about it, think about it, speculate about it, and then discover some time in the future that it had been accomplished, and take pleasure from that satisfaction.

The second type of autohypnosis is that accomplished as a posthypnotic suggestion. This type is more simply induced because it is taught to the patient during the hypnotic trance state. Consequently a specific objective can be reached in that manner. This method can be utilized frequently in the treatment of habit patterns such as insomnia, constipation, excessive smoking, overeating, anxiety states of a mild nature, etc. It can be utilized to reinforce the suggestions that were offered in the original hypnotic session.

Utilization of this type of therapy as an adjunct to indirect permissive symptom removal should be limited to those conditions which do not have a deep-seated root cause and are not conversion mechanisms. (See discussion in Chapter 8, General Medicine.) When the dynamics of the situation involved require more than mere reinforcing of indirect permissive suggestions, or re-education, or reassurance, or other relatively simple psychotherapeutic maneuvers, autohypnotic therapy cannot usually be used successfully.

The methods that may be utilized in teaching autohypnosis to the patient are varied. For example, the physician in general practice has patients come in to tell him they are too tired or upset by their day's activities to be able to fall asleep at night. This type of insomniac, owing to the enervating day he may have spent, tosses and turns for an hour or two or three. Actually, he does not have any constant psychologic pattern to cause his sleeplessness. It is not an unconscious desire on his part not to sleep. It is a habit pattern set up from the day's activities. This sort of individual is very readily treated by autohypnosis.

One can instruct a patient in the exercises by placing him in a hypnotic trance state. A light state usually suffices; if he goes into a medium or deep state, it will work as well or better. One tells the patient, "Now, as you are sitting here sleeping deeply and soundly, I'd like to present some points of interest to you. You might find it refreshing tonight, or tomorrow night, perhaps every night this week, to retire in the normal, usual manner and take the usual comfortable position in your bed. Close your eyes and in your mind's eye visualize a spot on the wall. Think of it as the same spot you saw here on this wall" (if that was the technique that was utilized to induce hypnosis.)

"And, as you lie there comfortably, you can really see yourself gazing very intently at that spot; you can find yourself going deeply and soundly into a very comfortable trance state, just as you did here. You have learned to do that here and you've learned to do it readily and rapidly and easily. You will find that you'll be able to do it readily and rapidly and easily in your own bed at home, at the proper time. You'll find that you are able to let your entire body relax, as you go deeper and sounder, just as you are relaxing now, as you go deeper and sounder asleep into the trance state. It's a wonderful, restful state. You'll feel just as you do now, or perhaps you'll go even deeper; you will be able to retain that feeling because it will be of very marked interest and desirable for you to do so. You can allow that comfortable situation to evolve into true nighttime sleep. You'll be able to experience a very comfortable night's sleep and awaken refreshed in the morning."

It is extremely important, as mentioned earlier, to be all-inclusive, particularly in the case of insomnia, and to teach patients what to do should they awaken during the night. You need to mention this carefully and cautiously because you do not want to give them the positive suggestion that they will awaken during the night. It might be phrased to the effect that frequently in the early learning process of remaining asleep all night, one needs to test his ability to awaken and to go back to sleep again. "Should that desire arise in you and should you find yourself awake during the night for that or for any other reason, you may repeat the same relaxing procedure, the same technique, and find that the next time it works even better. You may need to repeat this less and less frequently as you learn to remain asleep the entire night." You have given him a very positive suggestion that it will occur less and less each successive night.

For the utilization of autohypnosis in other habit patterns, such as excessive smoking, obesity, nail biting, and the like, the following approaches may be used. For instance, you have taught the patient certain patterns, certain habits, such as reminders of the proper prophylactic care of his mouth, the importance of brushing his teeth, washing his dentures, etc. Whatever the technique may be, where it is a pattern that needs to be properly learned by him, you can instruct him in words similar to these, while he is still in the hypnotic state:

"You may find it extremely helpful to utilize your new learning, to further your aims and your desires within the confines of your home. This will obviate the necessity for you to return here frequently for reminders. It is very simple for you to do this. You will find it very interesting to be able to do it, despite the fact that you are there and I am here. You are learning the method now of accomplishing this, even as you continue to sleep here, deeply and soundly. You will understand that you can produce an autohypnotic state, self-induced, a relaxing, comfortable state in which you are able to learn and remind yourself about certain things in your own time.

"You can do this by selecting any time during the day that you desire. Allow yourself two minutes or three minutes, one minute or five minutes, as much as is convenient. Just seat yourself in a comfortable chair and stare at an actual spot or an imaginary spot and allow your eyes to get heavy. As you sit in that chair, you will really get the idea that you are sitting here in this chair; you can almost feel or sense the fact that I am sitting opposite you or standing opposite you. You will really be able to visualize that without a bit of difficulty. Then, you will be able to hear the words as I have spoken them to you here today, or you will be able to hear your own voice repeating these words in a similar vein. You will be able to allow your eyes to get heavy and you'll feel your body relaxing, your arms and legs relaxing, just as they did here, and you will feel an intense desire for your eyes to close.

"Let them close, and you will find yourself going deeper and deeper into the hypnotic state; you will be able to go as deeply or even more deeply into the state of hypnosis or into the relaxed state or the sleep state, just as you have learned to do here. You may be assured of the termination of the hypnotic state exactly at the predetermined time."

It may be important at this point to make a specific explanation to parents of young children. During a normal night's sleep, a mother senses and hears her infant's cry, even though she is soundly asleep. She will continue to do this. Should a child cry out, or the doorbell or telephone ring, or should anything else arise that might require a total awareness of the situation, a parent needs to be assured that he—or she—will be aware of it, that he will react to it promptly and adequately, without any difficulty whatsoever. Patients frequently fear that they may not be aware of something when they are in the autohypnotic state. This is not so. They will awaken immediately, be able to take care of the situation very adequately, and also be able to return to the autohypnotic state shortly thereafter.

"While you (the subjects) are sitting here, you may find it

interesting to review the material that was covered during this session or any other material that may be related to it. You can think about a great many things and about different ways of handling them. You may wonder which way you will select to handle a given situation, knowing that you will handle it adequately and properly and in the manner that best suits you as an individual. These ideas can serve as reminders for you or reinforcements for you to help you achieve the goals you desire. Your trance can also be used as a review of thoughts or ideas directly or indirectly related to this situation. You will find it very relaxing to do this. You will arouse at the allotted time, just as you have done here, awakening in a very comfortable manner, feeling no drowsiness."

This is the kind of conversation utilized in the hypnotic state for instructing the patient carefully in how he may go about employing it in the autohypnotic state.

The same technique can frequently be used in the case of a mother, for example, who complains about the fact that her children nag and annoy her, or with women who have functional hypertensions, hyperacidities, and other tension states caused by the general dullness of ordinary housekeeping. They can be instructed to take a minute or ten minutes off, once or twice a day, just to sit down and let this comfortable feeling come over them. They must understand that they can rouse themselves from it, feeling ready to start over again for the day. This will carry them for several hours, or even perhaps for the rest of the day.

You can impress upon your patients the fact that they have tried to do this frequently in the past. They have been going to physicians or dentists for many years. The dentist or physician has said to them, "Now what you need to do is relax," but he never told them how. You can now tell them about a very simple way to achieve relaxation. They know they will be able to do it because they have already done it in your office two or three times.

The important thing to remember is the need for suiting the technique to the individual personality needs, for making the activities and the instructions as permissive as possible. You may read in the literature remarks by uninformed persons warning that autohypnosis may be dangerous to prepsychotics, neurotics, etc. But if you permissively grant an individual the possibility of autohypnosis, you will probably find little or no danger in its utilization.

Occasionally, we run across the schizophrenic patient, particularly the catatonic, who knows how to go into an autohypnotic trance of a pathologic kind. This is part of the schizophrenic process. It has nothing to do with any teaching the patient may have had and hypnosis cannot be blamed for it. The doctor needs to recognize that certain types of schizophrenic patients can go into autohypnotic trances, as can also a normal person. Occasionally, this type of schizophrenic patient can be taught, however, to use his autohypnosis in a much more satisfying way, to avoid the difficulties involved in the old, uncontrolled use of what the patients call their "floating fantasies" or their "withdrawal states."

The real difficulty with autohypnosis is that too many people try to use it consciously. Autohypnosis can definitely not be used to further a conscious plan. I will give you an example:

CASE OF ANNA Y.

Anna was a resident in psychiatry. She wanted to learn autohypnosis and she made inquiry about it. Since she was a good hypnotic subject, she was told that she would probably be able to learn. It was pointed out, however, that it should not be a conscious determined thing. Anna therefore decided that some day—she did not know just when—but some day when it was convenient, she would go into an autohypnotic trance. In that autohypnotic trance, she would do something that was interesting. She did not try to figure out exactly what she would do. She relied upon her unconscious mind to select both the day and the project.

One morning Anna got up. It was her day off. She started dressing for breakfast and stood in front of the mirror to put her hat on. Now this is the story that she told. "I was standing in front of the mirror, putting on my hat to go to breakfast. I had planned to go shopping in Detroit today. And then I turned to get my coat from the bed and, to my horror, the bed was all made and there was a pile of packages on the bed. And I wondered what had happened. I had gotten up only a little while ago and I'd put on my hat and I'd turned to the bed to put on my coat, and there my coat was—but there was also that pile of packages. Then I happened to notice that the sun was shining through the west window and that alarmed me. Then I looked at the clock and it said four o'clock. I rushed to the phone and called you. You said to come on over and here I am. What happened?"

Knowing that this was Anna's day off and knowing who else had a day off that day, I had an idea that if Anna went to town, she would undoubtedly go in the company of Jenny. I called Jenny and asked her to come to the office. I interviewed Jenny separately. Jenny said, "Well, I met Anna for breakfast. We had breakfast and then we both took the bus and we went downtown." She gave a detailed report of exactly what took place in downtown Detroit. She told about Anna's having met some old schoolmates of hers, having lunch at Hudson's Department Store, eating various items of food, and doing a lot of shopping. A full account was written out and then I saw Anna again. I asked her, "Well, Anna, do you want me to tell you what happened today, or do you want to find out all by yourself?" Anna replied, "Well, I've been thinking about it. Do you suppose that I went into an autohypnotic trance for the entire day?" I said, "It's quite possible. What shall we do about it?" Her answer was, "Well, I think you had better put me in a trance and tell me to remember it."

She was put in a trance and instructed to have a full conscious memory. Then Anna awakened and said, "I was standing in front of the mirror putting on my hat to go to breakfast and then I decided right then and there in my unconscious mind that I'd go shopping that day and spend the whole day in an autohypnotic trance." She gave the same account of the people she had met, the purchases she had made, the food she ate, that Jenny had given. She remembered the entire thing. Had Anna decided, "I'll go into an autohypnotic trance and I'll go downtown," she would have made it a conscious task. But she let her unconscious determine everything, instead. That's the best way of learning autohypnosis, to allow your unconscious to know that you are willing to have it take over at some convenient time to carry out some interesting project, but not to try to determine some conscious task that you can do consciously.

This account illustrates another factor that frequently troubles people. Suppose you are in a trance, what kind of difficulty can you get into? Anna walked downtown at the height of the Christmas season, shopping, dodging traffic, meeting friends, never disclosing, even to Jenny who knew her well, that she was in a trance state.

On a later occasion, I happened to walk into the Staff Room, where Anna was to present some case histories. One look at her face, her dilated pupils, her frozen features, told that she was in an autohypnotic trance. She proceeded to present cases and answer questions and so on for the entire staff and only I recognized that she was in a trance state. After the staff meeting was over, Anna lingered behind, turned while still in a trance state, and asked, "How did I do, Doctor Erickson? Do you suppose anybody suspected me?" I told her, "I was the only one who suspected you and I was interested in watching you. You made just one mistake, Anna. You never heard the telephone ring during your presentation. I happened to sit beside the telephone and I grabbed the receiver off every time, because you tried to talk right straight through the ringing of the telephone. You didn't make the normal response. In autohypnosis you try to visualize all the possible contingencies that might arise and you go into the autohypnotic trance knowing that you will meet any such contingency."

5
Clinical Applications of Surgical Anesthesia

Hypnosis, or suggestive relaxation, which is still another term for hypnosis, and chemical anesthesia have a great deal more in common than is generally recognized. Over 150 years ago, the chemist, Joseph Priestley, prepared nitrous oxide gas. About fifty years later, Sir Humphry Davy recognized the anesthetic properties of Priestley's gas. It was in 1844 that hypnotism indirectly introduced nitrous oxide gas as an anesthetic agent in this country.

Gardiner Colton, an itinerant chemist, was giving a demonstration of hypnosis in Hartford, Connecticut, on December 10, 1844. In order to ensure a successful trance induction, it is reputed that an assistant engulfed the subject in nitrous oxide while Colton made passes over the face of his subject. The subject fell and, while falling, hit himself violently against the chair without the slightest sensation of pain. Wesley Wells, the dentist, was in the audience and he noticed what had happened. Colton told him about the effect of nitrous oxide. The next day, Colton administered nitrous oxide to Wells for the extraction of a tooth.

Thus, when hypnosis was at its height, anesthesia was a curiosity. Wesley Wells spent five years trying to get his colleagues to use nitrous oxide, but met with such bitter resistance that the subsequent frustration made him commit suicide. Colton, who introduced nitrous oxide anesthesia to Wells, went to New York and opened up a school for teaching dental anesthesia. He was exploited by none other than P. T. Barnum. The paradox is that at the time hypnosis was popular, exploiters were pushing anesthesia. Today, after a century, the reverse is true. Now anesthesia is in general use, whereas hypnosis is being exploited by charlatans. This, unfortunately, is retarding scientific acceptance of hypnosis.

Pierre Janet stated, "If my work is not accepted today, it will be tomorrow when there will be a new turn to fashion's wheel, which is going to bring back hypnotism as surely as our grandmother's styles." This prophecy, made at the turn of the century, is now being fulfilled. It is evidenced by an ever-expanding interest on the part of the medical and dental professions.

Today only a sporadic application of hypnosis for surgical anesthesia is reported. It is also unfortunate that the advent of chloroform, ether, and nitrous oxide during the middle of the last century relegated hypnosis to undeserved obscurity and prevented it from being used as an anesthetic agent.

Hypnosis is still not entirely accepted by the medical profession, primarily because of the lack of training at the undergraduate and postgraduate levels, and the unfavorable cultural attitudes resulting from the association of hypnosis with entertainment. However, these resistances are rapidly being battered down as the result of more medical and public enlightenment. It is also of historical interest that nitrous oxide, chloroform, and ether were not utilized for many years. Physicians would not use these valuable agents because lay people were using them for "sniffing parties" and for "ether jags." Hence, at that time, respectable doctors would not use these pain-relieving drugs. Another reason for the profession's reluctance to accept hypnosis is that its ardent proponents, with their enthusiastic and extravagant claims, have indirectly done more harm in preventing recognition of its numerous scientific applications than have its opponents. For that reason we have stressed the limitations and the disadvantages of hypnosis in this text and with that precaution have set out to define its areas of usefulness. It is also gratifying that hypnosis is now in the hands of reputable scientists, who are using it in many areas, and expanding its scope of real utility.

Hypnosis may be a very valuable tool for allaying fear, tension, and anxiety, where chemoanesthesia is to be used. It should be emphasized that hypnosis will never be a complete substitute for present-day methods of chemical anesthesia. However, as an adjunct, it does have definite preoperative and postoperative advantages.

To one who has been interested in the advances of psychosomatic medicine, it is indeed gratifying that many anesthesiologists are finally becoming interested in the personalities of those who are going to be anesthetized. Psychiatrists are giving courses to anesthesiologists on the psychodynamics of the personality and many anesthesiologists are becoming interested in hypnosis.

Beecher studied the effect of preoperative medication and placebos. To a control group he gave atropine sulfate; to another, Demerol, sodium pentobarbital, and morphine. He asked experienced anesthesiologists to differentiate which patients had the sedative drugs and which the atropine. The anesthesiologists could not determine which patients had received the preoperative medication. He deduced that we are giving these drugs empirically and only because it is traditional. Since such drugs contribute materially to respiratory depression, it might be a good idea to eliminate them entirely. Beecher did not mention hypnosis, but one can readily see that hypnosis would be a very valuable aid for relaxing such individuals, thereby eliminating or reducing respiratory depressing preoperative medication.

With reference to "total" hypnoanesthesia, it is limited to about 25 per cent of selected obstetrical patients and to only 5 or 10 per cent of patients requiring major surgery. Hypnosis cannot be used in all patients for surgery without some sort of chemical anesthesia, regardless of how good the hypnotist may be; however, it has been the experience of some obstetricians and surgeons that, where this combined approach of hypnosis and chemoanesthesia is employed, the over-all amount of anesthesia given was reduced from 50 to 75 per cent for all types of obstetrical deliveries. This combined method naturally has a much wider application than hypnosis per se. The advantages to both mother and baby are obvious.

Hingson recently stated that a high percentage of cerebral palsy is due to fetal anoxia. Eastman, in a most interesting article, "Mt. Everest in Utero," showed that the condition of the fetus' brain in the uterus is analogous to that of an individual standing at the top of Mt. Everest. He contended that fetal anoxia is an important factor in the production of cerebral palsy, mental retardation, and epilepsy. The noxious drugs that we give our mothers, especially when they are given in large doses, may be partially responsible for the production of fetal anoxia. In the experience of some physicians employing hypnosis in labor and delivery, nearly all their babies are born "pink." They seldom require resuscitation.

Other possible advantages of this balanced anesthetic in surgery have been described. For example, one of the most interesting observations that many investigators since Esdaile have noted is that neurogenic shock is reduced in difficult surgical procedures performed under hypnoanesthesia. It is amazing that there has not been any research on this aspect of neurogenic shock, apart from recognizing the important role that the pituitary-adrenal axis plays in its adaptation to stress.

Postoperatively, atelectasis and pneumonitis are serious conditions. It is true that anesthesiologists know how to prevent these formidable complications by other methods; however, another excellent method would be added to their armamentarium if they knew how to induce hypnosis preoperatively, even where they are going to use an anesthetic.

To illustrate: When surgical patients wake up, they are usually afraid to cough because of the excessive pain; this is especially true of those individuals who have had operations in the upper abdomen. Now with properly prepared patients, this fear and frequently the pain may be eradicated by simply inducing hypnosis. The breathing and cough reflexes can also be regulated through posthypnotic suggestion. Hypnotic relaxation also facilitates the passage of a catheter, so that the anesthesiologist can suck out mucus deep in the tracheal-bronchial tree. Also pertinent to the postoperative aspects, wound healing can be facilitated. In a recent *Journal of the American Medical Association* article on the treatment of burns, there was a report on patients with severe third-degree burns, requiring large doses of opiates, who were hypnotized in order to reduce the need for opiates. As a result, the appetite was not suppressed and better healing ensued because of adequate nutrition. These same principles certainly apply to wound healing.

Because of the need for a close interpersonal relationship between patient and anesthesiologist, anesthesiology must of necessity some day take up its abode in psychiatry. Both specialties have one thing in common, namely, the production of psychic change to alter the conscious perception of and memory for pain.

It is not claimed that hypnosis is a panacea, nor is it felt that hypnosis will ever replace present-day methods of chemoanesthesia. Even though it has been around a long time, hypnosis is still a young science in its clinical applications and, contrary to popular opinion, it is a part of everyday life.

Hypnosis is rapidly becoming an accepted medical tool, perhaps more time-consuming than an injection, but certainly just as practical. Therefore, anesthesiologists who use hypnosis will certainly find new applications for this technique. It will help to bring insight into the numerous psychological factors associated with this specialty. Physicians would do well to direct their attention toward the subtle and reciprocal action of mind and body that is personality.

6

Hypnosis in Obstetrics

Indications and advantages of hypnosis in obstetrics

The induction of hypnosis in a patient is a very simple procedure; only a moderate amount of skill is needed to produce the trance state. Consequently, the physician can use it on almost all obstetrical patients. He needs to understand, however, that psychodynamic orientation is important because the constant interpersonal relationship between physician and patient is such that there is a marked emphasis of it in the hypnotic state.

One of the indications for using hypnosis is the understanding that respiratory and circulatory infection in the mother and baby with resulting anoxia is markedly decreased, perhaps even avoided altogether by the reduction or elimination of chemical anesthesia. Hypnosis also raises the resistance to muscular efforts. The fatigue that one frequently sees in the obstetrical patient in labor is therefore markedly minimized.

Whenever use of a chemical agent is contraindicated by virtue of a cardiac condition, tuberculosis, prematurity, etc., hypnosis may be used without fear of anesthetic danger to either the mother or the baby. It is generally accepted that any of the anesthetic agents used retard uterine activity; hypnosis does not. Another indication of the usefulness of hypnosis is that it can be controlled; if the hypnoanesthesia needs to be lightened or deepened, it can be readily accomplished by a simple suggestion on the part of the physician. When chemical or anesthetic agents are used, one can only counteract them by other drugs, by oxygen, or by time.

It is believed that capillary blood loss is diminished by hypnosis. This is probably due to a vasospasm or to some unknown effect on the coagulation time. Some experimental work has investigated this subject, but no definitive results have yet been attained. It is sometimes stated that bleeding can be stopped by use of hypnosis. This is questionable. The most one can expect is some sort of vasospasm, owing perhaps to a contracting of muscles along the capillaries and thus a diminishing of the bleeding in those areas. The claim has been made that bleeding in the sockets of the teeth can be stopped, but there again, it is probably by one of the two means mentioned above.

Another indication for the use of hypnosis is the reduced time element affecting both physician and patient. Previous antiquated methods used to induce hypnosis in obstetrics required the obstetrician to spend an excessive amount of time with the patient. He spent many hours training his patient to be a somnambulistic subject and developing anesthesia. When she went into labor, he had to hurry to the hospital to reinduce both the trance state and the anesthesia and remain with his patient all during her labor. It is understandable that obstetricians were not willing to use such a time-consuming method.

Changes in hospital attitudes and achievements by contemporary workers in the field have made the situation different today. Some hospitals, fearing legal difficulties, have prohibited the use of hypnosis. They have not been able to legislate against using hypnosis in the office, however. A use of posthypnotic suggestion and autohypnosis has therefore been evolved. The patient does her own hypnotizing in the hospital.

Actually, of course, using the recent techniques that have been devised, the time is considerably shortened. For example, the patient is comfortable during labor and therefore does not require the constant attention of her physician. Labor in primiparae is shortened by an average of two hours in the first stage; during the second stage, the patient is able to bear down more readily without extreme discomfort and expulsion can be augmented.

One other valuable indication is that with hypnosis there have been no reports of an increase in operative interference or of danger either to the mother or baby because of increased instrumental manipulation. These facts differ from the reports on almost all the other anesthetic agents.

An important point to bear in mind is that complete hypnoanesthesia may not be obtainable in a great many patients. But where a lesser amount of hypnoanesthesia is produced, as in light or medium hypnosis, there is still a marked reduction in the quantity of chemical anesthetics required. In every patient, therefore, in whom even a light or medium trance is produced, beneficial effects may be produced. This should include 95 to 100 per cent of the obstetrical patients. At the very least, the amount of chemical anesthetic agent the patient needs during labor is diminished with hypnosis.

Another good reason for using hypnosis is the postoperative comfort the mother is able to attain. She may be totally free of pain and, through this added comfort, the possibility of atelectasis and other dangers is also minimized or avoided.

Some obstetricians have reported that they can increase the secretion of milk in parturient patients by utilizing hypnosis and directly suggesting the filling of the breasts, or even better, by indirectly suggesting the feeling of well-being in the patient, with the mother looking forward expectantly to the wonderful child that she will be able to hold in her arms. Psychologically, this seems to cause an increase in the milk secretion.

Disadvantages of hypnosis

A primary disadvantage is the lack of training in hospital personnel. The patient enters the labor room and hears a woman across the hall or in the next room or even in the next bed crying out with pain. This upsets her and tends to break down her hypnoanesthesia. Similarly, a nurse or intern coming in to ask "How are your pains?" may bring back to her the idea of pain. This argument actually need not be considered too seriously. A patient who has been properly trained in the doctor's office, will understand that those things may happen, that some people have not had the advantage she has had of learning a technique. Also, patients properly trained hypnotically learn to understand that when the intern or nurse says "pain," what he or she actually means is "contraction," and are able to minimize the effect of the words on their hypnoanesthetic state.

The combined approach

The idea of using a combined approach of hypnosis and a chemical agent is the important consideration to keep in mind. Hypnosis is not an "all or nothing" principle. A physician should not utilize only those hypnotic patients capable of the somnambulistic state in which they can produce a complete and total anesthesia, and claim that these are the successes and that all the other obstetrical patients are failures. Hypnosis should be made available to every patient. Some will require no chemical anesthesia, others will require 10, 20, 50, or even 90 per cent as much as they would have required if they had not learned hypnosis. But even when the amount of anesthesia is reduced only 10 per cent, the patient is being treated in a better manner.

Patients should be allowed to learn other phenomena of hypnosis besides those of anesthesia and analgesia. The new learnings will assist in making the labor more comfortable so that the patient will look forward to the birth of the baby with less consternation.

The first visit

What follows is a step-by-step account of the author's procedure in utilizing hypnosis in obstetrics. At the first visit, the question of hypnosis is merely mentioned to the patient. If she knows little about the subject, she is given a booklet entitled, "An Old Art Returns to Medicine." [1] At the next visit, sufficient time will be allotted to cover the subject in a comprehensive manner.

The second visit

The initial discussion evolves around removal of the misconceptions of hypnosis. It is pointed out to the patient that she will not be asleep, that the hypnotized patient is not unconscious. The hypnotized patient can hear, feel, smell, sense, talk, and move around. [2]

[1] Heron, W., and Hershman, S. *An Old Art Returns to Medicine.* Chicago, 1958.
[2] Despite the fact that this is told to patients by their physicians, and read by them in the pamphlet, a percentage of them will say, following their first trance, "I wasn't hypnotized. I heard everything you said. I wasn't asleep. I felt everything." The fact that a patient has read the pamphlet and has had these ideas explained to her will not necessarily mean that she has accepted them com-

Following the removal of misconceptions by pointing out to the patient that she will not be asleep, that she will hear everything that is important, that she will feel relaxed, and that she will feel comfortable the patient should be advised that she can learn to eliminate extraneous distractions and become capable of focused concentration.

The percentage of people who go into a light trance, medium trance, and deep trance might be mentioned at this time for the patient must recognize that not all people can develop complete and total anesthesia. Also, the availability of chemical agents during labor should be mentioned. This must be done carefully. If one says to a patient, "In case this doesn't work, you will be able to get a chemical anesthetic agent," one is certainly giving a very negative suggestion, and the probabilities of failure increase. A physician does not advise a patient, "If this doesn't work, there will be other medications." One merely tells her the truth, and the truth is that she can learn hypnoanesthesia and hypnoanalgesia, and her unconscious mind can recognize that this is a different feeling, a different sensation, and during labor, her unconscious mind can recognize, too, that it might want to

---

pletely. She will listen intellectually, but she may not totally accept the statements made.

It is wiser not to challenge the patient's own feelings. If the patient claims she was not hypnotized, though she may actually have been in the somnambulistic state or in a medium or light hypnotic state, it is a good idea to say, "Very well, that is right. You may not have been hypnotized, but you certainly were relaxed, and you did develop an anesthesia or analgesia and you can use this without being any more deeply hypnotized than you were a few minutes ago." There is no reason to argue with the patient. One should respect the patient's wishes and her subconscious desires and needs. Attempts to meet her needs do not include forcing on her the acceptance that she was in a hypnotic trance.

compare the difference between this type of anesthesia and analgesia and chemical anesthesia or analgesia, or even no anesthesia or analgesia. Should her unconscious mind decide to test this difference, it is perfectly permissible. Once having made the tests in any way it chooses, the unconscious mind will select the one that it likes best, and immediately the patient can utilize that technique. This should be very carefully told to the patient so that she accepts the idea that should she awaken from the hypnotic state or if the hypno-anesthesia wears off, or if she would like to try no anesthesia or a shot or a "whiff" of gas, she may do so. At the same time, it should be made clear that she need have no guilty feelings about this idea, that she need not think she has failed for this is a perfectly normal situation that occurs frequently in many obstetrical patients.

Another point to be made at this meeting with the patient is that hypnosis is a teaching procedure; all the physician does is to teach the patient what to do. There is no possibility that the physician can fail. The doctor might say: "I have taught hypnosis for many, many years to hundreds of patients. Most patients are able to learn hypnosis very easily and very readily. Some patients learn it more slowly than others. There are different ways to gain knowledge. In learning to use a typewriter, some girls learn by listening to music as they type away at the keys; others learn by chewing gum very vigorously as they type; still others learn by keeping their eyes closely peeled to the typewriter. But as they are learning, *most* of them learn by making errors, by going back and correcting the errors, by indelibly implanting within their unconscious that particular error, and then proceeding with their learning."

The physician might continue with a discussion of the learning curve. This should be explained as simply as possible. "The learning curve is one of an ascending line, a leveling off, a little descending line, ascending again, a little plateau, a little descending, and so on. And that is the way you learn." As these things are being pointed out, the patient is acquiring a tremendous amount of knowledge to which she is entitled.

So far, this material has utilized ten to fifteen minutes of the appointment time. To review, hypnosis has been discussed with the patient. The patient has read the booklet, "An Old Art Returns to Medicine," and has received the answers to any unanswered questions. Of course, one must be careful to suit the phraseology to the intellectual and educational level of the individual patient. One cannot speak of learning curves to persons who have an inadequate education. One has to point these matters out very simply.

Step number two is teaching the patient how to go into hypnosis, and explaining to her the phenomena of the trance state. There is no preselection of technique here. The induction is begun when the patient sits down in the chair. One begins to talk to a patient and finds oneself using a technique that is suitable. It is a matter of clinical judgment.

There are two stages of hypnosis: the induction of the trance and the trance utilization. The trance utilization is employed to teach the patient certain ideas. Just as soon as the induction technique is begun, the physician can begin to mention items of importance. "As you go deeper into a trance, as you begin to relax more and more, I would like you to understand more clearly that the purpose of this is for you to learn some new ideas and some new thoughts so that you can look forward to having a very comfortable labor and delivery, so that you can look forward to having a perfectly healthy, normal baby." What is accomplished? The treatment of the patient, the therapy, is part of the induction technique.

This is extremely valuable for several reasons. Most physicians who have been sitting at a desk talking to patients for many years are aware of the effects they can produce. As one begins to discuss with the patient his or her particular problem, whether it be headache, asthma, a sore foot, or an abdominal pain, a trancelike state is accomplished. When one speaks to a patient very intently, very emphatically, impelling the patient to understand that every word is important, that the patient is all important, what happens? The patient's field of awareness is being narrowed; all externalities are being removed; thoughts are being concentrated only on inner feelings and inner sensations; a hypnotic trance is actually being induced.

Examining the patient during this period, a fixed stare of the eyes, a waxy immobility of the facial muscles, and a lag in muscular activity will be observed. Why? Because the patient is intently interested in the special problem at hand. She has forgotten virtually all else. She is interested, both consciously and subconsciously, only in this one particular item, and by definition has entered a hypnotic trance. This may be a light, a medium, or even a deep somnambulistic stage. Of course, most physicians are unaware that they have been inducing trances for many years.

Therefore, by using the patient's own needs and desires as part of the induction technique, e.g., "you can look forward to having a comfortable labor, you can know that you are going to be much more comfortable than other girls who do not have the privilege of this technique," the physician is helping to deepen the hypnotic trance.

The next step, after hypnosis has been induced, is to teach the patient to lose her fears and apprehensions of her impending labor by learning the normal processes of labor. One of the most common reasons for increased pain is ignorance, a lack of knowledge of what is going to occur, and the fear and tension that follows. This is frequently demonstrated by children. When they do not know what the physician is going to do, they cry, "What are you going to do? What are you going to do?" Their uncertainty increases their apprehension, their anxiety, and their pain. The same thing is true of a pregnant woman who has never had a baby. Let her know what is going to happen. Tell her what she is expected to do. Tell her what she should expect to feel. Tell her what happens. It takes only a few minutes. If she knows what to expect next, she may be much less apprehensive, much less fearful, and she will experience less pain.

The next step, then, depending upon the depth of the patient, is to teach the patient amnesia. One should not teach a patient amnesia by saying, "when you come out of this trance, you will not remember what I have said," because she may remember what was said. This is also an order that she may be unwilling to follow, though some patients do develop amnesia this way. Why not instead tell a patient as follows: "You have been learning a great many new things. Some of them were learned consciously and some subconsciously. The subconscious keeps on working and thinking all the time and you do not need to be aware of it. Now then, I would like to point out to you that it is not necessary for you to remember consciously everything that you hear. That is not necessary because all the information that you have ever heard, all the information you have read or seen, such as telephone numbers, names, and the like, is stored in the subconscious. This information is always available and when you are ready to use one of these learned facts, out it comes." One points out that the patient does not have to remember everything she has heard. She can remember some of the things now and less of them in an hour, and perhaps tomorrow not remember any of the things that have been said. That is all right. She should have confidence in her own subconscious ability and realize that the material will be stored to be utilized when necessary. In this manner, amnesia has been pointed out in a way that she can accept. She might not want to forget what she has learned, but she might be willing to experience the new idea that "maybe tomorrow I won't remember everything that was said, maybe next week I may not remember anything that was said." She is now giving herself positive suggestions and new ideas that have been presented on a permissive basis.

The next step is teaching the patient anesthesia. If one takes adequate time and does it painstakingly, glove anesthesia can be taught to almost every patient. The scoring scale found at the end of this chapter differs with the thinking of most other scoring scales. According to those scales, a patient must be in a medium hypnotic trance to develop a glove anesthesia. This scale places glove anesthesia in the realm of a light trance.

How glove anesthesia can be transferred to other parts of the body must be pointed out to the patient so that she can understand that the anesthesia may be transferred to the abdomen, the back, from side to side, etc. The area to be anesthetized should extend from the nipple line to mid thigh. The patient can learn to develop anesthesia in that entire area.

If there is any time left during this appointment, one can teach the patient other phenomena depending upon the depth of her trance. A posthypnotic suggestion is given to help her recognize that she has learned something new. She now has done it once; the second time, it is obvious that it will be easier and will be accomplished more readily. She may also be told that she will be able to go into a deeper trance the next time.

This should not be interpreted to mean that at this visit the patient has been able to develop a complete and total anesthesia in the abdomen, the thigh, and the vagina so that she is capable of undergoing normal labor without pain, although this may sometimes occur. Rather, the patient now has the idea of what is going to be accomplished during her training period. All this only requires from one-half to one full hour.

Subsequent visits

At the next appointment, the patient is seated, a trance is induced, and she is told to review her new ideas and learning. She can reproduce the phenomena and almost without exception will be able to accomplish them more readily and more rapidly. At subsequent visits, repetition of these techniques is practiced. Obstetrical patients are usually seen every three weeks until the last month, when they are seen every week. The periodicity of the obstetrical patient's visits need not be changed if hypnosis is used.

When the patient enters the hospital, the physician may reinduce the trance and repeat the above or transfer the "rapport" to the intern or husband, who then may continue to reinforce the anesthesia, etc. Recent revision of this technique has obviated the necessity of the presence of the physician in the hospital. The training of the patient in the office is the same except that even before the patient has demonstrated her ability to produce all the desired phenomena, she is taught autohypnosis.

Techniques

Autohypnosis may be utilized by the patient as a method of practicing and thus increasing the level of anesthesia.

The patient may also be taught to reinduce the trance when distractions interfere. This may be suggested as follows: "I would like you to understand that if you practice your lessons well, they will be easier for you. You can practice producing anesthesia, etc., by yourself at home. It will only take a few minutes each day. This is the way you go about doing it. Seat yourself comfortably in a chair in the living room, kitchen, bedroom, or wherever you find it most comfortable. The chair you select is very similar to this chair—it has two arms, four legs, a back, and so on. Then I would like you to look at a spot on the wall (or put your hands on your thighs or whatever technique you have used) because that spot is similar to this spot and really all spots serve the same purpose."

What occurs is that the patient sits down in that chair at home and equates it with *this* chair in your office, and that situation is like *this* situation so that in effect, she feels as though she is in your office and can reproduce the hypnotic circumstances.

The patient should be told that after the trance has been induced (whether it be for a preselected time of one minute, two minutes, or more) she will find that when the allotted time has expired, or when her attention is needed elsewhere, she can end the trance voluntarily.

The patient should be taught that she can practice hypnoanesthesia. She can practice producing it in her hand and testing it, and then she can place her hand on her abdomen and feel that "dull feeling" leaving her hand and spreading out over her abdomen and thighs and back. Another method is to teach the patient to produce the anesthesia directly in the defined areas. She can practice either method at home once or twice a day for one, two, or three minutes and when she returns for her next visit, she can recognize that the practice has helped extensively.

It should be emphasized that it is the patient who has accomplished this learning. She is the one who controls the sensation or lack of it when she enters the hospital, and when she feels the contractions getting stronger, she can induce the trance state and alleviate the discomfort. This, as previously mentioned, makes the early presence of the physician unnecessary. Instead of keeping the rapport or transferring it to an intern or to the husband, what is effected, in this case, is a transfer of the rapport to where it really belongs, that is to the patient. She may control her sensations in her own manner because each patient has different needs and desires; it is unfair as well as improbable to expect all patients to follow one system of hypnotic conduct.

A slight variation of this technique is to teach the patient to accomplish all her new learnings as a posthypnotic suggestion without the need for formal hypnotic induction. She may, however, use autohypnosis if necessary for deepening the anesthesia, amnesia, etc.

One other method is the "feedback" technique, which consists of having the patient tell you at the nonhypnotic level and also at the hypnotic level what she would like to experience, what she would like to feel, and what she thinks she will feel, and use this to feed back to her in the hypnotic state with repetition; e.g., "you say that you would like to be wide awake at the actual time of the birth of the baby, and you really would like to see the baby and then go to sleep. Well, you are able to do that, and you can look forward with anticipation to a very comfortable delivery." Thus, her own ideas, subconscious needs, and wants are utilized, and she is learning that she can have the kind of labor that she would like to experience.

Finally: The technique that each physician should use is a combination of all or any of the above; that is, he should use the technique that will best suit the particular patient. Actually, the patient should be the one who selects the technique.

Questions and answers

The following are frequently asked questions involving the use of hypnosis in obstetrics.

1. *What about the patient who has the idea that she cannot induce the trance in herself unless the physician is there?*
Point out to the patient that if this were so, she would be a most unusual patient. She is certainly as capable of accomplishing autohypnosis as is any other patient. Demonstrate to her that she can do so: "I am going to step out of this room. I will be right around the corner in the next room. You go right ahead and follow the instructions, and I will be back in a minute or two." Now you *are* there and yet you are *not* there, and this will allow the patient the dual situation she needs.

2. *Does one tell the patient that she is going to have a normal labor and a normal child?*

Using care in the selection of words is important. Do not tell the patient, "You will have a labor that will last one hour, or one hour and twelve minutes." Rather tell a patient, "You can look forward to a normal delivery. You can look forward to a normal child, and you will be very happy after the delivery." And she can *look forward to* a normal labor.

3. *Should there be a nurse present at the first induction?*

Probably not, because offices usually have several rooms and there is enough activity so that the patient knows there is someone there. One no more needs a nurse present for the induction of hypnosis than for a vaginal examination. Most patients do not want a strange woman looking on. But some physicians use nurses for vaginal examination, and some physicians use nurses when they induce hypnosis. That is a matter of personal choice.

4. *What about the woman who doesn't want her husband to know that she is being hypnotized or wants to surprise the husband, and who goes home to practice hypnosis and has the husband walk in on her?*

Several patients who have been trained for hypnosis in obstetrics were having another physician deliver their babies. The delivering physician refused to have hypnosis used, said it was valueless. These patients wanted to have hypnosis and asked what could be done. It was pointed out that whether or not hypnosis was used was their personal decision. These patients went through labor and delivery without any anesthesia, the obstetricians often attributing it to their own ability. Many patients mimicked a state in which they looked as though they were not hypnotized.

The same thing can be accomplished at home. The physician can tell the patient, "should your husband walk into the room, there are several things you can do. You will know he is coming. You can let your eyes close and let him think that you are asleep or you can immediately rouse from the trance and thus keep the information to yourself." And she can do that readily.

5. *Is it possible that the hypnotized patient will fail to recognize the onset of labor?*

No. Precipitate delivery by a hypnotized patient is no more frequent than that by a nonhypnotized patient. Most physicians have had experience with a precipitation. Because the hypnotized patient is so acutely aware of her inner feelings and her body activity, she will feel labor contractions beginning long before the nonhypnotized patient, but they need not hurt. Hence the danger of precipitation is negligible. When false labor consisting of contractions occurs, the patient will recognize the uterine contractions as "different" and will not define them as term contractions.

6. *When should one begin the use of hypnosis in an obstetrical patient?*

Primiparae should learn hypnosis in the third or fourth month and multiparae in the fifth or sixth month.

7. *Should one charge an additional fee for using hypnosis?*

There need be no additional charge for using hypnosis. The hypnotic patient is usually much easier to handle and frequently requires less time spent in the hospital by the physician during labor.

8. *Has labor ever been induced with hypnosis?*

One experiment was reported several years ago. A multipara who was a good somnambulistic subject was placed in the labor room, hypnotized, and revivified to her previous labor. It was pointed out to her that in a few minutes she would get the same contraction that she got at that time. According to the report, labor was induced in a hard closed cervix, and the baby was delivered in "an hour or two." Very frequently as one reads reports on hypnosis, one wonders whether it was the reporter or the patient who was hypnotized.

9. *What about group hypnosis in obstetrics?*

Group hypnosis in obstetrics has been used by several physicians in this country. The proponents of this type of treatment utilize the idea of competition. They feel that every woman likes to compete with other women and, therefore, will be a better hypnotic subject and will develop anesthesia more quickly when trained in a group.

Objections to this method are readily found. My own opinion is that each patient would prefer to be treated as an individual. Just as she would like to deliver her baby in a room by herself without a group of women looking on, she would like to learn hypnosis by herself. She doesn't want to be offended or embarrassed by having others watch.

Although those who use group hypnosis state that they often do so as a means of saving time, this argument can be easily refuted. When one takes into consideration the delays, the interruptions, the repeated questions involved in training a group, it is readily seen that no more is accomplished than would have been in individual sessions.

The decision to use or not to use group hypnosis, however, is a matter of personal preference.

10. *Can hypnosis cure nausea and vomiting in pregnancy?*

Statistics are not useful on this subject because one cannot measure emotions in the laboratory. It seems logical that by virtue of the fact that hypnotic patients have a diminution in their minds of fear and anxiety regarding the birth of their baby, because they have learned to relax and be comfortable and to look forward to a perfectly normal labor, there is a markedly reduced amount of nausea and vomiting of pregnancy.

My own experience of a limited number of cases per year has revealed the following: Before utilizing hypnosis, nausea and vomiting were reported by a large percentage of pregnant patients. Today, there is rarely a patient who does not obtain relief by simple breathing exercises, placebos, etc. Obviously, these figures are not conclusive because they are small, but they indicate the type of results to be expected if hypnosis is utilized.

HERSHMAN'S CRITERIA FOR ADEQUACY OF HYPNOTIC STATES

(Common Order of Learning)

LIGHT TRANCE

1. Relaxation
2. Eye lid catalepsy
3. Eye closure
4. Beginning limb catalepsy
5. Slowing and deepening of respirations
6. Immobilization of facial muscles
7. Beginning catalepsy of limbs
8. Sensation of "heaviness" in various parts of the body
9. Glove anesthesia
10. Ability to perform simple post-hypnotic suggestions

MEDIUM TRANCE

11. Partial amnesia (some subjects)
12. Definite lag in muscular activity
13. Ability to accomplish illusions and simple hallucinations
14. Increased "detached" feeling
15. Marked catalepsy of limbs
16. Ability to perform more difficult post-hypnotic suggestions

DEEP TRANCE

17. Ability to maintain trance with eyes open
18. Total amnesia (in most subjects)
19. Ability to control some organic functions (pulse, blood pressure) etc.
20. Surgical anesthesia
21. Age regression and revivification
22. Positive and negative visual and auditory hallucinations
23. Ability to "dream" meaningful material
24. Ability to perform all or most of the above in the post-hypnotic state

PLENARY OR STUPOROUS TRANCE

25. Manifested by marked slowing of all organic responses and almost complete inhibition of spontaneous activity.

NOTE: *It should be apparent that despite the categorical delineation of the trance states, extensive variation is to be expected in any individual. Any of the above phenomena may be present in other than the described order, depending upon the experiential life of the subject, the nuances of the operator, and individual learning capabilities.*

7

Hypnosis in Children

The history of hypnosis in children starts with Mesmer. One of the first patients he treated was seventeen-year-old Maria Theresa Paradies, a blind pianist, whose sight he restored by direct suggestion. Her blindness was apparently hysterical in nature. Cases like this in 1777 and shortly thereafter quickly established Mesmer's reputation and great popular interest was aroused in mesmeric phenomena. Another important case of that period was that of Victor Race, a twenty-three-year-old shepherd boy, who was treated by the Marquis de Puysegur, one of Mesmer's students. Victor was a somnambulist and his case is of particular interest in that it makes the first mention and description of somnambulism, as it is still defined. Interestingly enough, Victor was able to determine what type of treatment should be used with him and how he could go about getting better. The story is included in most of his historical texts.

Elliotson, the man who introduced the stethoscope to England, also treated children with mesmerism. Even before this he was an advocate of guidance aimed at parents. After gaining experience with hypnosis, he used it in parent guidance, as well as in psychotherapy with children. Somewhat later Liébault used hypnosis for the treatment of children at the famous Nancy School of Hypnosis. In 1889 Bertillon spoke at the International Congress of Hypnotism in Paris on the subject, "The Value of Hypnosis in the Treatment of Vicious and Degenerate Children." He stated that many carefully observed facts proved the therapeutic value of suggestion in the following diseases of children: incontinence, nervous twitchings, nocturnal terrors, enuresis, onanism (by which he meant excessive masturbation), blepharospasm (tic of the eyelid), and other functional disturbances of the nervous system. In this address, he also mentioned the value of hypnosis in the treatment of lying, cruelty, idleness, and cowardice.

Suggestibility

It is very interesting to observe that the early writers on the subject of hypnosis in children all agree as to its simplicity, the ease of induction, and the high percentage of results.

Bertillon, for example, reported 250 cases where, he stated, he had an 80 per cent success in inducing hypnosis on the first attempt. Wetterstrand reported on a great number of cases, with subjects ranging from three to fifteen years of age—actually the youngest was two and a half years old. He claimed 100 per cent results with hypnosis. Liébault treated twenty-three cases up to age seven, where he obtained 100 per cent results; sixty-five cases from seven to fourteen, with 100 per cent results, and eighty-seven cases from fourteen to twenty-one, with 90 per cent results.

Many hypnotists today will find that they can get almost identical results. Children in general are imaginative. It is easy to get them to utilize most of the required techniques. They are keenly interested and hypnosis can be produced very rapidly.

Therapy (medical considerations)

In the therapy of children, particularly from the medical standpoint, it is usually unnecessary to have a very deep hypnosis. Their vivid imaginations and visual memory make gains possible on other levels. Children can be induced to see ball games, listen to concerts, and do all sorts of things while the physician or dentist is working on them, usually with satisfactory results. Gordon Ambrose reported extensive hypnotic work as a psychiatrist with children in a child guidance center. He stated that there are three cardinal rules that should be kept in mind when using hypnosis in children: (1) gain their confidence; (2) tell them what you are going to do; (3) use any technique.

RESPECT FOR THE SELF

In approaching the child hypnotically, either for the correction of habit patterns or for education in any particular regard, one needs always to bear in mind that the child must be taught to respect himself and, in respecting himself, not only to respect his own mind and his own body, but to respect very thoroughly and completely his own capacities to behave, his own capacities to learn.

In the following examples, hypnotic trances were constantly employed.

The most effective technique in child hypnosis is that of speaking simply and earnestly to the child, in such fashion as to fixate his attention. In this way a light to medium trance can be induced, in the process of offering therapeutic suggestions.

SOME SPECIAL PROBLEMS

Enuresis

One of the most important things one needs to accomplish in treating enuresis is to improve the child's confidence in himself, to get him to stop worrying about his failures. Thus it is better to persuade him—and more particularly, to persuade his family—to stop talking about a "wet bed" and start discussing "dry beds." In simple language, one must help the child to an understanding of what aggressions are, what parental attitudes are, and so on. Of course, it is frequently very important to include the parent or parents in the treatment.

CASE OF MARY ANN L.

When the young girl, Mary Ann L., was brought in for consultation, her parents complained that she wet the bed 365 nights per year. For the initial three weeks of her therapy, she was asked to bring in a report, not on how wet her bed was, but on what percentage of her bed was dry. Some nights one corner was dry; some nights the bed was one-third dry; at other times, it was half dry. At the end of the three-week period, the girl who had previously wet her bed seven nights per week was now wetting the bed twice a week, that is, she had a dry bed five nights a week. Now, after five or six months of therapy, Mary Ann has a dry bed from twenty-five to twenty-eight nights a month and she is no longer worrying about the problem.

Sometimes if one can get children to understand by indirection that wetting the bed is an aggression against the parents, the aggression itself may be employed to curtail the bedwetting. One can say, for example, "Just think how mad mommy and daddy will be when they come in in the morning and find your bed dry! That will really cause a commotion!"

Anxieties

With the childhood anxieties, such as shyness, nightmares, fears, somnambulism (sleep walking), nausea and vomiting, constipation, etc., one needs to discuss with the child the meaningfulness of the activity, the reasons for it, and the purposes served by it. This should be done at the child's intellectual and educational level. The attitudes involved should be discussed with both child and parents.

The following case report is given in considerable detail, to illustrate at some length the actual comprehensive approach to the child.

CASE OF VICTOR J.

Until the age of three, Victor J, a seven-year-old boy had evidenced no unusual fear of thunderstorms. At that time, however, an early teenage lad was brought into the home for foster care. He and his mother, now deceased, had spent a number of years as Japanese prisoners of war and, as a result of his war experiences, the boy had become highly neurotic and subject to numerous fears.

During his initial months in the foster home, the ex-internee showed almost uncontrollable terror during an actual storm, or even when one threatened. Gradually his apprehension was communicated to the younger child. Victor's lack of fear was replaced by much the same terror manifested by the foster brother.

Two additional incidents contributed to the smaller

child's attitude. One evening the mother, during a violent wind and rain storm, had opened the door to the carport, preparatory to going outside to secure some porch furniture. A strong gust of wind jerked the door out of her hand, caused her to slip on some wet concrete and, thus unbalanced, she was thrown under the car parked in the carport. The little boy began to scream with terror. It was very difficult to quiet him and assure him that his mother was uninjured.

Some time later, Victor and his father were out driving when a sudden desert duststorm arose, making visibility nonexistent. The father was forced to stop the car and park at the side of the road, as a safety measure. The wind rocked the car noticeably as the two sat in it, unable to see out, waiting out the storm. Following this episode, the child's fears intensified.

The parents had tried numerous measures in an effort to reassure him. They had quietly talked to him about the necessity for rain and what it meant, especially on the desert. He had had stories about rain read to him, and had been taught poetry about rain, wind, and storms. Although he enjoyed the rhythm of the poems and retained the content of the stories, his apprehension did not noticeably decrease. He insisted that the curtains be drawn when there was rain, or even an indication of rain, and he often asked to be put to bed, where he huddled fearfully under the covers.

The psychiatrist who was consulted had known the family socially over a long period and consequently many of their family traditions and practices were familiar to him. He was aware that the child still retained his belief in Santa Claus; it was the practice of the parents, from time to time throughout the year, to give the child small presents, crediting Santa Claus with having brought them. When the parents came into the office about the problem, the psychiatrist advised the parents to continue their practice of discussing with the child the need of flowers, grass, trees, and the earth for rain, and of teaching him poems about rain, but he suggested that they also tell Victor it was just possible Santa Claus might leave him a gift if the thunder became loud enough. The little boy was also seen in consultation and was told earnestly and emphatically that Santa Claus would probably have a surprise for him the next time it rained.

The child listened most attentively. When the next storm occurred, he was induced to peer out between the slightly parted curtains from time to time, to check on the brightness of the lightning, the loudness of the thunder, and the volume of the rainfall. He was persuaded to listen expectantly for each thunderclap, to determine whether, in his own mind, the noise was loud enough. He was also given pennies for each flash of lightning that he counted. He went to bed happily, in anticipation of Santa Claus' visit, and was delighted to find the promised gift the next morning.

A little later the parents reported that Victor had spontaneously begun to ask when it might rain again and whether, because of the rain, Santa might not use a boat instead of his customary sled.

He was seen casually on a number of social occasions and comments were made reinforcing the association of Santa Claus with storms.

Gradually, from his initial tentative peeking out between the drawn curtains at the rain, he has come to insist that the curtains not be drawn in bad weather. During a recent heavy rain, which had been preceded by a dust storm and considerable wind, the child accompanied his grandfather to the outside porch and happily played on his swing there despite the surrounding downpour.

A comparable example is that of three children, literally terrified by thunder and lightning, whose mother followed the psychiatrist's instructions to the three children in a light trance state, that they were to vie for prizes on the first discovery of lightning and the first hearing of thunder.

Stuttering

Another area in which pediatric hypnosis is useful is in stammering or stuttering. The early cases are, of course, the most easily managed. Long-standing chronic stuttering is frequently extremely difficult to handle, involving a tremendous amount of time and effort in working through the child's ideas and attitudes. Here again, one needs to build up the ego of the child, to give him a feeling of importance about himself, to get him to develop hobbies in which he can take a strong interest, and to discuss the ideas of the aggressions that he may feel.

One can discuss with him: Against whom does he have this feeling? Is it everybody, or is it just one or two people? Is it necessary to cause these people the additional work involved in listening to him and trying to determine what he is saying? Does he want everybody to have that additional work and effort? Does he want them to have it all the time, or just part of the time on certain days? One can produce a marked alleviation of symptoms by working this way. One does not try to take away the symptoms forcibly; one merely tries to limit them and restrict them and make them actually useful to the person. As soon as the symptoms become consciously useful, rather than expressions of unconscious defensive mechanisms, the patient has the opportunity of altering them to fit his total personality.

The stammerer may be convinced by his parents, his teachers, and everyone else that he cannot possibly talk without stammering distressingly. Yet, one can convey to the child an understanding that speech itself is only one form of communication. One can demonstrate to him that writing is another form of communication, drawing still another. He may be given a good understanding of this by showing him how a child learns to write. He takes a pencil and sticks out his tongue, twists his shoulders, contorts his face, even wiggles his feet. The patient can draw a parallel between the young child's physical behavior in learning to write and his own physical behavior in stuttering. The doctor can point out that as the writing becomes more proficient, the child no longer sticks out his tongue, his leg and shoulder movements cease, and his facial contortions are no longer evident. From this parallel, the young patient gets the idea that there is a possibility of alteration. This is the basis of any therapeutic development.

CASE OF NORMAN C.

Norman C, an eleven-year-old boy was treated hypnotically for his stammering. He was seen briefly for daily sessions over a period of less than a week, never for longer than one hour per day. His stammering, in addition to his actual speech difficulty, involved much grimacing and an uncoordinated writhing and twisting of his body. Watching his efforts to talk, one was forcibly reminded of the efforts made by a small child striving laboriously to learn how to write.

As an approach to his therapy, he was asked while in a light trance state a question about his handwriting—which was exceedingly illegible—and a parallel was drawn between his speech and his writing. The suggestion was also made that he would discover his speech improving when he found that his writing was changing for the better.

After a week's interviews, all conducted in the light trance state and during which the question was repeatedly raised as to which body movements were necessary for him in speaking, Norman was dismissed. He returned to his home in another state, with instructions to write a report regularly on his school and social activities.

When he was seen a year later, Norman was greatly improved. His facial grimaces were restricted primarily to an elevation or a depression, in rather uncoordinated fashion, of his eyebrows. Almost all the writhings of his body had disappeared.

His progress was praised, again during a light trance. The improvement in his handwriting was particularly complimented. The expressiveness of the facial muscles in speech and the actual possibility of communication by gestures were also discussed.

By another year, all of Norman's adjustments were greatly improved. His general attitude was that he was at liberty to stammer if he wished, or not to stammer if he wished, that he had entire freedom to stammer once a day, once a month, or once a year, to whatever degree was necessary.

In any therapy of the child, regardless of the problem, there is a need to understand the child, to utilize constructively whatever symptomatology he presents, and to integrate the behavior of the child, symptomatically and otherwise, into a coordinated, expressive, and useful totality.

Nail biting

Another frequently encountered problem in children is that of nail biting. The precipitating trauma is frequently insecurity, with masturbatory gratification in the form of oral comfort, followed by the development of a habit pattern. One often finds that it also denotes a masochistic tendency, the child turning his aggressions inward, toward himself. It may also be a lever against dominating parents. Again, one needs to discuss with the child on his own level the particular dynamics involved. One wonders which fingernail he needs to bite most. How much? At what time of the day? How much blood does he need to taste? Just a little, or a lot? One might wonder whether, instead of biting all ten nails, he would like to bite one nail ten times as much, or two, five times as much.

The mother can teach a child not to bite his fingernails by patiently painting the nails with polish. Of course, the polish is soon bitten off and the mother paints them again. It comes off again. The mother paints the nails after a little delay this time, because she is very busy making a cake. The child stands around waiting for the nails to be repainted. Mother has a brand new bottle of polish and the child is very anxious to have it applied. But now, of course, mother has to get dinner started and she can't do it immediately. The child begins to wish and wish that he hadn't chewed off that polish. Nobody has told him to make that wish, but the child automatically is going to wish he hadn't chewed his fingernails.

Another approach is to get the child to be very pleased with all the biting he has done on one nail, while the observer is interested in the beauty of the other nails. The important thing is to get him to yield the symptom by biting only one nail, or two, or even five, instead of ten. He has then tacitly implied permission for further manipulation of the symptom. And one can eventually get him to eliminate it entirely. The problem is primarily that of transforming without attacking.

Thumb sucking

Far too often, the problem of thumb sucking is handled by the parents, the physician, the dentist, and the teachers with all manner of threats which do no good at all. A child's need to suck his thumb must be respected. The child feels the need, demonstrates the need, and will react with antagonism, resentfulness, and uncooperativeness if threatened. A person might be perfectly willing to give up something of his own if asked for it. But bullying and name-calling will yield only a rightful resentment. The thumb-sucking child's reaction to threats is the same.

On the other hand, if one gives the child an understanding that he may need to suck his thumb and that he really ought to suck it enough, one has introduced a certain element of doubt and questioning in his thinking. Does he suck it enough? Does enough mean more or less? One can point out that he obviously gets pleasure out of sucking his right thumb. One can then point out, "Perhaps the fourth finger is pretty good. Possibly it's bad, but why not try it out?" He discovers that the fourth finger is bad. In other words, inserting a digit into the mouth is really bad. Of course, it just happens that this particular digit is the bad one, but then he soon finds out that another is bad, and another. Soon there have been eight bad ones and eight bad ones give a questionable two good ones. The idea there is something more in life than just thumbs has been introduced. One can wonder with him how long he will need the thumbs and one can recount the case history of a six-year-old who always sucked his thumb because he was growing up and, as soon as he got to be seven years old, he would not need to because he had grown enough. Of course, the fact that the patient's birthday is not for another three months means he can still suck his thumb because he is still growing up. One has set a definite limit to the thumb-sucking with the young patient, though he does not realize it.

CASE OF BOBBY G.

Six-year-old thumb-sucking Bobby G was asked, "What would really happen to you if you stood there in the corner and didn't suck your thumb while the clock moves from here clear down to there? The clock hand moves awfully slow—that's an awfully long time—but what would happen if you waited while the hand moved from here to there and you just stood in the corner without sucking your thumb? I wonder what would happen. I wonder if you wonder what would happen."

He stood there and watched that minute hand on the clock, wondering what would happen and nothing did happen. And that fact was emphasized, "Nothing happened and you stood there. That was an awfully long time for you not to suck your thumb. Do you know what really happened? Your found out that you didn't have to suck your thumb at all. That's what happened." That little six-year-old accepted the idea. The next day he insisted upon standing a whole half hour in the corner, and it was promptly pointed out, "In that corner? What about the corner over here?" Pretty soon there wasn't any place in the house where Bobby couldn't stand with his thumb out of his mouth. It had simply been spread all over his home, all over the yard, all through the environs of his daily life.

CASE OF MARIA F.

How do we deal with the child who sucks the thumb at night, or sucks the finger tip? Maria always went to sleep sucking her forefinger. She would jam it down her throat and choke repeatedly. The question was raised with her—which part of the finger could she feel best, this part, or that part? Of course, the dice were loaded in favor of the tip of the finger. Now, which part of her mouth could she feel best with? Was it the back of the tongue, the middle of the tongue, the gums, the tip of the tongue, the edge of the tongue, the gingival margins, the inside of the lips, the top of the lips, or just the border between the ordinary skin and the mucous membrane? Equivalent terms were used that she could understand.

That little three-year-old really got curious about it. Then the therapist wondered if, in her sleep, she would be able to feel that border nicely and whether she wanted her finger wet when she touched it or whether she wanted it dry. She could wet it nicely by using the tip of her tongue, so it graduated from the back of her throat on down to that. Later the question was raised, "Do you need it all the time when you're asleep? Or do you need to do it only when you are going to sleep?" After that, a trance was induced and the suggestions made that she would lie there and feel herself sleeping in the middle of the night and that she might try out those different feelings. Of course, it was a light trance, but she actually had the opportunity of measuring her satisfactions. She was won over. There was no reason for the need itself to be attacked. It is a false and peculiarly perfectionistic theory of therapy that demands that behavior be abolished rather than changed.

Tics

Other symptoms for which child hypnosis may be recommended are the tics, such as winking, tongue noises, blinking, and other such habit patterns. The treatment generally used is to re-educate the child, build up his ego, and reassure him. Of course it is frequently important here, as elsewhere in dealing with children, to treat the parents as well.

Therapy (dental considerations)

As a general procedure, the dentist's limitations in carrying out experimental procedures using hypnosis and in practicing psychotherapy are recognized. But there are certain problems where the use of psychotherapy by the dentist is definitely indicated.

SPECIAL PROBLEMS

Bruxism

The dentist may see the child who comes in and grinds his teeth, and that is the only particular symptom that this child shows—bruxism. The dentist may advise the parents to take the child to a psychiatrist, but the parents are certain that there is no problem except the bruxism and may be reluctant to seek psychiatric advice. In such a case, the dentist is well within his province as a dentist when he handles the bruxism. If that bruxism is the symptom of an underlying neurosis, the dental treatment will not suffice. The neurosis will become more apparent in other ways and the parents may become more amenable to the idea of taking the child to a psychiatrist. But as long as the child is showing neurotic behavior exclusively in bruxism, then it remains a dental problem.

How does one train a child to give up the bruxism? The treatment is the same for child and adult. One teaches the patient to go into a deep trance. One tells him that every time he grinds his teeth, he will awaken from sleep and that he will be angry at being awakened by the grinding of his teeth. But one also gives the posthypnotic suggestion that he can feel very happy because he can go right back to sleep. The idea has been to tie an anger reaction to the bruxism and a pleasure reaction to going right back to sleep. Merely telling the patient, "You'll awaken every time you grind your teeth," without giving the posthypnotic suggestion of comfort in that he can go right back to sleep, will lead to insomnia. The sense of accomplishment about the bruxism is the positive and important factor. One can also teach the child, as one does with adults, something about relaxing the jaw and keeping the teeth separated.

Another method is teaching the patient to tie some sponge rubber on the palms of the hands and showing him how to squeeze it. One builds up an association between the jaw muscles and the hand muscles, thus relating the bruxism to the gripping movements of the hands. Sponge rubber will protect the fingers and give the fingers resistance and one gets the bruxism transferred to the hands. Very shortly, the patient will cease the bruxism. The sponge rubber habit is not too well established and wears off. It is a perfectly safe procedure. The worst that can happen is the achievement of a good hand grip.

Tongue thrust

The same approach is used with the tongue thrust where the child insists on trying to shove the front incisors out of the mouth. Certainly, one can threaten the child with fear of malposed teeth. On the other hand, if one teaches a child to use the tip of the tongue to count the teeth and then raises the question of counting the cusps of the teeth, so that he can really identify them, one has put that tongue thrust all around the mouth, above and below, and taught the child that there are other experiences in the mouth that are just as important. One can then teach him how to curl the tongue and how to feel the roof of the mouth and get him interested in that experience.

Techniques of induction in children

THE USE OF IMAGERY

Earlier in this presentation it was pointed out that children, as a general rule, are exceedingly responsive hypnotic subjects. Since they usually have no difficulty in drawing on their imagination, a hypnotic approach employing visual imagery is frequently successful.

Demonstration 14: LIGHT-SWITCH TECHNIQUE

This method requires a patient old enough to understand the concept of electricity traveling through wires. The verbalization can then be as follows:

DOCTOR S (*demonstrating*)

When one turns a light switch one way, the electricity is on and the lights go on. When the switch is turned the other way, the electricity is off and the lights go off. We have wires in the body that connect to switches in the head. These wires are called nerves. When the switches in the head are on, we feel pain; when the switches in the head are off, we don't feel pain. Would you like to learn how to turn your pain switches off?

SUBJECT

Yes.

DOCTOR S (*demonstrating*)

O.K. Close your eyes. I want you to pretend that your right thumb is transparent, that you can see through it. (Showing the child a cellophane bag prior to this procedure is helpful.) Tell me, what color is your wire or nerve?

SUBJECT

Red.

DOCTOR S (*demonstrating*)

That's right. Now pretend that the arm from the thumb to the elbow is transparent and see the nerve in the arm. Now you can see it all the way to the elbow. Is it getting bigger or does it stay the same size?

SUBJECT

It gets bigger.

DOCTOR s (*demonstrating*)

Now pretend that the part from the elbow to the neck is transparent. Is the nerve still the same size?

SUBJECT

Now it is.

DOCTOR s (*demonstrating*)

Watch it as it connects with a little box about the size of your thumb in the middle of your head. Do you see the box?

SUBJECT

Yes.

DOCTOR s (*demonstrating*)

On one side of the box are a few switches. Are they on the left or right?

SUBJECT

On the right.

DOCTOR s (*demonstrating*)

How many are there?

SUBJECT

Five.

DOCTOR s (*demonstrating*)

Fine. Four switches are of one color and the other switch is different. What color are the four switches?

SUBJECT

Blue.

DOCTOR s (*demonstrating*)

What color is the different switch?

SUBJECT

Yellow.

DOCTOR S (*demonstrating*)

In your mind, reach over and turn off the yellow switch. Have you done it well?

SUBJECT

Yes.

DOCTOR S (*demonstrating*)

You have now turned off the electricity to your right thumb. The hurt to the thumb is now disconnected. See the left thumb is connected and it still hurts. (*Test with sharp stimulus.*) You can feel the right thumb but the hurt is gone. (*Test.*) Isn't that right?

SUBJECT

Yes.

DOCTOR S (*demonstrating*)

Anything you touch with a disconnected thumb also gets disconnected. (*Have patient demonstrate his ability to disconnect pain in various areas.*)

The above technique with only slight change in language is also applicable to adults.

THE USE OF IDENTIFICATION

The following technique can also be employed with children. You can take a recalcitrant two- or three-year-old, put her in her crib, take her favorite toy along, then tell her that you are going to let the toy animal go to sleep. "The toy is now going to sleep. He's very tired and little sister had better lie quiet; she might wake the bunny. See, the bunny is really tired and sleepy. You can see that the bunny's leg is loose." You then pick up the leg of the toy, let it loose and it falls down. Then you pick up the other leg and the leg falls down in a relaxed way; you pick up the toy's floppy ear and that falls down—perfect relaxation. "And, little sister, be very careful to let the bunny sleep." So little sister does let the toy sleep, but in the process of helping the toy to sleep, little sister gets very much relaxed and goes into a nice trance state. One cannot, of course, expect a great amount of hypnotic phenomena from a two- or three-year-old child. The child has not lived long enough and has not had enough experience. But a young child can show such phenomena as catalepsy, restricted awareness, and anesthesia.

To summarize, children are generally more amenable hypnotic subjects than adults, although one cannot expect a very wide range of hypnotic phenomena in youngsters. Almost any technique that can be used for the adult can also be used for the child. In working with children, as with adults, we must never lose sight of the fact that, regardless of our hypnotic purpose, the subject must be taught respect for himself, his mind, his body, and his capacities.

The eidetic imagery capacity of the child, the tremendous hunger for and need to seek new experiences and understandings, and the need to exercise and to repeat experiences enable the child to be a most receptive and responsive subject.

8

Clinical Applications of
Hypnosis to General Medicine

In one of his lectures William James remarked that every scientific theory goes through a classical career of stages. First it is attacked as absurd. Then it is admitted to be true, but obvious and insignificant. Finally it is deemed to be so important that its adversaries claim they were the ones who discovered it. Hypnosis is at present in the second of these stages, with indications that the third stage has begun in certain areas. Some of our colleagues believe that its use should be limited to the psychiatric field. Others still feel that hypnosis is of no consequence. A few think it is absurd. Actually, none of these opinions is valid. Hypnosis has a practical application in almost all fields of medicine and its allied professions. It can and should be used by general practitioners and anesthesiologists, pediatricians, dentists, clinical psychologists and, obviously, psychiatrists.

Hypnosis adds speed and directness to psychotherapy, but it is not a panacea. Where the therapeutic goal has a time element involved, where an exhaustive rehabilitation of the individual is not essential, a short-term therapeutic maneuver utilizing hypnosis may restore the individual's capacity to meet the rigors of his inter- and intrapersonal relationships. This utilization of hypnosis may also help in the development of a motivation to continue further treatment in the psychiatric realm with the total reintegration of the personality as the goal.

Wolberg emphasizes that the history of hypnosis demonstrates conclusively that it is no miracle method but that, shorn of extravagant claims made for it by some of its adherents, it is an important and useful therapeutic tool. The late Robert Lindner contended that hypnoanalysis can be the equivalent of surgical removal of barriers and hazards in that it pierces the psychic substrata and raises the repressed to the level of awareness. Brenman and Gill state that in the induction of hypnosis, the various illusions or even hallucinations a patient may go through are due to a change in the ego, which leads to a minimization of the importance of external reality and to alteration in bodily sensation and body image.

In April 1955, after eighteen months of intensive study, a subcommittee of the psychological medicine group of the British Medical Association reported the following:

1. Hypnosis is of value and may be the treatment of choice in some cases of psychosomatic disorder.
2. It is valuable for revealing unrecognized motives and conflicts.
3. As a method of treatment, it has proved its ability to remove symptoms and to alter morbid habits of thought and behavior.
4. Doctors do a disservice to themselves and medicine by making communications to lay audiences and the lay press in a manner inconsistent with medical ethics.
5. Description, therapeutic possibilities, and limitations of hypnosis should be taught to medical undergraduates.
6. The clinical use of hypnosis should be taught to medical graduates, particularly psychiatrists, obstetricians, gynecologists, and anesthesiologists, as well as to others who practice in any of the fields of psychological medicine, which actually includes all people in the therapeutic field.
7. University departments and research foundations should institute more research along clinical and experimental lines.

Background

The utilization of hypnosis in modern medicine began, as we well know, with Mesmer. Probably all the proponents of hypnosis utilized direct suggestion to produce anesthesia and a direct removal of symptoms to effect their medical "cures." Esdaile, Elliotson, Charcot, and others described the necessity of making suggestions forceful, strong, dogmatic, and repetitious. Some of them used flowing robes, austere surroundings, and a dramatic showmanship in an attempt to elicit the sensations of awe and fear and to heighten their prestige with patients. Apparently, if one can accept their reports as valid, these procedures did work on a large number of patients. It is difficult, however to determine whether the use of hypnosis resulted in a "cure," or whether prestige suggestion might have had the same results without the production of the trance state.

Major techniques

Five main techniques are utilized in hypnotic treatment. First, and most rarely used, is the prolonged, deep hypnotic trance, where the patient is placed in a deep hypnotic state and kept there for a period of hours or days. This treatment has been utilized for some fifty years, particularly in some of the neuroses, e.g., the vomiting of the gastric neuroses. It has also proved some value with some of the emotionally based tics.

The second method, also utilized for some time, is indirect suggestion. Here the technique employed is that of indirect, permissive suggestion, or indirect permissive removal of symptoms. The suggestions must be very detailed. For example, in treating an insomniac and teaching him how to go to sleep by means of posthypnotic suggestion, one must bear in mind that he must also be told that if he should awaken during the night for any reason, this teaching will also include the ability to return to sleep.

Direct hypnotic suggestion constitutes a third method. This particular technique can be effectively employed in a small percentage of cases, but it requires especially careful handling of the patient to avoid arousing resistance.

The fourth method of treating patients hypnotically is the use of a cathartic hypnotic state wherein, as Breuer stated, the hypnosis diminishes the inhibitions and repressions and releases the emotional block. This is a psychiatrically oriented type of therapy.

Hypnoanalysis, the fifth type of therapy, constitutes an approach in which analytic techniques are utilized on a psychiatric level, the hypnosis constituting an adjunct to shorten the therapeutic course.

DIRECT HYPNOTIC SUGGESTION

Kline's expression "directive hypnotherapy" as a term to replace "direct suggestion" is very well taken. The terms may be considered synonymous; however, they have different connotations. Despite the fact that it is called "directive hypnotherapy," the best type of therapy would actually be one that is utilized as an indirect suggestion in therapy— not a means of directly attacking the problem or symptoms or directly suppressing them with orders, but rather a technique bringing about a condition within the patient that can lead him to evaluate more productively the effectiveness of the activity, and resulting in a behavioral response more adequate for him as a total personality.

Two elements are requisite to the elicitation of productive activity in the hypnotic subject when direct suggestion is used. One is the depth of the hypnosis required; a somnambulistic state is probably necessary for most psychophysiologic conditions. The second requisite is adequate understanding by the patient of the purposes to be served and their relationship to his personality needs.

Direct suggestion will probably never be as efficacious as indirect suggestion, which can eliminate some of the natural resistances of the patient. As one might expect, resistances increase in proportion to the neurotic needs of the patient and the resulting altered state of psychologic and neurophysiologic functioning. In a patient with fewer neuroses and less neurotic behavior, there is more willingness to comply with direct suggestion.

INDIRECT PERMISSIVE SUGGESTION

An adaptation of the second hypnotic technique, indirect permissive suggestion, is probably most important to the general practitioner and the one with which we shall concern ourselves primarily in this discussion. The internist or the general practitioner is not usually qualified to give extensive psychiatric therapy to the patient, but he can utilize many of the techniques of indirect permissive suggestion to render the most satisfactory treatment to his patient. Most physicians have been treating symptoms by giving aspirin for headaches, codeine for coughs, and in many of these cases merely treating the symptom without getting to the underlying cause. With the utilization of hypnosis, one has a valuable therapeutic adjunct. This type of therapy frequently presents the best opportunity for application and is usually the most effective in the ordinary complaints presented to the physicians.

Such suggestion can be employed (1) to obtain the deepest possible state of hypnosis within the time allotted to the patient, directing the symptoms and the suggestions with all eventualities considered; (2) to repeat these things frequently to the patient, thus reinforcing them.

Of course it is also important, before determining the type of suggestion to offer a patient, to get a well-oriented history without necessarily going into a detailed psychiatric history. It is important, as well, to utilize the patient's questions, both in the induction stages and in his treatment.

The depth of trance is probably not too important in the treatment of the minor neuroses that the average practitioner handles providing the doctor can clear up the mental state of the patient. Frequently, definitive results can be obtained. Schilder and Kauders claimed that they could obtain results in from one to four sessions. Of course, this may not suffice for a permanent cure. Many persons learn by slipping or erring and some patients need to experience this. Treatment should be continued subsequent to this "slip."

Severe neuroses generally require more extensive hypnotherapy and many more sessions are usually indicated. The therapist may find that it is important to the patient to learn the purpose of his symptoms, when they do serve a purpose for him. It is not necessary for this awareness to be on a conscious level, however; the actual purpose may never become consciously recognized, but the patient's realization of the possibility that his symptoms may be important may lend itself to a revaluation of his symptoms. Consequently, substitutions may be evoked on the part of the patient through permissive suggestions, allowing for an improvement of the total personality. Schilder and Kauders also state that medical hypnosis helps the patient to rebuild his personality on the basis of an increased ability to adjust himself and to accept reality. This reconstruction takes place under the direction of the physician.

It is important also to note that reassurance, persuasion, re-education, and the like, which are certainly of value in the nonhypnotized patient, will have increased value in the hypnotized individual. These measures can be used effectively with even a light trance.

In the production of the trance state, the utilization of indirection allows for a better acceptance on the part of the patient; it removes the possibility of defenses that are a normal response to a direct ordering away of either a physical sign or a symptom.

DIRECT AND INDIRECT APPROACHES CONTRASTED

In contrasting the two methods, one might employ the following direct approach to the production of hypnotic deafness: "When I count to ten, you will find yourself getting more and more deaf, until finally, at the count of ten, you will be unable to hear anything at all."

On the other hand, the indirect approach might proceed in this fashion: "I wonder how it feels to a person who is about to lose his hearing? I wonder if he notices the fact that sounds seem to grow very, very slightly less distinct at first, if he finds that they seem to be fading off into the distance? And I wonder if the person then sits in his chair, leaning forward toward the sound? Does he cup one ear or both ears, or does he test his hearing by putting a finger in his ear to see if there is an obstruction there? Does he find himself straining more and more and holding his head to the side, all in an attempt to try to get an accumulation of more of the sounds? Does he find that, despite this, the sounds continue to fade farther and farther into distance? Do things finally sound as though they are only being whispered? Then does he notice despite the fact that he can see the speaker's lips moving, that he is unable to hear anything except an occasional noise coming through? I wonder if this is distinguished by a slight buzzing noise, or if there is no buzzing noise? Then how does he feel; how does he look at one? Does he gaze intently, staring at people in an attempt to read their lips?"

All the while, of course, as this is drawn out very carefully and in detail, the speaker can be reducing the volume of his own voice, to help in the realization of the situation. In a careful, indirect procedure of this sort, one can produce hypnotic deafness. It will stand all the tests of physiologic deafness, because the subject was allowed unconsciously to utilize his own feelings, his own sensations, and his own knowledge of things, in order to limit and de-limit his ability to hear sounds and the spoken word. He did not experience the normal resistances evoked by order-ing him directly not to be able to hear. This type of pro-cedure should also be used in the production of the hyp-notic trance state. It should be employed in the treatment of any of the ailments where hypnosis is utilized.

General therapeutic approaches

SYMPTOM REMOVAL

Several general types of therapy can be used by the general practitioner in medicine. First are symptom-removal tech-niques. These utilize a direct hypnotic approach, similar to that described earlier. There is probably little place in the modern concept of dynamics for this particular type of technique for despite careful planning on the part of the hypnotist, the procedure can again result in evoking the resistances of the patient.

SYMPTOM ALLEVIATION

The second type of treatment is the alleviation or ameliora-tion technique. By inducing changes in perceptions, changes in reception of stimulation, and changes in sensations, a large portion of the treatment procedures can be accomplished. Relaxing mechanisms of the physical as well as the emotional state can be utilized in this type of technique and anxiety symptoms can frequently be lessened.

SYMPTOM SUBSTITUTION

The third technique is a replacement or change in the symptoms. Actually, this amounts to a substitution of the symptoms. While it is frequently stated, particularly by psychotherapists, that direct removal of one symptom will result in another symptom, many workers have found that if the suggestions offered are indirect and permissive, frequently a symptom will not be substituted. One needs also to bear in mind that the therapist can manipulate symptoms, causing a patient to accept a substitute that is less disturbing.

CASE OF MR. THOMAS A.

One such case was reported by Erickson. He described a patient, Mr. Thomas A, with a functional paralysis of one arm. The paralysis was gradually maneuvered by the therapist to the point where the patient agreed to have it placed in the right little finger.

The patient still satisfied his neurotic needs by having a hysterical paralysis; however, it is located in such fashion that it does not prevent his carrying out his normal activities. This is a very specialized therapeutic maneuver, but one that can readily be accomplished by many therapists familiar with hypnotic techniques.

SYMPTOM MANIPULATION

Another technique is that of yielding the symptom to the therapist. Initially the therapist may be permitted only to increase the symptom, but this carries with it a tacit permission on the part of the patient for it to be further manipulated. Thus the symptom can be gradually reduced, or finally eliminated.

In treating a patient with migraine headache, for example, one might tell the patient that there is a possibility that his headaches could become worse, that temporarily, in a limited situation, they might not only become more severe but more frequent. When the patient allows the therapist to make his headaches worse, he is surrendering a measure of control. The implication is that if the therapist can make the headache worse, he can also make it better.

Symptom manipulation can be effected with the use of hallucinations and other sense-modality changes, such as age regression and time distortion. These processes, it must be remembered, do not cause a change in the self-understanding or insight processes of the patient directly, but they may be employed directly to affect and ameliorate the patient's distress. It would seem, however, that there must of necessity be some re-evaluation of symptoms, at least on an unconscious basis, for these results to be permanent in character.

HANDLING RECURRENCE OF SYMPTOMS

Brief reference has been made to the fact that some persons learn by slipping or erring and that some patients need this experience before a permanent cure is effected. Patients ought to be made aware of such a possibility and should be instructed to report back to the office following such an experience.

Patients are usually told that everybody who learns something learns it in a different manner. Sometimes the example of the typist is given. She may learn to type by making errors, going over and over those errors, correcting them, then making still others, until she finally learns exactly where her fingers should be in relation to the keys. They are also told that people are frequently able to remove symptoms in themselves, but then they may need subconsciously to know how it was before they removed the symptoms. Thus they can sometimes reproduce the symptoms subconsciously, merely to test them and decide whether they want to continue with them, or whether they want to remain free of them. In that manner, patients are prepared for the fact that they may have a recurrence, but the information is given without positively suggesting the recurrence. Consequently, when they do find the symptom recurring, they do not simply give up, feeling that everything is hopeless.

CASE OF NANCY B.

Nancy B, a girl of fifteen who had severe dysmenorrhea and excessive bleeding, was put in a deep trance and discussed with the doctor her first menstrual period. This had occurred at the age of eleven or twelve. There was excessive bleeding, although she experienced little pain. A great furore was raised about it, however, and she was hospitalized and given hormones by mouth. This was a very exciting experience for Nancy. Since that time, all her periods had been accompanied by very severe pain and an unusual amount of bleeding.

The fact was discussed that often young girls of eleven, twelve, and thirteen do not have a standard body reaction: thus, some months they need to have excessive bleeding; other months they need to have little bleeding; some months they need to have more contractions, and others, fewer contractions. Following the discussion, the patient was told "Now you're a grown girl and, of course, your body should have learned by now. It can learn within the next thirty days exactly which mechanism is necessary."

Nancy's next period was painless and she bled about 60 per cent of the amount she had previously, probably the normal amount for her. She came back to see the doctor after that period and the possibility of the body learning things first one way and then another was discussed. The second month she again had a relatively painful period, although not as painful as originally; furthermore, she lost almost as much blood as she had been doing. It was pointed out to her that this actually could be an excellent thing, since she was experiencing various ways of learning.

Her third period was entirely normal and free from pain. Nancy was told that she might "slip up" again. She was also told that, since she was going to be menstruating for many, many years, it was almost inevitable that she would miss some periods because of illness, accidents, or pregnancy, after which she would start to menstruate again. These things were explained in detail to allow for the possibility of their occurring without disturbing her emotionally to the point where she would revert to the old painful and excessive bleeding pattern.

Areas of usefulness

The use of hypnosis in general medicine can be put together and classified under the systems. Under the respiratory system we might treat colds, asthma, hay fever, and the like.

The gastrointestinal system will include ulcers, hyperacidity, constipation, plain old-fashioned bellyaches, heartburn, perhaps gall bladder diseases, and ailments of that nature. Under the genitourinary system, such problems as enuresis, impotency, and premature ejaculation would be included, along with others discussed under obstetrics and gynecology.

In regard to the nervous system, apart from matters handled by the psychiatrists, one could use hypnosis for such disturbances as anxiety, insomnia, and migraine. Also, questions of excessive smoking, nail biting, stammering, obesity, and the like can often be resolved by the nonpsychiatrist.

FEARS

Many persons have a fear of the unknown or a fear of something known, without understanding that there is probably some reason for it; sometimes such fears persist, even when the person understands that these feelings may be based on traumatic events of early childhood. One such type of patient is the high school or college student, more often the graduate college student, who comes in with a fear of failing an examination, for which he admits he has read adequately. Or he may be one who was too restless to study very much for the examination and is now exhibiting marked concern.

One needs to teach such persons in the hypnotic state the necessity of respecting the unconscious. One needs to teach them that all memories are stored in compartments within the subconscious or the unconscious mind, and that when students read for an examination, they need not read with the idea of memorizing but only for the purpose of understanding the material. It can be impressed upon this particular type of patient that if he reads with understanding, his knowledge will be retained within his unconscious. Of course, it takes longer to discuss it with the patient than it does to review here the few general broad statements that are made.

One needs to teach these patients that if respect for the unconscious has been properly developed by the doctor and by the patient, they need merely sit down when they go into the examination with a feeling of well-being, with a feeling of satisfaction, with a knowledge of the material being there within the unconscious and of its being forthcoming at the proper time.

Two different mechanisms are involved here. One concerns itself with posthypnotic trance states, since the subjects tend to go into light trances while they are writing the examinations. The other mechanism has to do with the fact that by putting the pen on the paper, the patient is allowing the unconscious to rule. The unconscious, having a knowledge of the material, can allow it to pour forth and the patient will frequently write an excellent paper. One patient, a law student, after taking the bar examination recently, reported that he sometimes didn't even know how the information got on the paper, that he didn't know how he knew the law involved, yet he wrote a passing examination.

Other patients will come in, complaining of fear of airplane trips, and resulting airsickness. One could readily take a patient with this fear and, if he is a good hypnotic subject, let him experience a pleasant sensation on an airplane trip, hallucinate it, and learn to enjoy it, then give him the memory for the experience. One could also explain, basically and simply, while the patient is in the hypnotic trance, the pleasure of looking around and seeing the broad expanse of sky, looking down and seeing the minuteness of the cars, the people, the houses, etc.

Fear of not falling asleep is another frequently encountered problem. One could produce a hallucination of normal sleep within the patient. One could also treat insomnia by teaching the patient autohypnosis, as previously mentioned.

PAINS

We are naturally faced with the problem of handling pain in general medicine. It is generally accepted that suggestion probably results in alteration of the vasomotor apparatus, not only in the circulatory system, but in the entire system of the individual. For the production of deep surgical anesthesia, it is probably necessary to produce a somnambulistic state in the patient. For the alleviation of pain in dental situations or in minor surgical procedures, a light or medium trance will frequently suffice. Some of the conditions for which this type of hypnoanesthesia or hypnoanalgesia has been utilized are: suturing of minor lacerations; instrumental examination, such as cystoscopy or urethroscopy, laryngoscopy, and proctoscopy. Even the discomfort of a vaginal examination in a tense, fearful patient can be markedly alleviated by the production of a light hypnosis, followed by suggestions of relaxation and the elimination or reduction of pain.

Other painful conditions where hypnosis has marked value in general medicine are: removal or reduction of pain resulting from arthritis, myositis, bursitis, traumatic injuries of not too severe a nature, sprains, fractures, and the like.

CASE OF MARIAN D.

One case, interesting particularly from the orthopedic standpoint, is that of Marian. It may perhaps answer some questions about the possibility of harming patients by removing symptoms.

Marian came in one day with a severely sore ankle, which she said she had twisted. The ankle was x-rayed and it was found that no fracture was present. She was therefore given an anesthesia for her sprained ankle. The existing pain was removed at one or two o'clock in the afternoon; at about seven o'clock that evening she called and said that the ankle was hurting her severely. She was instructed to come to the office. The ankle was examined and, since it presented a somewhat different appearance than it had earlier, it was re-x-rayed. The new films disclosed that she now had a fracture. Apparently some time after leaving the office, she had reinjured the ankle and this time had broken it. Despite the fact that she had been given a total anesthesia for the ankle, this condition represented something different. The sprain was not a necessary pain; the fracture was a necessary pain, and therefore her pain returned. The fracture was set, a cast was applied, and she was again given her anesthesia. She responded very well.

The question has been raised concerning medicolegal liability in this case. The question can be answered by saying that the patient did not break her bone because she was hypnotized, or because she had an anesthesia for a sprained ankle. Suppose the girl had been treated by an injection of Novocain in the ankle to enable her to walk on it. That is acceptable treatment by some orthopedists. The patient would have no pain. Now, assuming that she broke her ankle, there would be no case against the doctor for having used Novocain. Similarly, a psychologic anesthesia for the sprained ankle was produced here but it had nothing to do with the fracture.

PHOBIAS

Hypnosis is useful in the treatment of certain phobias, such as those which result, for example, from present-day fear-provoking advertisements concerning cancer and similar matters. It may be possible to suggest to the patient that the frequent repetition of these ideas of cancer, of polio, and so forth, really constitute a hypnotizing of the individual and a suggesting of such symptoms.

UPPER RESPIRATORY INFECTIONS

Hypnosis has a value in the treatment of upper respiratory infections and the ordinary cold. It is a common expression that colds will clear up, if left alone, in a week; that with the utilization of any of the modern medications, they will clear up in seven days. This humor notwithstanding, it is firmly believed that the symptomatology of the common cold can be markedly alleviated and often completely removed within a very short time with the utilization of hypnosis. A technique that may be utilized is as follows: One can tell the patient in detail exactly what his rhinitis, his laryngitis consists of; how, in the case of rhinitis, it is an edema of the tissues, a swelling owing to inflammation, with consequent obstruction of the normal air passageways; that these are symptoms of which the individual must be aware, so that he can protect himself from overexposure. But, of course, these symptoms have already made themselves known. The patient is now aware of the fact that there is an inflammation in the throat and in the nose. He has known that for 24 to 48 hours. That is why he came to the physician to seek treatment.

Therefore, what is the need of retaining these symptoms? How important is it for these symptoms to be present constantly? It is possible, perhaps, now that the patient is aware of them, that it is unnecessary for them to disturb him any longer. Could he find that he might allow a shrinkage of those tissues? Could he have a feeling and a sensation as though there were being poured on those tissues a chemical such as is used in nose drops, causing shrinkage of those tissues and bringing them back to their normal condition? The patient knows that for the next week he is going to be careful not to have any overexposures, because he knows the cold will persist for four, five, six, or seven days. Despite the fact that he will not feel the symptoms as severely, if at all, he will continue to take care of himself for the next week. He will partake of sufficient fluids, but he can go about his daily activities with the knowledge that the treatment is going on, the normal, natural care that the human body gives is occurring. This type of approach, suggesting a sensation of freedom in the head, a lack of pain, and easing of other discomforts can result in marked alleviation.

MULTIPLE SCLEROSIS

Multiple sclerosis can sometimes be helped through the utilization of hypnosis. Of course, one must be careful not to make extravagant claims about curing multiple sclerosis, which has the usual periods of remission. One needs to be able to differentiate between a remission and an alleviation brought about by hypnotic suggestions. It is recognized that there is often a prevalent psychogenic factor in multiple sclerosis. By guidance, reassurance, and the development of proper attitudes, many of the symptoms may be alleviated.

TICS

Before the turn of the century, it was advocated that the patient should practice the suppression of tics before a mirror. Brissard recommended that the patient could start out with only a few minutes, but he emphasized the fact that the suppression must be complete. This type of treatment, if one is willing to accept it, can be markedly helped by the utilization of hypnosis and the teaching of the autohypnotic state. One can also discuss the meaningfulness of the tics, the need for utilizing them on all occasions, and whether or not the patient can be satisfied with an occasional utilization of them. Sometimes, too, an individual can be helped with a transferring of the tic from an obvious one to one that is not as obvious, as, for example, a clenching of the fist, or the clenching of one little finger, or perhaps merely a slight twitch of the little toe.

CONSTIPATION

Physicians frequently see patients with constipation who have run the gamut of all the cathartics and other medications to relieve the constipation, all to no avail. One can set up a reflexology in such patients. For example, with the production of the trance state, one can discuss with the patient the possibility of setting aside a certain time convenient to the patient each day, and utilizing that period for the emptying of the bowel. One can employ that training program, allowing the patient to use the same period every single day merely to sit and speculate and wonder as to whether the bowel movement will be a full one or a partial one. One can build up within the patient a feeling of satisfaction, a feeling equated with "healthy," with any of the reflex features that one can utilize, depending upon the patient's personality. In this manner, one allows for the reflex conditioning that may result in daily bowel movements to take place.

INSOMNIA

The treatment of insomnia can be discussed in terms of a particular case.

CASE OF DONALD E.

Donald E, age twenty-four, presented himself with the major symptom of insomnia and a secondary symptom of fear about making decisions. The fear had been growing increasingly more severe. In the light hypnotic state, Donald discussed the fact that he woke up tired, could not take criticism, and that he was 4-F in the Army examination because of hypertension. He stated, too, that he never dreamed, that he was tired and sleepy in the morning when he awakened, that all through the night, ideas were constantly turning over in his mind. He kept reversing whatever decisions he made and hadn't been able to keep a girl friend for more than one or two dates. A brief history elicited the information that, whereas his father was very critical and strict, his mother was easygoing. He described himself as a "borderline neurotic." He stated that he felt tight and tense, as though he were "ready to break." He never relaxed. He utilized all forms of barbiturates and other medications in an attempt to break his insomnia, all to no avail.

He was taught autohypnosis. He was also trained to take one of the nonbarbiturate types of sleeping pills, with a strong suggestion that this pill was exceedingly valuable and useful, that it could have a very marked effect, that its effect was very rapid in action, that it took usually less than fifteen minutes to begin to work, and that its effects lasted from six to eight hours in most individuals. Utilization of this type of suggestion with the medication described resulted in a marked improvement in his ability to sleep.

Further examination in the hypnotic state revealed that many years ago, while there was conflict in his home and a discussion of parental divorce was under way, a fire had occurred. The night following this fire in his home, Donald's insomnia had begun. It was pointed out to him that this fire had occurred many years ago, that actually it was all over now, and one could wonder whether it was necessary for him still to have the same fears of going to sleep that he had had at that particular time. He understood the type of suggestion that was offered; he retained a memory of all that took place in the trance state, since he had specifically requested no amnesia of the trance experience; nevertheless, the insomnia condition improved markedly.

THE TREATMENT OF HABITS

As has been indicated earlier, habits are more easily treated than neurotic or psychosomatic manifestations.

Smoking

The problem of smoking is of importance to many persons now because of the current cancer scare. In the January, 1956 issue of the *Journal of Clinical and Experimental Hypnosis,* some of the methodologies that may be used with various types of individuals are discussed in detail. The particular approach depends upon the given individual's verbalizations. One utilizes what the patient himself has to say concerning his motives for quitting smoking, how he feels about it, what ideas he has on the subject, employing these both for trance induction and trance utilization.

Obesity

Obesity is a relatively similar problem, differing only in components. It is handled similarly by discussing the body image of the individual. These techniques are simple and do not always involve analysis of the root cause of the problem. In some cases, of course, it is necessary for the psychiatrist to intervene, employing age regression, free association, or other analytic types of techniques, in order to try to determine the causation and to allow the patient to gain insight into the problem in an effort to alleviate his pattern of overeating or oversmoking.

In treating problems of obesity the general practitioner attempts to get the patient to work at building up a control. Simply to put a patient on a diet and say, "You stick to that diet and you reduce so much per week," is to approach the problem backward. The patient needs to be interested in what the pleasure of eating is. The pleasure of eating lies not only in the taste of food, but in what food does to the body. We raise the questions: What is the patient's attitude toward his body? How can he discover his attitude toward his body?

CASE OF PHYLLIS C.

Phyllis C, a girl in her early twenties, sought help because she had become some forty or fifty pounds overweight. She was encouraged to go into her favorite store frequently and look at a size twelve bathing suit. She went in to look and she really built up a strong motivation to buy that particular suit. It took her about nine or ten months to reduce to the point where she was able to get into it, but eventually she was able to wear it. She got a great deal of pleasure out of that accomplishment.

Nail biting

Teenagers are usually the patients who present the greatest nail-biting problem, although all ages may be encountered.

CASE OF ROSEMARY K.

Rosemary K was graduating from high school and she was embarrassed because she still bit her nails. She wanted to stop. It was very important to her, she said, and yet she had tried and tried and had been unable to quit. The patient and her therapist discussed many things, among them the matter of fees. It was learned that Rosemary had saved $500 as a college fund. The question was raised concerning the possibility of using her as an experimental subject, about whom an article might be written. If she gave permission for this and quit biting her nails, the fee would be her permission to describe the "successful cure of a case of nail biting"; however, if she did not quit biting her nails, since a great deal of time would have to be spent with her, the fee would be the $500.00 that she had saved. At the time of Rosemary's second visit, it was noted that her nails were beginning to grow. She was a very happy girl. On each subsequent visit her nails were a little longer. She experienced no further difficulty in keeping them nice. She is now in college.

This particular technique is often effective, because it provides a motivation that the patient can understand. He feels that he is literally being paid to get well.

Enuresis

Indirect hypnotic approach to the problem of enuresis has been discussed under the section on pediatric hypnosis. Similar techniques are often successful, even with adult enuretics, where the pattern has been long established.

CASE OF MR. AND MRS. J.

A detailed report of this case was published some time ago.[1] A young couple, both of whom were very religious, came to the office most hesitantly, stating that their problem was that each of them wet the bed. Briefly, their story was this. When they got married, each kept it a secret from the other. The morning after the wedding night, they were both very polite to each other and never said a word about the wet bed. For nine months, things coasted along in that manner. Then, one of them said to the other that it would be nice if they had a baby on whom to blame the wet bed. That led to their discovery that they were both bed wetters. They continued to wet the bed every night for another three

---

[1] Erickson, Milton H. "A Clinical Note on Indirect Hypnotic Therapy," *J. Clin. & Exper. Hyp.*, II, 3, July 1954, pp. 171-74.

months before they made up their minds to seek therapy.

After the doctor became acquainted with them and learned their story, he discovered that they had no money at all. An offer was made to treat them on an experimental basis. The fee would be the satisfaction of curing them; however, if time were spent with no resultant cure, then they were to be charged the standard psychiatric fees.

The method used was a very light hypnotic trance, in which they were told that they had to obey all the instructions given them, no matter how absurd, ridiculous, or outrageous they might seem. Their deep religious feeling made it a certainty that they would obey a solemn promise. The promise they had to execute was this: Every night they were to go to the bathroom at six o'clock. They would drink a glass of water before going to bed. They were to go to bed with the door to the bathroom locked. They would get into bed, kneel hand in hand facing their pillows on the bed, and proceed to urinate and get the necessary bed wetting over with. After that they could lie down with the certainty that the bed wetting had already been accomplished and be able to sleep the rest of the night without worrying about what time of the night they had wet the bed.

They were made to promise to do this for two weeks, at the expiration of which period they could take a night's vacation; they could go to bed without first wetting the bed. Next morning when they awakened, as they threw back the covers and *only* if they saw a wet bed, would they know what to do next. The implication was that they would have to see a wet bed to know what to do next but, of course, when the time came for their "vacation," they felt so happy to lie down in a dry bed that they slept all through the night without wetting the bed. After all, they had *had* two weeks of practice sleeping *through* the night without wetting the bed! When on Monday morning, they threw back the covers and saw a dry bed, it left them rather confused. They had been instructed not to discuss matters with each other. As they described it later, since they didn't know what to do, they turned off the light that night and sneaked into bed. They awoke on Tuesday with another dry bed. On Tuesday night, they sneaked into bed once more. At the end of three weeks, they returned to the office. They had been told that they would return in a specified number of weeks with an amazing story. When they arrived, they were still confused and uncertain about what had been happening to them. They had had a dry bed for three whole weeks and, they said, they did not know what to do next.

Seemingly casual matters were discussed with them for a while and then the statement was made, "Next month is May," and they were literally shoved out of the office. In May they returned to report that all was going well. A year later they came in proudly to introduce their baby, stating that now they could have a wet bed any time they wanted to, but it would be a cute little wet spot.

The indirection of that approach, not letting them know, making them work for their own good, and forcing them into a situation where they had a bed that they did not wet during their sleep built up in them the realization that they could have a bed they did not wet during their sleep. Of course, they wet it before they went to sleep, but that was another matter entirely. That was a controlled thing; they controlled it. They also controlled keeping the bed from being wet more during the night. Thus they learned to have a dry bed.

Stuttering

As mentioned in the chapter on child hypnosis, the earlier phases of stuttering are relatively easier to handle. With older patients, one is likely to encounter more difficulty. One can raise the questions: When is it necessary to stutter? Do you need to do this to satisfy your needs and desires every day? Or could you do it four days a week, or three days a week? Could you do it merely when seated at tables, when in a standing position, or while you are in the bathtub? You can sing or whistle in the bathtub, so you can certainly stutter in the bathtub. Or, you could stutter while you are brushing your teeth. You could even stutter to yourself while reading a book silently, then find when you are reading it aloud that you do not need to stutter. One might also inquire: If your stuttering represents aggression, against whom do you want to utilize this aggression? How often? When?

CASE OF MICHAEL O.

Michael O decided on his own, through indirect permissive suggestion, that it would be an excellent thing to utilize his stammering every day whenever he was in his bathroom. He stutters diligently in the bathroom as he shaves and washes, but he is relatively free from stuttering the rest of the time.

The tendency of medical men to come full face against a problem and to try to overwhelm it, smack it down, or assault it, as though it were some enemy that ought to be conquered all at once, requires a good deal of reconsideration. The better medical approach is simply to recognize the kind of problem it is, then consider how it can be reduced to something the patient can use. Stuttering in the bathtub is just as good an activity as singing in the bathtub. Why shouldn't the patient really discover that he can control his stuttering by controlling it in the bathroom? He can take his stammering there, use it there, and leave it there. He can take a shower any time he pleases and stutter all he wishes. Treatment has thus gratified, but limited or circumscribed, a neurotic need.

THE TREATMENT OF OTHER PROBLEMS

Allergies

There are many reports on the treatment and "cure" of asthma or hay fever with direct suggestion hypnosis; however, here again the preferable method seems to be indirect permissive suggestion, where the patient is allowed to employ any of the techniques he feels may be satisfactory to him. The unconscious understands that something can be done about the problem and something is usually accomplished.

Generalized urticaria

General practitioners see many patients with giant hives, generalized urticaria from foods, and the like. These conditions are frequently emotionally based.

CASE OF CHARLES H.

Mr. Charles H came in recently, complaining of giant hives. He had been breaking out with marked itching, which had been coming and going for many weeks. He had already been to half a dozen doctors and had tried a variety of medications, including hydrocortisone, with no relief. Initial treatment consisted of discussing with him a "newer medication." He was assured that it worked much better than any of the others and one of the interesting things was that it worked differently with each individual. With some patients it took only a minute for it to take effect; with others, it took five minutes; with still others, it took as long as an hour for all the hives to disappear and to remain gone. Mr. H was asked only to wonder how long it would take for this new medication to work with him. Since it had worked in only a minute on some people, he was determined that he would not be beaten by anyone else. Therefore, it took a little less than a minute for the placebo to become effective!

CASE OF MARTIN D.

Martin D, an eleven-year-old child, was suffering from a bad case of hives. He would break out after eating chocolate or eggs, after walking through a wheat patch, playing with animals, etc. He was hypnotized and told that he could now eat chocolate and eggs and play with animals, without worrying about breaking out in hives. He was given a chocolate bar. He ate it and did not break out. He came back a month later, however, saying, "You know, I ate some tomatoes and broke out in hives." The suggestion concerning tomatoes had been overlooked. He was therefore hypnotized and told that he could now eat tomatoes.

Martin D was used as a demonstration subject, at which time he had been free from all hives for about nine months. One of the doctors present asked, "Do you think you could make the hives return?" The child was therefore hypnotized and given an amnesia for the fact that he had ever been previously hypnotized. Again he was given a chocolate bar which he ate. He had been told that in exactly fifteen minutes he would break out in hives. Fifteen minutes later he broke out in generalized hives. One of the doctors then inquired whether it would be possible to remove a particular hive from the child's cheek, pointing to the one he had in mind. The subject was then told that in fifteen minutes this particular hive would disappear. The hive did disappear. Martin was then rehypnotized and told that he would never have hives again; the amnesia for the fact that he had been previously treated was removed. He has been free from hives ever since.

There was a good deal more control over that experiment than is apparent in this description. The boy sat in front of some fifty persons. He himself was not sent out for the chocolate bar. Someone else went for it. He ate it in front of everyone present. His hands were watched to see that he did not touch his face or his body. He just sat there, ate the chocolate bar, and the hives were produced. The same conditions prevailed during their removal.

Dermatologic conditions

Hypnosis has a marked value in dermatology. As the skin is the largest organ in the body, most of the skin diseases have some emotional overlay. One needs to approach the individual personality to alleviate the emotional aspects of the skin disorder. By removing the emotional aspect, one can allow the physiologic functions of the skin to return more quickly to normal.

CASE OF MARJORIE B.

One patient was seen complaining of a marked neurodermatitis with typical distribution. She was a seventeen-year-old girl who had been suffering this way for twelve years. Apparently she had had an infantile eczema that resulted in the neurodermatitis. She lived in Pennsylvania and was visiting her sister, who was pregnant and about to deliver her baby with hypnoanesthesia. The sister asked if hypnosis could possibly help her younger sister, Marjorie. When Marjorie was seen she described the violent attacks of itching and burning, accompanied by a sensation of heat that would spread over her elbows, in the inner aspects of her knees, around her neck, and elsewhere. Marjorie was able to go into a light hypnotic state very readily. In this state she was taught how she could convert the feeling of heat into a cooling sensation. With the disappearance of the heat, of course, the itching might also disappear for itching is usually associated with warmth. She was taught how to go into an autohypnotic state at home whenever she felt sensations of heat beginning and itching coming on. She would thus be able immediately to remove the discomfort. She also was given some bland ointment to apply, only for reinforcing the suggestion. She was seen about six times over a three-week period. At the end of that time, merely by a blink of the eyes, she was able to remove the heat and the itching and produce the feeling of cooling and comfort. Her autohypnotic trance was a light one and lasted only momentarily. Marjorie returned to her home in Pennsylvania. Her sister has since reported that Marjorie rarely has an outbreak of neurodermatitis any more.

Ulcers

One disability with which hypnotherapy has been successful is that of ulcers. It is generally recognized that there is a typical emotional pattern resulting in ulcers. Many patients have been seen whose radiographic examinations confirmed the presence of an ulcer. They were treated with suggestion, with discussion, and other hypnotic techniques and it was often found that within six weeks the ulcer had disappeared. This was checked by x-ray studies. No change was made in the diet of these persons and they were given absolutely no medication. Discussion was held concerning their attitudes toward life, toward their jobs, toward their families; how one should think about these matters, how much and what kind of thinking served to aggravate the ulcers, what relaxation is, and how one can go about relaxing, even momentarily. Many of them were taught to go into autohypnotic trance states, lasting about sixty seconds, several times a day. They were told just to relax and to think about whether it was important to have these problems bother them for just the sixty seconds in question or for the entire day or week in question.

CASE OF MISS ELIZABETH R.

It is important to utilize one's knowledge of the personality of the patient in the treatment of ulcers. Miss Elizabeth R, a nurse, who sought help, was an individual who dominated everyone and everything. She was finally forced to drop out of the field of nursing because no doctor could work with her. She insisted upon dictating to the doctor absolutely.

Miss R came in with the report that she had a half-inch crater in her stomach wall. X-rays confirmed her statement. She demanded that she be put in a trance. She was accordingly told that she could go into a light trance, that she could use whatever techniques she understood to induce that trance. When she felt she was in a light trance, she was to nod her head. The therapist purposely avoided inducing the trance for her. A dictatorial personality does not usually tolerate that well.

As soon as Miss R nodded her head, the doctor burst into

laughter. She waited, becoming more angry by the minute. When he stopped, she wanted to know what had been so funny. She was told, "Well, at long last, you've got yourself into a situation where *you* can be dictated to. Your stomach ulcer is now going to dictate to you very, very thoroughly." At that, she set her jaw and discussed how she could dictate to that ulcer. A month later, she had a clean x-ray. She never went on a diet. As a matter of fact, she was Hungarian and she went right on eating the highly spiced foods she was accustomed to having. But she simply was not going to be dictated to by an ulcer. What was done, in effect, was to arouse all her antagonism, then direct it into a useful channel.

CASE OF MRS. ELEANOR K.

Mrs. Eleanor K also came in with a history of an ulcer. On hypnotic induction it was found that she was a somnambule. As she started going into the somnambulistic state, she began to shout, "I can't; I can't; I can't; I can't." She was asked in a quiet tone, "You can't what?" She replied, "I can't stand those kids. I can't stomach them." Therapy after that consisted of discussing attitudes toward children; what is normal in children; how much they should be allowed to run, scream, and yell, and whether they could be invited to do it outside, or how and when they should have the run of the house. She can "stomach" her children now and her ulcer has disappeared.

Migraine headaches

Hypnosis offers another approach to the treatment of migraine headaches. Some migraines, it is true, have very deep-seated psychologic bases and it may be necessary for an analytically oriented doctor to handle these problems. But there are times that the general practitioner can handle them.

CASE OF MRS. KATE B.

Mrs. Kate B came in, complaining of migraine headaches. She was a very staunch Catholic, as was her husband. They had a child, who was about four or five years old, with whom they seemed to be having a problem. Both parents felt unable to handle him. Whenever they told him to do something, he could be depended upon to do exactly the opposite.

After several interviews it was discovered that there was a time element involved in Mrs. B's headaches. They would usually—in fact, almost always—occur prior to her going out on a social engagement, or when they had invited guests to their own home. After some discussion, it was discovered that when the couple went out for a social evening or when they had guests in the home, the husband would have a drink or two. Each time he drank, he became amorous. They were strict Catholics and Mrs. B was very concerned about becoming pregnant. Of course, the migraine headaches kept her from going out on a social engagement, kept her from having people in her home to join her husband in a drink; so she was able to avoid pregnancy in that manner.

The problem of the boy was also explored. Proper behavioral attitudes and the handling of children were discussed. Her son was seen on one occasion. He was a nice child who was not being handled properly. Both parents learned how to get along with their son. The father made a special point of including the boy in his household projects, letting him hold hammer and nails, discussing ideas with him.

It didn't take long for the woman to start losing her migraine headaches. She began to suffer less and less frequently. Then, much to her amazement, she discovered that she was unable to become pregnant again. Since that time she has adopted two children. Now, she rarely has a recurrence of her migraine. When she does, it is very mild. She has a full social calendar and she is a most contented wife and mother.

Tinnitus and dizziness

Two extremely distressing symptoms, particularly in young people, are tinnitus and dizziness. One question recently raised has been whether a block could be interposed that would effect equilibrium, so that one would get away from the actual production of the symptom of dizziness. Probably if the dizziness is functional in origin, one can treat the symptom and teach the patient to become less and less aware of this malfunction. If it is an organic dizziness owing to arteriosclerosis or to a Ménière's syndrome, one can get at the functional overlay that is almost always present in Ménière's. Rosen has cited several case histories in which he made a diagnosis of Ménière's disease. Some of the patients were scheduled for brain surgery. With hypnotherapy, he was able to discover that many of the symptoms were functional in origin. He was able to clear them up without operating.

An approach to the handling of tinnitus can be illustrated by the following case report.

CASE OF DR. FRANCIS Z.

Dr. Francis Z, attending a seminar in a professional capacity, sought help from another doctor. He asked to be hypnotized to help him get rid of the persistent ringing in his ears. Previous attempts at hypnosis had been unsuccessful. The ear problem was functional. All the routine tests revealed that there was nothing organically wrong. At the time he made his request, he was told that an attempt would be made to hypnotize him if he would be kind enough to wait until there were a few spare moments. Late the same afternoon, he asked, "How about now?" The reply was made, "Sorry. I can't do it just yet." The next morning, he again asked, "Well, what about now?" The reply was, "No, not yet. You'll be told when." That afternoon a most interesting case report was being given. Dr. Z listened carefully, intensely interested in every single word that was said. He was motioned outside and was told, "I want to get back in there and listen to that, too. Now you just sit down in this chair and you go into a very deep trance, just exactly the way you put your patients in a trance. I'm going back in there for a few minutes." He sat down in the chair and for the first time very promptly went into a somnambulistic state, within just a few moments.

The procedure whereby one might go about blocking out sounds from an ear was then discussed with him. He thought about that for a bit and said, "Well, if you don't want to hear something, you can put your finger in your ear, can't you?" The therapist replied, "Well, that might be done." He promptly put his finger in his ear. Then he was told, "Of course, if you want to hear part of it, you press lightly and, if you don't want to hear any of it, you press harder with that finger. It would probably be possible for anybody who didn't want to hear any sounds in his ear to press as hard as is necessary to remove that sound." He promptly proceeded to press very hard on his ear with his finger. Then the possibility was suggested that as soon as the particular sound that he didn't want to hear was gone, he could remove his finger and with it remove whatever cause emotionally had produced that sound, that he might be able over the next few days just to wonder about it and understand it and perhaps get it back occasionally for practice, in order really to understand about that sound.

He sat out there for a total of about three minutes, then took his finger out of his ear. This occurred a little over two years ago. He has had that ringing in his ears three or four times in the intervening period, but when it occurs he puts his finger in his ear, blocks it out, and in a moment it is gone. In this case the patient was prepared over a period of two days; in effect, two days were spent hypnotizing him and he finally was maneuvered to a point where he had to go into a trance, because that was his last chance to be hypnotized. When hypnosis was induced, he certainly had no difficulty in figuring out subconsciously how to remove his tinnitus.

Angina

An angina patient is usually an individual who is extremely overanxious and tense about things. One must teach this kind of patient techniques of relaxation, continuing with this type of instruction until a response is obtained. Then one can proceed to deeper hypnotic induction. "Now you've learned to relax very thoroughly and it is pleasant, is it not? Now that you are relaxing mentally and emotionally, of course all the activities of your body are relaxed and your heart muscles and the vessels of your heart are all relaxed." It can subsequently be explained to the patient that angina is a tension situation, and he can be told about the narrowing of the vessels, etc. At that session or the next the patient can be taught autohypnosis, how he can sit down in a chair or lie down on a sofa or a bed, then go into an autohypnotic trance, allowing the necessary relaxation to occur. He can learn to do this very rapidly, so that he can obtain the relaxation within a minute, then within thirty seconds, then within ten seconds. Finally, he can learn to do it merely by thinking about it for an instant.

One starts out by teaching a patient a technique that he consciously practices. Then it becomes a subconscious habit with him, just as the anxiety state has become a subconscious habit, though that may have started with a root cause. As the habit formation is altered, one frequently can get a marked alleviation of symptoms.

Emotional hypertension

The same thing is done with emotional hypertension where there is no organic cause. Every physician is probably aware that he can see a patient in his office with a blood pressure of 220 and, just by calming the patient for a few minutes, bring the pressure down to 160. One can obtain similar results with hypnosis, if one teaches the patient how to relax whenever he feels the need. "When you get excited and upset about something, take thirty seconds off—you can certainly spare thirty seconds—and just let yourself relax and forget about whatever it was that bothered you; then go on to your next piece of activity." One is upsetting the old habit and starting a new one in the individual; and the new habit will eventually become subconscious.

HYPNOTHERAPY IN CHILDREN WITH SPECIAL DISABILITIES

Polio

In the treatment of children who have had polio, one will often find that the child is convinced that he can never move again, walk again, never even lift a hand again. He is confronted with a rather horrible understanding of his future. In the trance state one can get him to recall exactly how it felt to lift his hand, how it felt to close his hand. Then he can be told to come out of the trance state into a waking state, with the memory of how he used to close his hand, or how he used to lift his arm. In this way past memories and understanding are being utilized and the child can reorient to his present somatic feelings in terms of past somatic feelings.

It is somewhat similar to the man who comes in with complaints concerning a phantom limb, saying that it is all cramped up, that he can feel it, and he suffers a lot of pain. He can be put in a trance and reoriented in time so that he can feel his foot move, or his hand open and close. Then satisfactory feelings can be built up in him concerning his forearm, his upper arm and shoulder, or his leg, as the case may be, so that he no longer need have that phantom limb. One tries to treat the patient as a total creature, as a total personality, to utilize memories, feelings, understandings—everything he has.

Cerebral palsy

The question often arises as to what particular techniques are most effective in trance induction in the cerebral palsied child. One always has to work on the level of the intelligence of the particular child. In cerebral palsy we have a wide variation of intelligence from the very alert, intelligent youngster all the way down to the levels of idiots and imbeciles. The doctor works with him on his own intellectual and educational level, using any induction techniques that seem best suited to the personality. In general, they appear to work well with cerebral palsy.

Questions and answers

Adequate histories

QUESTION

We are all medical men in one field or another, but I think in busy practices we are all prone to make one mistake. I think it would be well to emphasize the fact that before we attempt to cure a suspected psychosis in a patient, it is of prime importance to do not just an adequate, but a supremely adequate history and physical examination.

ANSWER

That's right. A conscientious doctor cannot really practice medicine at all unless he becomes exceedingly well acquainted with the patient, both historically and physically.

Use of the term "hypnosis"

QUESTION

What about the advisability and effectiveness of inducing any degree of the trance state without mentioning it as hypnosis? Even if you do not mention it to patients, some of the more intelligent ones are going to deduce what you are actually doing. Moreover, some of them might resent the word if you did mention it, through some pre-existing prejudice.

ANSWER

There are several approaches that can be used. There is one in which the term "relaxation" is used, instead of "hypnosis." Occasionally there will be a patient who will jerk out of the trance and say, "You hypnotized me, didn't you?" Your reply can be, "What I was attempting to do was to teach you how to relax. Now the deeper stages of this relaxation have been called hypnosis and it is perfectly all right for you to go into a hypnotic state if you want to. But you don't need to; you can just go into the deep, relaxed state without going into hypnosis." It is not necessary to disguise the technique very often. It is better to tell patients that an attempt will be made to use relaxation in a hypnotic trance state, which is called medical hypnosis. They are told: "It's a very different type of hypnosis from what you may have seen on the stage or TV. We don't go through any antics; we don't order you to do anything. We merely ask you to sit there in a chair, as you are doing now, and go through some simple learning processes to teach you how to be able to give all your awareness to the things that we are discussing here. The purpose of your coming here was to have this accomplished. There is no point, therefore, in having you sit there and wonder about whether dinner will be cooked on time, or what the children are doing, or whether your boss will care if you miss a half hour from work. To get all these things out of your mind, you do just as a person does who goes to a concert—he closes his eyes so he can hear better and he takes his thoughts away from everything but the music. That is what I am going to ask you to do, to learn how to close your eyes involuntarily, to learn how to take your thoughts off everything except the situation at hand." There is usually no objection to that approach.

The only time hypnosis is disguised is when indirect induction is being employed on a mother, father, brother, or other person when actually that particular person is not the avowed patient. Even then, the individual in question knows that hypnosis is being used, but believes it is being employed only on the ostensible patient. He is not actually being fooled; he is merely being included, given the opportunity to go into the trance state if he desires.

Trance depth and effectiveness of suggestions

QUESTION

Does a deeper trance fortify posthypnotic suggestions?

ANSWER

It will, if the posthypnotic suggestion is very unusual, but if one provides the patient with a rationale for a posthypnotic suggestion, he can get it accomplished with a very light stage just as well as with a very deep stage. Many patients are treated in the light and medium stages. With those patients who go readily into a deep stage of hypnosis, depth techniques can be employed that are almost the same, except that more of the phenomena of hypnosis can be elicited. Such patients can be given a little more complicated or difficult instructions to carry out. The light and medium stages work almost as well, however, and since about 95 per cent of people can go into the light stages of hypnosis, that is the stage that one should learn to utilize.

Medical uses for deep trance

QUESTION

Are there any medical objectives to be obtained by going into an extremely deep trance?

ANSWER

The only purposes for which deep trance phenomena would be required would be age regression, experimental work, the uncovering of techniques, or the production of major surgical anesthesia.

Handling physical disorders (scalenus anticus syndrome)

QUESTION

With the patient who has had scalenus anticus syndrome, has had it for several years, and is using it psychologically, particularly with the idea of not having it operated on, would it be wise to remove it if possible?

ANSWER

He might be offered three possibilities. First, he could be told he might just go on the way he is, having the discomfort, if that is the thing that satisfies him most. Second, he could be offered the possibility of minimizing the discomfort so that he could carry on his daily activities with some knowledge that it is there, perhaps really feel it only at night just as he gets into bed and have it disappear when he goes to sleep. Or he might feel it in the morning, just when he gets up, then have it disappear, or feel it when he is eating—just at mealtime—then have it disappear. He could also be offered the third possibility of wondering just how this might be after surgery.

Actually what one can do with a good hypnotic subject in that particular situation is to use time distortion age progression. Progress him to six months following his operation and see how he feels about it then. Or progress him to six months following his decision to have it occur only once or twice a day and see how he feels about that. An excellent impression can be gained from him in that manner. Then he can be brought back to his present conscious awareness. When he is reoriented back to the present, one often gets some very sound decisions made by the patient.

Terminal carcinoma

QUESTION

Will you say just a little about the treatment of terminal cancer cases and their symptoms?

ANSWER

Unless you are willing to spend a great number of hours producing a somnambulistic state, you may have difficulty alleviating the organic pain; however, in one to several sessions, the emotional part can be removed. You can prepare the patient to understand that there are certain organic changes occurring, that they do produce sensations, that the sensations may be uncomfortable, but there is no need for these normal physiologic sensations that are occurring to be disturbing enough to cause him to go through the distress that many manifest.

9
Clinical Applications of Hypnosis to Psychiatry

The role of hypnosis in psychotherapy

Hypnosis is no miracle. It is primarily a method of approaching a patient, a means of securing his attention and cooperation; therein lies its significance. Nor is hypnosis a cure-all. It is a tool, an instrument, an adjuvant to any medical or psychiatric procedure one wants to employ. It can be used as a means of making the patient feel at ease within himself and at ease in the situation in which he finds himself. Furthermore, in trying to deal with the patient as a personality, the use of hypnosis allows the patient to develop a certain amount of competence and security in his relationship to the therapist. This is the first orientation of hypnosis in the areas of medical and psychiatric problems.

PSYCHIATRIC EXPLORATION AND HANDLING OF PATIENTS

In trying to explore and investigate a patient psychiatrically for the purpose of bringing about changes in his personality, one has to map out the personality and get some understanding of the individual. Having secured that understanding, therapy proceeds in accordance with the patient's needs.

Need of unconscious to express aggression

One sometimes encounters a patient who has directed aggression toward himself, his family, his total life situation. It is evidently necessary for this patient to express aggression toward someone. Therapy can help him to direct it in more constructive channels.

CASE OF MARGARET E.

Margaret E, a hysterically paralyzed girl, was asked during a deep trance why she no longer walked. In answer, she merely set her jaw. She had been approached directly and most indirectly. The girl's reaction to the very indirect approach was, "He is probably getting at something. I can't see how but I know he is getting at something."

She was therefore usually allowed to think that the indirect approach was on some irrelevant matter. Frequently, when she was sitting in her wheelchair, the psychiatrist sat directly in front of her. She often became so irritated with him that she raised her paralyzed legs and kicked him on the shins, without realizing what she was doing. Since it was exceedingly important for her unconscious mind to express the aggression, the doctor carefully chose that position for himself.

Need of patient to retaliate against hypnosis

In hypnosis, one must respect the need of the other person to retaliate in some way. Each time one tries to use hypnosis on a psychiatric patient, a psychoneurotic patient, a psychosomatic patient, one is rushing in on a personality defense. It is a disordered personality defense, but nevertheless a defense that the patient has established. When something is taken away from a person, he does not like it.

Consider the small child with a knife in his hands. If the mother tries to take the knife away from the child, even when it is cutting the child, he lets the mother know that she has not that right. The child needs to be approached in such fashion that he willingly accepts something else in place of that knife. So it is with the psychoneurotic or the psychosomatic patient. He must be given something in place of the neurotic defense that he has. Furthermore, the therapist must have it clearly in mind that what he is going to give him is something that will increase the patient's satisfactions as a personality.

Practical orientation to psychiatric problems

One never really reaches into the mind of a patient and says, "This is the problem." Actually one never quite knows what the problem is until it has finally been corrected. One factor may be part of the problem. Another may be in some way related to the problem.

Too much has been written lately about the need for the unconscious to be made conscious. Many a patient prefers to get well without consciously knowing the reasons why. One of the purposes hypnosis and hypnotherapy should accomplish is to make plain to the patient that he has not only a past that is highly important to him; he also has a present that is more important, and a future even more so than the present or the past.

Many patients think that the experiences they have had in their lives before they come to therapy are the only things that are important. The essential objective is their adjustment at the present time and in the future—if they are to be happy—with whatever understandings they can achieve of the past. They must start making plans for the present and the future with a willingness to abstract from the past only what they need to promote their current and future adjustments.

Psychotherapy sometimes seems overoriented to an academic understanding of the past. Consider the girl with claustrophobia, who can't stand to be in a small room with the door shut. Perhaps her grandmother did lock her in the closet to punish her; that entire history can be obtained from her in the trance state. But is that really where her claustrophobia started? Her claustrophobia actually started, while she was locked in the closet, when she heard her mother's footsteps going down the hall, down the steps, and down the sidewalk. That tied into every other situation in which her mother had deserted her. Being locked in the closet by her grandmother was only the creation of the situation where she could sense and become keenly aware of the various desertions that her mother had committed.

When certain traumatic incidents are uncovered in therapy, it is important to discover what the associations are in relation to the incidents. It is the way the traumatic incident is used that determines whether or not there is to be a neurotic response and the building up of neurotic habit patterns.

Therapy of habits

One ought to be alert to the fact that many a problem is no more than a habit. It may have started originally as a profoundly neurotic response. As the years passed, it became a physical habit.

MAKING A HABIT TOO PAINFUL TO RETAIN

CASE OF WILLIAM A.

Seven-year-old William had a very distressing habit. About once every minute, all day long, he made a noise that sounded like "eek, eek." His mother, father, teachers, and everyone else were frantic. But it was no more than a habit pattern. Treatment consisted of regarding it as such.

In this case, therapy was achieved in one week's time. A psychiatrist, a friend of the family, happened to be visiting. He sent the boy to his room with the understanding that, instead of once a minute, he was to make the sound twice a minute. He had to make the sound twice a minute before he could come out of his room.

When the boy finally got impatient about being locked up in the bedroom, he gave up, agreed to make the sound twice a minute. What was he actually doing? He was voluntarily taking control of a habit. One entire day went by with that "eeking" twice a minute, with his mother and the psychiatrist insisting that he ought to watch the clock for if he didn't practice the "eek" twice a minute, he would have to be sent back to his bedroom.

The next day he was asked, "How about three times a minute? How about four times a minute?" The boy knew that the question was completely serious. The doctor was explanatory, reassuring, telling him it was important to find out why he made the noise. The boy could understand that a doctor makes examinations and studies results. The psychiatrist, he thought, was very stupid to need so much time, but he could see where his own days were going, practicing that "eek" sound. Within a week's time he had deliberately taken control of the habit. He did not dare to have it.

That was several years ago. He hasn't "eeked" since then, nor has he developed any other symptomatology.

USE OF A PAINFUL TASK TO DISCOURAGE A HABIT

CASE OF MR. VINCENT C.

Mr. Vincent C, age sixty-five, sought help, explaining that he had lost his wife the previous August. He felt very much lost and alone, though he was living with his son, a bachelor. He explained further that he had been suffering from insomnia for the last fifteen years. He had been taking barbiturates. Gradually, over the years, his dosage had increased. The death of his wife had stepped up his nightly dosage from twelve to fifteen grams of sodium amytal; he had just visited his family physician to get a nightly increase in allowance to eighteen grams. He took the medicine at about midnight, slept for about an hour and a half. For the rest of the night, his sleep was completely unsatisfactory.

The psychiatrist listened to his account of his wife and of how much he missed her. He also listened to Mr. C tell how he went to bed at 8 o'clock, rolled and tossed, and wished he could sleep without drugs; Mr. C always weakened and took that excessive dose of sodium amytal, drifting off to his hour and a half of sleep, then rolled and tossed again until it was time to get up in the morning. The psychiatrist spent perhaps two or three hours with Mr. C, explaining that it was perfectly possible to learn to sleep all night long without sedation. When Mr. C was asked if he would really give his cooperation, he was led along that line of thought until he had committed himself unreservedly to cooperation. Then he was given the explanation that cooperation and the correction of his insomnia would be a bit expensive, not financially, but in the way of effort. Mr. C agreed; "Hang the expense," was his attitude, "I'll do anything."

In taking the history, it had been discovered that Mr. C abhorred the housework. He did the cooking for his son, but the son, in turn, did the dishes and all the waxing of the floors. Mr. C always went outside when the son waxed floors; he could not tolerate the odor of floor wax. The psychiatrist told Mr. C, "Tonight, you get out the floor wax and some rags. You have hardwood floors in every room in your home. You start at 8:00 P.M. That's the time you usually start to toss and roll in bed. You will wax the floor all night long, over and over again. It will only cost you an hour and a half of sleep—that's all. You are going to wax the floors and you can hate it all night long, just as you can hate me all night long. You can actually enjoy hating the floors and hating me, but do it." The old man said, "Well, you've talked me into it and I'll do it." He waxed the floors that night. He waxed the floors the next night. He waxed the floors the third night.

On the fourth night, at 7:30, he lay down on the bed with his shoes on, "just to rest my eyes." He awakened at 7:00 A.M. He has been sleeping every night since, without any sedation. He had promised that any time he couldn't get to sleep within half an hour, he would get up and wax the floor all night again. He preferred to sleep.

Specialized techniques

PATIENT PROTECTION

Psychiatrically the matter of guarding the interests and needs of the patient is most important. Actually, it is equally important in the practice of obstetrics, dentistry, dermatology, or the general practice of medicine.

Being put to test

In experimental work with college students, graduates in psychology, or medical students, workers in the field of hypnosis have been put to the test many times by naïve hypnotic subjects.

CASE OF BARBARA L.

A psychiatrist demonstrating at a midwestern university was looking for a hypnotic subject. Early in the afternoon he was introduced to a number of graduate students, among them a girl named Barbara. He looked her over, chatting with her in that group situation, and decided that Barbara would make a good hypnotic subject. He induced relaxation and a very light trance, just to find out how she would react. Then he asked Barbara if she would serve as a demonstration subject that night. She replied that she would be delighted. When she was asked if an experimental procedure that might interest her could be carried out, she willingly gave her consent, both in that light trance state and in the waking state.

The doctor suggested automatic writing. He instructed her to write automatically some harmless little sentence that she would be willing to have him read, and everyone else who would be present. He placed her at the end of the table and took his position at the other end of the table. Barbara looked at him with a smile, then proceeded to write something automatically. After she had written (which she did without her own knowledge), the hypnotist walked over, picked up the sheet of paper, and turned it face down without looking at it. He asked Barbara if he could read it. She asked, "Read what?" He replied, "You did some automatic writing on that sheet of paper." Barbara looked down and stated there was no writing on it. She was told, "No, I turned it over." The doctor told her he had no intention of reading it until given permission to do so. She granted that permission, but then he suggested that perhaps they had better just take that sheet of paper and fold it. He took it, folded it so that she could not possibly see the writing, and told her that she had better put it away. She looked at him, shrugged her shoulders, and put it in her purse.

When she was asked to do some more automatic writing, she wrote, "This is a beautiful day in June." After she had written that, she was asked if it could be read. She extended it to the doctor so that he could read it. He asked her immediately, "May I pick it up and read it? When she replied "yes," he picked it up and read, "This is a beautiful day in June." Then he told her in the trance state, by inducing another trance, that there was that folded sheet of paper in her purse, that she had better keep it there absent-mindedly. Some time later she might want to read it.

She came to his lecture that evening and said, "During this afternoon, I had a feeling that I could trust you to do anything, so feel perfectly free to experiment with me during the course of the lecture, because I really trust you and I don't know why."

About two weeks later she came in to see the doctor. She said, "I've found a folded sheet of paper in my purse. It has a rather curious message on it and I recognize it as my own automatic writing. I also know this, that I wrote that unconsciously, automatically, to find out if I could trust you. I know that you didn't read it. I know you don't know what's on that paper. But you were willing to let me write it and you were willing not to read it. Now I can trust you as a psychotherapist." And she showed the psychiatrist that sheet of paper. On it was written, "Will I marry Harry?" She said, "I don't understand that, because I'm engaged to Tom. We're going to get married next summer. I don't even know a Harry, or Harold." She was told the question related to something in her unconscious, that if she wanted to let it come to the foreground, into her consciousness, gradually, systematically, at a rate she could understand it, then she would know what, "Will I marry Harry?" meant.

Some time later she came in and said, "I have broken my engagement to Tom. I don't know why, but I just can't stand that man. He's a nice guy, but personally I can't stand him, but I don't know any Harry." Still later, she reported that she had met a man named Harry. Barbara married this man Harry, whose real name was Harold.

Barbara had actually met Harold previously, had formed

her own unconscious impression of him, noted that he was commonly called Harry, but had then "forgotten" him. She had also realized unconsciously that she was not in love with Tom. Thus, she put the whole problem in a nutshell on a sheet of paper. As visiting lecturer, the psychiatrist did not have the right to intrude upon her personal life. But she thought he might be a competent therapist, and she tested him.

One protects the patient in every regard. One does not intrude upon his personal life. One merely expresses a willingness to help the patient—and only at the rate he can tolerate.

When deep trances are needed

One of the things a hypnotist must bear in mind is that there is sometimes a need for a deep trance, no matter what the situation is. One should be able to induce a trance that may help uncover factors related to a patient's particular problem.

Rehearsal

Rehearsal is important not only in the general practice of hypnosis, but as an uncovering technique. It is a procedure that can be used with many types of problems. One particular patient may go into a trance. He may say that he is perfectly wide awake, that there is no point in time at which he can not awaken and walk out of the room, engage in conversation, or the like. He has been taught to go into that light trance, as *he* thinks it is, by counting to twenty, and to awaken when the therapist counts backward from twenty, in the manner demonstrated in Chapter 4, Demonstration 14. The result is that he rehearses awakening and going to sleep. Although the operator follows this "rehearsal" with the patient, the patient is responding to the situation and cannot follow the maneuvering. As a result, the patient can give most adequate information in this trance state and the doctor has a very effective technique.

Rehearsals can be used to teach a subject to go deeply asleep, to establish different trance states in which the patient can behave differently, to give more information or to give better responses. The anesthesia in the first trance may not meet the wishes of the doctor or the patient. Another trance state may be induced by a rehearsal technique and that one develop much more satisfactorily.

Rehearsal is important both in teaching subjects to go into a trance and for utilizing a trance state.

Use of "new" trances

Perhaps the patient does not wish to tell something in today's trance. If the therapist believes it important to uncover a particular fact, he can induce a trance, then bring the patient out of it. That is the end of today's trance. The patient is then put back into a trance. The second trance that has been created is an entirely different trance, one in which he can talk. The therapist uses this "new" trance as his uncovering technique.

Illogic of the unconscious

One needs to try to understand what hypnotic experiences mean to the subject. The unconscious is often illogical in its behavior. The hypnotist needs to understand what may often seem illogical expression in relation to its meaningful-ness to the subject.

Anesthesia by dissociation

CASE OF RALPH G.

Ralph G, a dental student, volunteered as a hypnotic sub-ject to be demonstrated to a group of dentists. The problem was: "How could an anesthesia be induced in a dental sub-ject without ever mentioning anesthesia?"

The hypnotist and the subject sat in chairs in front of the audience. The student was asked to look across the room. He was told that it would be very nice if he could see a little doll over there, one that he would like to pick up and play with. He looked at the designated spot very intently and said he could see a doll there. It was suggested that if he looked again, he would see a little boy named Ralph. The little boy would be playing with the doll that was there. Since he was over there, he could be asked (sitting in the chair beside the doctor), "What are you doing?" He re-plied that he was playing with the doll.

While he was doing that, his hand was taken and the fingers squeezed in on themselves, a very painful procedure.

The subject felt nothing since he was over in the corner playing with the doll. This inanimate, senseless, insensate body in the chair just could not feel the pain.

A dentist came up with an instrument, jabbed it around the boy's mouth, got no pain responses; the little boy was still playing with his doll. In other words, what had been done was to bring about, in that indirect fashion, a dissociation.

On suggesting with conviction

When the hypnotist looked over at the doll, he tried to give the impression that anyone else could also see it there. He gave the suggestion not only of the presence of the doll, but of the feeling of enjoyment that anyone could have in playing with it, as well. Of course, if the subject enjoyed playing with a doll, he could hardly be a six-foot tall dental student. He had to be a genuine little boy, thereby making use of his actual psychologic memories, his actual personal experiences. He regressed back to the time when he was a little boy playing with a doll.

Use of regression

A dentist who learns how to induce regression can have his patient sitting comfortably in a chair, looking at or concentrating on a doll or any other object on the other side of the room, while painful work proceeds. Psychiatrists can use the same technique to explore the mental life of a patient. Regression, as a hypnotic phenomenon, can be used to meet the varying needs of the individual patient.

The patient who wants to watch her childbirth can be brought to see herself on the other side of the room painlessly watching "that woman" giving birth. She will not realize that she is using her mental images to visualize herself. She is merely watching that other woman, with whom she feels a warm sense of kinship, have a baby. Actually, she is dissociating her delivery as a physical experience, but enjoying it as a psychologic experience in which she is dissociated from her physical self.

TIME DISTORTION

CASE OF JOSEPHINE D.

There are various types of dissociation. Josephine D went to a dentist who did not believe in hypnosis. "It's pure nonsense, you know—just a silly idea." The patient had previously been instructed, posthypnotically, to look through the narrow windowpanes in the dentist's office, out into the courtyard beyond, to look at the trees, the shrubs, and the grass and really enjoy being out there, really to have a good time. She sat down in the chair and suddenly found herself a little girl wandering around on the ground out under those two silk oak trees. She didn't know the place. All she knew was that she was a little girl, having a perfectly fine time. It was fall. She was kicking up the leaves and she was very, very puzzled about something. Somebody was burning leaves—she could smell it. She looked all around, but she could not find those burning leaves.

Then finally, the dentist, back in the office, far removed from the scene, said, "That will be all." She turned and looked at him and said, "What do you mean, that will be all?" He said, "Well, I'm through. Things went a lot faster than I realized that they would." She looked at him and said, "You're all through?" He said, "Yes, it took an hour and a half, and I'm surprised at the way you got through this, because you did everything exactly right." She didn't tell him that she had been in a trance.

When she came to see her hypnotist, she told him about the burning leaves. It was, of course, the smell of the drill.

It took three trips to that dental office for the patient to discover that there were not two trees in that courtyard. There was only one. She was asked to draw a picture of that courtyard several times. Each time she brought it in, she would say, "I know this is wrong, but I went over it very, very carefully." Now, she goes to the dentist, sits down in the chair and "immediately" gets out. Actually, her visits take an hour. She has simply distorted time very satisfactorily.

And she has dissociated herself, regressed herself, taken herself out of that situation of a dental chair, out of the situation of a physical experience, and put herself in a psychologic frame of reference where she deals with the things that belong to that psychologic frame of reference. Similarly, a person who kicks the covers off his bed on a cold night may be too tired to get up and put the blankets back over his feet. He dreams, therefore, that he is walking for miles and miles through the snow and the cold, with freezing feet, until finally his body can't take it any longer and he wakes up and covers himself. The dream is a protective dream. In the dental chair there can be any choice of past experiences from which one can select something to enjoy, dissociating oneself in this way from the dental experience.

REGRESSION

Regression is that psychologic process by which one develops an amnesia for current things, for the relatively recent things —a total, blanket, all-comprehensive amnesia, going back in life until a certain age level is reached. A good hypnotic subject can be regressed to a much earlier period in life. A good regression, one that can be tested in the psychology laboratory for validity, sometimes needs several hours of preparation. A patient successfully regressed to the age of six will act and talk as a six-year-old does. He will not act as though he were trying to be six years old.

Age-regression experiment

In an age regression experiment that Erickson undertook, he used a number of doctors, nurses, and occupational therapists as subjects, age-regressed them back to eight years of age, took their IQ's, made them nine, ten, eleven, twelve, thirteen, fourteen, fifteen, sixteen. When he regressed one to the age of ten, the next time he might regress him to the age of thirteen; the next time to the age of eight; the next time to the age of fourteen, etc. Then he plotted the IQ's. The subject always tested higher than his suggested age level. At a suggested level of eight, his IQ was higher than it should have been. At a suggested age level of nine, it was relatively even higher. As the age progressed upward, the IQ increases paralleled it. Erickson then took those same subjects, and had them respond to intelligence tests *as though* they were eight years old. He told them to do everything they could to give eight-year-old answers, to reflect an IQ that would be fitting for an eight-year-old. Every one achieved an incorrect IQ. Subjects read a question, decided that they couldn't answer that one at the age of eight. Of course, at the age of eight, they could not actually even have read the question. In the hypnotic trance, there was an effort to read the question, then the realization, "I don't know how to read that question. I can't read it and I don't know the answer."

CASE OF MARGARET R.

What can one expect to accomplish in regression? Margaret R sought help, stating that she had a phobia for the color black. She had shut herself up in her room, allowed no darkness in her room at all, no color black. She had gas light, electric light, and candles there, burning day and night. When she finally decided to seek therapy, she inquired about the appearance of the psychiatrist. She stated that he would have to wear a towel over his black hair, adhesive over his mustache and over his eyebrows. He had to be dressed completely in white, including shoes and socks. Eventually she was hypnotized, regressed carefully, and her story secured.

At the age of six she was playing on the sidewalk in front

of her home when a big dog came along. He reared up on her in a playful, friendly fashion, putting his paws on her shoulders. His weight was too much for her, however, and she fell to the sidewalk. He straddled her and licked her face in apology. That was the real situation. Her mother came out at just that time and saw the great black dog apparently eating her daughter's face. She screamed. Her screams alarmed the entire neighborhood. People screamed, brought out brooms, chased the "child-eating" dog away. They terrified the little girl, who had been enjoying the friendly dog up to that time. Eventually, the child was convinced by her mother and the neighbors that she had been almost eaten alive.

She had forgotten the experience by the time she was ten. Then, when she was about twenty-one, a frightening thing happened. She saw one speeding car crash into another. A little girl and a little black dog were thrown out onto the sidewalk. Both lay dead in a pool of blood. She took one hasty look at that horrible sight and rushed past. By the age of twenty-five she had repressed that episode. When she was thirty-five, her mother died and the house was draped in black. Everything was in black. Finally, after the estate had been settled, she began to discover that she was overwhelmingly afraid of black. That went on for three years until she came in for treatment.

Through regression the therapist was able to let her unconscious mind recognize the true meaning of the original experience, link it to the accident when she was twenty-one years old, link that, in turn, to her mother's death. Then her unconscious mind was encouraged to let her conscious mind remember a little, a little more, still more, until her conscious mind remembered and understood every part of the total experience.

REVIVIFICATION

What is meant by revivification? It is the reviving of past experiences enabling a person to see them, understand them, and feel them, while still recognizing them as past experiences. In regression, the patient exists in his understandings and feelings of that time; in revivification, he recognizes his response as a memory of things, even though a very strong one.

As a means of canceling posthypnotic suggestions

Revivification is often a very useful technique for inducing hypnotic trances. A subject may come into the office who says, "I was hypnotized by So-and-So, who told me never to let anybody else hypnotize me. So, Doctor, while I need hypnosis, I feel that you can't give it to me." A patient cannot be hypnotized if he is acting upon a contrary posthypnotic suggestion. But he can be given the suggestion, "Tell me about the original time when you were hypnotized and told not to let anybody else hypnotize you." He revivifies the experience very intensely and, as he revivifies it and tells all about it, the further suggestion can be inserted, "You were told never to let anybody else hypnotize you, but that probably meant for entertainment purposes and things of that sort. Do you suppose the original hypnotist meant that you should never use hypnosis again for a legitimate medical or dental need?"

With subjects who have suddenly lost their ability to go into trances, one can use revivification, get them to remember how they used to go into trances, utilize their memory of how they used to do it. Thus, they can again learn how to go into a trance.

VISUALIZATION

Another technique useful to both dentists and psychiatrists is visualization. Here one can employ a portable movie screen for patients to look at. Or the patient can be induced to hallucinate the screen.

Just as the dental patient looked through the narrow windowpanes out into the yard and found herself psychologically and emotionally playing on the lawn as a little girl, so the hypnotist can use the movie screens and let his patient, medical or dental, observe himself in the screen. The patient is given another frame of reference in which to think and to feel about himself.

One hypnotic phenomenon can be used to induce another. The movie screen can be employed as an uncovering technique. The patient looks at it, sees his past, or the past of somebody in whom he is interested. It is a form of projection. He can look at the screen, lose his own identity, and observe various traumatic experiences that occurred in his own life experience. He can describe those experiences and give full information that may be much more reliable than his conscious account of things.

CASE OF ARNOLD M.

Arnold M reported that his dog had been run over when he was a little boy. It sounded like a perfectly reliable memory. But on the movie screen, what did he really see? He saw the dog dead and the deputy sheriff standing there with a smoking revolver. The deputy sheriff had shot his dog. At the time, the patient wished that the dog had been run over; that would have been an accident instead of a deliberate and to him senseless execution. His wish colored his subsequent conscious memory; on the movie screen, however, he could really see the dog lying dead and the deputy shooting it.

On another movie screen, the patient saw himself at a later age; on another, at a still later age—all the way from five years of age on up to thirty-two. He could compare similar traumatic events in his life. Setting up the screens was no problem at all. The patient could fix the visions on each screen so that he could look at them and compare them. Then he was allowed to set up another screen where he could see himself as he hoped to appear next year. Thus he was led to recognize what he wanted in his future, what was meaningful for him in that future.

PSEUDO-ORIENTATION INTO THE FUTURE

That technique has been called pseudo-orientation into the future. Just as one can orient a patient back to the past, so one can project him into the future in accordance with his own motivations and desires. A girl considers herself too unlovely ever to attract a man. She will not believe that any man can ever become interested in her, refuses to recognize that she may be an exceedingly attractive girl to some man, refuses to permit herself to speculate on having a home, a husband, and children. In the hypnotic trance one builds up the situation in which she can see herself in the future, in a life situation that she herself projects on that hallucinatory movie screen. She projects her own ideas, her own wishes—not what the therapist might wish, but what she really feels, deep within herself. Thus, she is forced to recognize on the movie screen what she feels. It is a projection of her own needs, desires, wishes and hopes. She may say, "Well, that's myself I see up there. I do have a husband and that's a baby. I can't quite see its face, but I know it is a baby and I have the feeling that it's mine. I can't see my husband's face, but I know I've got a husband. I can feel it." She entertains the feeling that she can achieve all those things in a definite future. She begins gradually to accept the possibilities of such a future for her.

The dentist can use the movie screen by having his patient look at the screen and see himself, for example, in his first gagging experience. He can understand that *this* situation is not *that* one, that he is here in the dental office only to have his dentures fitted. Therefore, he need not gag the way he did there. He can look at another movie screen and see himself wearing those dentures correctly. The dentist is not doing any deep psychotherapy here. He is helping his patient to meet the problems of wearing his dentures. This is not a personality problem requiring psychotherapy but it is a problem important to the patient and one in which the dentist's assistance is often necessary.

AUTOMATIC WRITING

Automatic behavior is employed in many ways. In writing we all take up a pencil and inscribe marks—sometimes meaningless—on a sheet of paper. The hypnotic subject, however, can pick up a pencil and start writing without necessarily knowing that the hand is writing. There can be a dissociation of the hand from any personal awareness of it. The unconscious of that person is governing and directing his hand.

Automatic writing can be employed with many patients to help them write out conflicts, fears, anxieties, clues, and cues that will assist in their therapy. Sometimes the therapist recognizes what those writings mean; sometimes he does not, but he has enlisted the aid of the unconscious mind in communicating. The dentist who can interest a recalcitrant patient in trying automatic writing has introduced a technique that may interest the patient in developing other hypnotic phenomena. The dentist is interested not in the content of the automatic writing, but in using that and other techniques to teach that person to be a good dental patient.

As an induction technique

A person who uses automatic writing has a peculiar script that belongs to him as a hypnotic subject. One can take a person who has never been in a trance, has never seen a trance, and slowly and systematically train him to be a good automatic handwriter. His normal waking script can then be compared with his hypnotic script. Automatic writing is usually in a rather childish form, with block letters, written much more slowly and spaced differently on the paper.

Economy of unconscious response

The hypnotic subject also tends to show an economy of response. How does one spell the word "Yes"? There's only one letter that defines the answer "Yes." That is the "Y," which is essentially a vertical letter. The word "No" is written essentially in a horizontal fashion. Naïve subjects have been used in experiments where they have been taught automatic writing. Instead of writing the word "Yes," or the letters "No," they have spontaneously responded with a vertical line, meaning "Yes," or with a horizontal line meaning "No." There is a definite economy in other behavior responses of the hypnotic subject, as well. Noting these patterns, a hypnotist develops a clinical judgment about when a subject is in a trance, when he is not yet in a trance, and how far along he may be in the trance.

POSTHYPNOTIC SUGGESTION

In every posthypnotic performance, either just before, during, or immediately afterward, the subject goes into a brief, temporary trance, that is essentially identical with the trance in which the posthypnotic suggestion was given. It is another sign that the subject is responding to posthypnotic suggestion.

One can discuss a variety of topics with a patient. A topic might be the life of Benvenuto Cellini and what the patient remembers about it. During the discussion, one gives the patient a posthypnotic suggestion to be carried out next week. Then, one induces another trance. This time, the discussion might be about the life of Michelangelo. One gives another posthypnotic suggestion, arouses the patient from the second trance and, after a while, puts him in a third trance. During this trance, one might discuss the intricacies of playing chess, interrupted by a third posthypnotic suggestion.

The following week, at the cue provided in the original trance, the posthypnotic suggestion is carried out. One arrests the subject at the moment that he starts to carry out the posthypnotic suggestion and he shows catalepsy; he is in the trance state. Then one says to him, "I forgot what you just said," or "I didn't quite understand. . . ." He now starts talking about Benvenuto Cellini. One finishes that discussion as though it were last week and awakens the patient. A little while later, one gives the next posthypnotic cue. He carries out the posthypnotic suggestion, again arrested in the trance state. Then one awakens him and gives him the second posthypnotic cue. He carries it out. One proceeds as before. "I don't quite remember that. Can you tell me the instance?" "Well, it happened when Michelangelo was so old." When the hypnotist remarks, "I don't quite follow you," the subject says, "But, of course, when you move your queen here, that's going to lead to checkmate." Obviously, he is discussing chess.

In other words, it seems to the subject that he is back in the original trance carrying out all the activity of that original trance in which the posthypnotic suggestion was given. Therefore, within the practice of medicine or dentistry or psychiatry, the posthypnotic suggestion should be used especially in connection with some very pleasant thing. One gives the patient a posthypnotic suggestion at the time that he is feeling very happy about his new dentures, really enjoying feeling them fit into his mouth, or looking in the mirror and enjoying his smile. One gives a posthypnotic suggestion in that connection. The next time the patient comes into the office and executes that posthypnotic suggestion, he reverts to the happy mood in which he was enjoying looking at his very nice smile. Of course, that use for the posthypnotic suggestion serves to bring about a good trance to reinforce all the good learnings of the previous trance and to accelerate the learning of the next trance.

REORIENTATION

Just as one can reorient a patient to the past or to the future, one can reorient him in relation to his body. An amputee, for example, who cannot adjust to the fact that he has suffered an amputation, can be put into a very deep trance and reoriented to the time when he did have both legs. The problem can be discussed of how he would possibly react if at some time in the future he did happen to have an amputation. "Nobody really knows, but it can happen to anybody, even to you or to me." One can discuss how he would adjust to a future in which he suffered an amputation. One can learn a great deal about his fundamental rejections and raise with him the various questions of adjustment that may develop. These can be discussed as hypothetical problems and, since they are hypothetical to him in that state of disorientation, he can discuss them without too much anxiety or fear or distress, mapping out a way in which to meet the actual problem of the existing amputation.

THE PATIENT'S ABILITY TO RECALL TRANCE EVENTS

The patient may remember or he may forget information and understandings obtained in the trance state, in accordance with his own personality needs. The most important thing to keep in mind is that the hypnotic subject is able to carry out suggestions in his own particular way.

Getting patient to recall at his own pace

Deeply repressed experiences may be uncovered in the trance state, and the patient instructed to remember them consciously at some future date at that rate of speed that is most conducive to the patient's welfare.

REPEATING THE SAME DREAM

For the patient who needs a great deal of therapy, one can suggest that he dream a dream; he can make it as symbolic and obscure as he wishes. Then he can be told, "Dream the same dream, with the same meaning, the same emotional significance. But this time, dream it with a different cast of characters." When he has done this, he is told to repeat it with still another set of characters, etc. Each time, the dream becomes more and more obvious. Eventually, the patient himself will readily recognize the actual meaning of the dream.

CAPABILITIES OF THE HYPNOTIC SUBJECT

Anybody who uses hypnosis must recognize that he is dealing in the trance state with a human personality able to do any of the things he can do in the waking state, in any order and relationship possible in the waking state. The patient in the deep hypnotic trance is fully as competent and capable as that same patient in the waking state. He can be even more attentive to the performance of a task because he is not distracted by the externals of his environment.

CASE OF PROFESSOR H.

Professor H, a specialist in art, was brought by a hypnotist to a state hospital to lecture to the staff psychiatrists. They wanted hypnosis demonstrated. The professor gave an excellent lecture on the utilization of art in the occupational therapy of psychotic patients. The audience was fascinated.

After the lecture, Professor H was aroused so that the staff could realize that he had been in a trance, had lectured to them, illustrated his lecture with a chalk talk, and discussed composition of pictures and their significance with them while in this state. Then he was awakened with a complete amnesia and with the belief that it was one o'clock. He had been told very carefully that it was one o'clock while he was in the trance state. His watch had been set back so that it read one o'clock. He flatly refused to believe it was four o'clock; he thought everyone else had watches that were wrong. He had a total amnesia. Looking at one of the pictures he had sketched on the blackboard, he commented very freely, "A rather talented person developed that composition." Then he showed why it was good. Later the hypnotist saw that same picture in his studio. Professor H explained that the composition had come to him all of a sudden. It was much like one he had seen that some state hospital patient had sketched! Finally, he was told what really had happened.

Indirect suggestion

The topic of indirect suggestion has been discussed rather comprehensively because of the great effectiveness and value that it has in dealing with all sorts of problems, from the simplest to the most deep-seated. Some of its more comprehensive and subtle applications can be illustrated by case examples.

A young girl comes into the office suffering from dysmenorrhea. The usual tendency is to hypnotize her and encourage her not to have any more painful menstruation. Actually, one should consider who that girl is, what she is, and something about her future as a person. Just to stop her having painful menstruation and to bar it from the rest of her life actually means allowing her to encounter the future without adequate preparation. She is not interested in discovering the cause of her painful menstruation and she does not want to go in for a prolonged analysis. The approach should therefore be one that is decidedly comprehensive and also indirect.

In all probability, a girl who has painful menstruation has it because of lack of understanding, fears, or possibly a traumatic experience in her life. She does not like it. One may therefore suggest this understanding to her: Menstruation is a phenomenon that is going to repeat itself many times in her life. There are also going to be interruptions, presumably, if she lives a normal life. She may marry, become pregnant; she may become seriously ill and have her menstrual cycle interrupted. One can also give her an explanation of what menstruation is. An astonishing number of women actually have no real understanding of what menstruation is. They can be given an adequate understanding of that, of what congestion is, and the sensation of congestion. In the hypnotic trance, the patient can learn to distinguish between a sense of congestion and a sense of pain. When these are not differentiated, a patient very often mistakes congestion for pain.

CASE OF AMELIA L.

Amelia L came into the office recently to state that she had decided to have a painful menstrual period. She could not figure out any other way of escaping from the surgeon's office where she worked as an assistant. She did not want to be there on a certain day when the surgeon had a series of operations scheduled. She decided to have painful menstruation to get out of a lot of work that she didn't want to do. That was her choice. She deliberately chose painful menstruation, a pattern with which she was familiar in the past.

In other words, painful menstruation may be developed as a result of various factors. During the course of a lifetime, it may come to have other meanings and values. When one attempts to abolish all pain, a patient may rebel. The first time a patient rebels against a suggestion of a painless menstrual period, hypnotic therapy has lost its significance and its value to that patient. It is better to suggest to the patient, "You may want painful menstruation from time to time. I don't know. You may want a little pain. You may get married and want to get even with your husband for something. Just remember that while you want painless menstruation now, there may come a time when you may possibly want pain, perhaps a little, perhaps a lot—whatever you, as a personality, decide upon." Thus she is indirectly given permission to have a painless menstrual period, one with a little associated discomfort, or one with a great deal of discomfort.

PREPARING THE PATIENT FOR RECURRENT EXACERBATIONS

In dealing with an arthritic patient, for example, in teaching him how to use his involved extremities and giving him freedom from pain or minimizing his discomfort, one has to make him aware of the fact that he must eventually expect to have more trouble. He should be prepared for future recurrent exacerbations, so that the first rain that comes along does not serve to negate the effect of hypnotic suggestions for freedom from pain.

CASE OF MR. JOEL M.

Mr. Joel M, one such arthritic patient, occasionally gives his psychiatrist a call to find out how *he* is getting along, but really to report on himself, too. He has about three days in bed every January and August (the peaks of the rainy season in his home state of Arizona). He fully expects to be laid up, but the hypnotic suggestions that were given him several years ago are still as effective now as they were at that time. He has the feeling that each new January and August rain serves to reinforce the suggestions given hypnotically for control of his pain.

COMPREHENSIVE SUGGESTIONS

In giving suggestions, the real question should be: How much of the symptomatology does the patient really need? Does he need all of it? A part of it? One raises the questions in the trance state; then one might suggest that it be cut down until he has only the amount of symptomatology that is useful to him. It is a way of winning a patient's cooperation. The therapist is not asking him to transform himself completely as a person. He is merely trying to help the patient keep what he needs, whatever truly belongs to him.

10
Hypnosis in Dentistry

Even professional persons frequently become confused about what dentists achieve with hypnosis as compared with what they can achieve with drugs. It is true that sedation can be accomplished chemically. But there has never yet been a chemical that can re-educate the patient, help him to respond more positively to dental treatment. Many dentists use drugs to get the patient into a relaxed condition, and must continue to use drugs each time the patient returns. After employing hypnosis for five or six sessions, however, a dentist frequently finds that the patient no longer needs it (hypnosis). He has learned a new pattern of response to the stimulus of dental treatment.

Advantages of hypnosis

FOR THE PATIENT

In reducing patient apprehension

The person whose dental office behavior is not what one would like it to be frequently reacts as he does because of the apprehensions he has about treatment. Even the patient who appears stoic usually has some manner of demonstrating his fears apart from actual flinching from treatment. Many dentists have begun to discontinue placing a cup of water at the side of the patient. The tendency, in so many patients, is to spend an inordinate amount of time in rinsing. Such patients are not wasting moments washing their mouths because they have no appreciation of time; they are employing a defense mechanism to postpone the dentist's resumption of treatment.

CASE OF MR. EDWARD B.

It is common dental experience that as soon as one removes his fingers and instruments from the mouths of some patients, the patients will almost invariably bring their heads forward and away from the headrest. Thus, each time the dentist returns to the patient, he must reposition the patient's head. But Edward B demonstrated a new variety of delaying tactic. He not only brought his head forward; he also had to perform certain compulsive gyrations before returning it to the head rest. What in essence did these represent? Nothing more than a postponing of dental treatment. The induction of only light hypnosis is usually enough to handle such cases. If there is any fear in the dentist's mind that he is going to spend so much time using hypnosis that he won't have any time to practice dentistry, he can be assured that with a patient like Mr. Edward B hypnosis will be the most time-saving method he can employ.

In anesthesia

Hypnoanesthesia can be employed in dentistry as a substitute for, or as an adjunct to, chemoanesthesia. While many patients never reach the depth of hypnosis at which hypnoanesthesia may be obtained, it seems logical to use it when they *can* reach that depth. It certainly *must* be attempted in those individuals for whom all other varieties of anesthesia are contraindicated. In general anesthesia, the amount of anesthetic may be significantly reduced when it is augmented with hypnosis.

Some persons are motivated to study hypnosis in dentistry because they expect to be able to find a substitute for anesthesia. They hope that in hypnosis they will find a medium which will allow them to throw out their syringes, their ampules, and their inhalant anesthetics. One seminarian once announced, "The only reason I came here is to learn to pull teeth with hypnosis." One doesn't extract teeth with hypnosis. During hypnosis, however, routine dental procedures are facilitated.

In gagging and nausea

Gagging and nausea can be controlled or minimized during hypnosis. (See demonstration of the technique to be used on a patient with an exaggerated gagging reflex, page 390).

In eliminating patient fatigue

Even where hypnosis is no longer needed for elimination of apprehension, it does offer an additional advantage in that it may be employed to reduce or eliminate patient fatigue. Without hypnosis, the patient is often fatigued by long-drawn-out sessions in the dental chair. In this regard Erickson has mentioned the studies made in laboratories of the hypnotized patient's ability to keep his arm elevated for extended periods. The same thing is accomplished by the dentist who suggests to the patient that his open mouth can lock in that position. The mouth does lock and the patient is completely unaware of any resultant fatigue. In Erickson's work on time distortion, he has shown that the patient frequently has a completely distorted idea of the length of time his mouth has been open. An hour and a half of dentistry may be accomplished, but as far as the patient is concerned, he may feel that his mouth has been open for only five minutes.

In postoperative healing

Much has been written about the possibilities of facilitating postoperative healing. The verbalization following tooth extraction may be as follows: "Mrs. Patient, your tooth has been removed successfully, but I want you to relax for a little while longer as I talk to you. The socket from which your tooth was removed is clean and the gum seems to be in fine condition. I believe that when you return here next you will tell me that you had uneventful healing following removal of a tooth."

FOR THE DENTIST

As an aid to ordinary procedures

Some dentists approach hypnosis with the idea that perhaps they will be able to cancel, through a knowledge of this art, the effects of defective inlay margins, incompletely filled root canals, overextended borders, or premature contacts in dentures. Hypnosis is not going to substitute for good dentistry.

If, however, the dentist approaches hypnosis with the idea that it is another method for amplifying the good he can already do, he has the right approach. There are areas in which hypnosis can be used in varying degrees on most patients: removing fears and apprehensions, persuading the patient to accept the treatment he fears, helping to obtain impressions and bite registrations, and for suggestions (post-hypnotic) to ensure correct follow-up by the patient in the management of dentures, orthodontic appliances, and oral hygiene. In other words, a dentist can do far more good for many more people if he accepts hypnosis as an adjunct to, and not as a substitute for, any technique of dentistry. Correctly viewed, hypnosis is a means of assistance in performing the dentistry that one already does, a means of doing it more easily, more quickly, and more comfortably, both for the patient and the dentist.

As an aid to reduction of tension on the part of the dentist

The dentist who works on tense and nervous patients absorbs these tensions. The cumulative effect of working on several such patients is detrimental to his health and emotional stability. A dentist who teaches his patients to relax and also applies the techniques to himself will preserve his health and prolong his usefulness. At the very least, he will improve his relationships with his patients and his family.

Hypnotic orientation

FOR THE DENTIST

How should the dentist approach induction procedures? In the first place, every normal person can be hypnotized under proper conditions by a skilled operator. But the dentist must clearly realize that the patient who resists hypnosis cannot be readily hypnotized. This should be emphasized with the patient; he should know that he actually hypnotizes himself and can do so when hypnosis is indicated and when he is working with a qualified operator. In stressing this point, a better relationship is established with patients.

FOR THE PATIENT

Reactions to the term "hypnosis"

Some patients do not feel at home with the word "hypnosis." Some dentists feel the same way. They are afraid that if they use the word, they may antagonize their patients. If they feel this way and use the word with this feeling, the probability is that they will prejudice their patients. They need to find a euphemism until they can get over this feeling. One doctor in Illinois was so uncomfortable about "hypnosis" that he renamed the process. He told his patients, "You seem to be tense. I am going to teach you countertension." He taught his patients "countertension" successfully. During a recent meeting, he was asked, "How are you getting along with countertension?" "Oh," he replied, "I don't use that term any more. My patients like hypnosis!" His patients began to understand what it was; more important, the dentist came to understand what it was.

Using relaxation as an avenue to hypnosis

If patients are apprehensive, it is better not to talk directly about hypnosis. One merely observes that they are nervous and gives them a reason for it. The patient might be asked, "Wouldn't you like me to show you a way of getting rid of that tension, so that you can have your dentistry done without pain?" When they say "yes," they can be started off with what is described as a relaxation technique. It is a trial run on hypnosis. The disadvantage in this approach is that a patient may not cooperate as fully and the technique may be a little slower. On the other hand, some of the usual interferences and resistances may not be encountered.

Obstacles may present themselves. A patient may say, "Did you use hypnosis on me?" The reply could be, "The extreme of this *could* be hypnosis. Perhaps, though, you weren't in hypnosis. Were you unconscious?" The patient answers, "No." "Could you have opened your eyes and awakened any time you wanted?" The patient says, "Yes, I could have." Then the answer might be, "It was a nice feeling, wasn't it? Do you feel any harm as a result of relaxing so completely?" By this time, the patient gets the idea and drops the subject. He is usually very happy, even if it was hypnosis.

Patient doubts about hypnotizability

Patients will come in and ask, "Can you hypnotize me, Doctor?" The answer should be, "No, but I can teach you how to go into hypnosis," or, "I can teach *you* hypnosis." Remember that the patient should be in readiness to be hypnotized before one starts the actual technical procedure. Ensure his readiness through orientation and through re-r. oval of his doubts about going into hypnosis.

Conserving time in patient orientation

The phrase "mind-set" appears frequently in the hypnosis literature. It usually refers to the creation of a favorable atmosphere for the induction of hypnosis. The expression infers power by the hypnotist over the individual. On the principle that the responsibility for entering hypnosis belongs to the patient, the term "patient preparation" or "patient orientation" is preferred. It seems better to think in terms of achieving "a state of readiness" to be hypnotized. Once this state has been reached, entering hypnosis is quick and simple.

Achieving a state of readiness can be a time-consuming affair. In the dentist's early use of hypnosis, he may find himself tempted to spend two or three, sometimes more hours giving patients education and orientation on hypnosis. The use of informational booklets can minimize the time factor. The booklet entitled "An Old Art Returns to Dentistry" by William T. Heron is especially useful.

The doctor states: "The answers to any question you may have on this subject are contained in this little booklet. Take this copy of 'An Old Art Returns to Dentistry' and read it. When you have finished, call me for an appointment and we will discuss it."

Trance induction

HOW TO PRESENT HYPNOSIS TO THE PATIENT

One's own attitude in approaching the patient should be that of strong, firm, positive conviction. Do not say to patients, "Would you like to try hypnosis?" or, "Maybe we'll try hypnosis and see if that will work for you." That is about as negative an approach as can be made. There should be no question in the dentist's mind that hypnosis is going to work on the patient. "We will use hypnosis" expresses the attitude that should be taken.

THE SEMANTICS OF HYPNOSIS

A dentist using hypnosis must exercise unusual care in his choice of words. People often say one thing and mean another. In ordinary conversation, that is generally understood and no harm or confusion results. But in hypnosis one must take into consideration the literalness of the subconscious. A concrete illustration is: "Doctor, do you mind telling me your name?" He will almost invariably answer, "Doctor Jones." Actually, his name was not requested at all. He was asked if he would mind giving his name. If he were in hypnosis and he were asked that question, his literal subconscious would probably say "yes" or "no." He would have to be asked directly, "Tell me your name." Only then, would his reply be "Jones."

In working with another patient, the dentist could not induce a trance and the effort had to be abandoned finally. He was told later why his patient would not go into hypnosis. The dentist had told her that her legs were getting heavy and she was at that plump stage where she did not want to be reminded of this fact. Many personality factors need to be taken into consideration in the choice of words to be used.

VALUE OF SIMILES OR ILLUSTRATIONS

The use of simile or illustration: Phrases vivid with simple imagery, such as, "Your arm as straight and stiff as an iron bar," "Your arm as if floating in the air like a feather on a breeze," "limp as a wet dish cloth," "limp as a piece of tired lettuce," are of great value in trance induction.

VARYING APPROACH TO SUIT PATIENT

No one stereotyped approach should be used in trance induction. It is necessary to vary hypnotic technique from patient to patient. Even with the same patient, different situations may demand variations in approach. If, for instance, the patient will not levitate his arm after an attempt has been made to get him to do so, there are other ways of developing hypnosis or deepening his trance. The patient who refuses to produce an arm levitation may have some sub-conscious concern about his arms.

CASE OF MRS. GERTRUDE F.

When Mrs. Gertrude F was regressed to her childhood, it was found that she had a vivid memory of a housemaid employed by an old aunt. The maid was sixty or seventy years of age and carried her arm in the Kaiser Wilhelm II paralysis. As a child the patient had been fascinated by this arm. In the hypnotic treatment of Mrs. F, the dentist met absolute refusal whenever he tried anything in the way of arm levitation. The patient seemed to equate arm levitation with arm paralysis.

ONE SPECIALIZED TECHNIQUE (PEN FLASH)

Various methods of trance induction have been presented in the earlier chapters. One doctor worked out his own variation of the eye fixation technique. He uses a pen flashlight, with a little light bulb on the end as a fixation point. When he sees that the patient's eyes are getting ready to close, he says, "Now, just watch the light; closer and closer; your eyelids are getting heavier and heavier; soon, you will see two lights. When you see two lights, close your eyes and be deeply relaxed." As the patient reaches the point of muscular divergence, he does have a diplopia, of course, and he does see two lights.

INDICATIONS FOR PRESENCE OF NURSE

For the dentist's own protection, his nurse should be present. It is true there are some nurses who appear to work against hypnosis by making themselves too obvious. They stand in front of the dental chair, or a little to one side, watching the patient as the operator is working. Many people resent the presence of a third person during the trance induction. One possible compromise is to see to it that the nurse is in the room immediately adjacent to the one in use at the time, and that she makes little, calculated noises. She may open or close a door—just to be sure that the patient senses that someone else is in the area. After the desired depth of hypnosis has been obtained, the nurse can be called in for direct assistance at the chair side. It is best to warn the patient about the nurse's impending arrival, merely by announcing, "And now the nurse is going to join us."

Trance maintenance

Operations should be carried through to completion before arousing the patient. Many dentists make the mistake of bringing the patient out of hypnosis at the end of cavity preparation, for instance. They then place the matrix band $\frac{1}{16}$ inch into the soft tissue and wonder why the patient didn't have an entirely enjoyable experience. There is no reason to hurry. Let the patient stay in hypnosis as long as there is any possible need for it. Hypnosis is not a general anesthetic and does not impose the time limits of a general anesthetic. Maintenance of trance depth does not require a continued flow of words from the operator. An occasional "That's fine" or "Sleep deeply" will suffice.

LEAVING THE PATIENT FOR A SHORT TIME

The question is often asked, "May I leave the patient alone, or will the trance state be interrupted if I am called from the room?" Of course, the patient can be left alone, but if the dentist does not announce that he is leaving, it is very possible that the patient will arouse himself. When he misses the dentist, the rapport may be broken. The situation can be handled very simply. One need only say, "And now, Mrs. Patient, you won't hear my voice for the next two minnutes," (or five minutes—whatever it is going to be) "and in the quiet here in the office, you will find that you will be able to relax even more deeply. Remember, I will be back in five minutes." It is important to get back within the time limits set.

Trance termination

HANDLING PATIENT RESISTANCES

Sometimes the patient is given a signal to awaken or a suggestion to alert himself, and he does not respond. A prepsychotic or abnormal patient may sometimes use the hypnotic state as an excuse or as a means of withdrawing from a situation, but such patients are encountered relatively rarely in the dental situation. More often seen are those normal patients who enjoy the hypnotic situation so much that they do not want to leave it and in not wanting to leave it, they may become refractory in following suggestions for awakening.

Making use of the resistances

Erickson has mentioned that patient resistances can often be used to help the patient. He reverses the procedure by saying, "Well, you are trying to stay asleep and I don't think you *can* awaken; try to awaken, but you can't. The harder you try to open your eyes, the more difficult it becomes." Because he is now refractory, the patient may say to himself, "I'll show him. He can't make me stay asleep if I don't want to," and he awakens.

Appealing to the patient for cooperation

One can put the matter on another basis. The patient can be told, "Mr. Smith, we are using this technique because it is a cooperative venture. We need 100 per cent cooperation at all times. If you refuse to cooperate, we can no longer use this technique for you in the future." Here, of course, one risks the possibility that hypnosis may have to be discontinued with that patient in the future.

Charging the patient for extra time

If one attempts to awaken the patient and he just smiles as if to say, "I'm going to stay right here, because I'm enjoying it," one can then say, "You are perfectly welcome to stay in this chair and enjoy the situation as long as you like, but my next patient is already here. If you choose to use his time, it is all right but you will have to pay for it." Patients usually arouse after this statement.

POSTHYPNOTIC SUGGESTIONS

For reinduction

Inquiry has been made as to what kind of posthypnotic suggestions can be given and when they are considered most useful. One of the most important is some type of signal for reinduction of the trance. The signal should be, first of all, one that suits the practitioner. Further, it should be a signal that can be used for everyone. If one uniform signal is employed, the dentist doesn't have to think, "Now what did I tell Mrs. Jones? Was it the following of a finger, or the touch on the shoulder, or the counting method?" The signal can be a simple touch on the right shoulder. Or, one might prefer to say, "When you sit in this chair—every time you sit in this chair—and your head touches the headrest, you will be reminded of what it is that you need to do to become deeply relaxed, go into a comfortable state where you can enjoy your anesthesia, or your dentistry."

For transfer of anesthesia

Posthypnotic suggestions can be given so that the anesthesia that a patient has been able to induce in one area can be transferred to another any time that it becomes necessary.

For removal of discomfort on waking

Another suggestion given is for the purpose of ensuring comfort on awakening. For instance, "In a few moments you will receive the signal to alert yourself; you will then proceed to become wide awake, feeling fine in every respect. This has been a completely enjoyable experience." If the patient was given eye strain in an eye fixation procedure, if he has catalepsy, or if he has remained a long time in a fixed position that may produce bodily fatigue, one must be sure to suggest away that fatigue.

For time limit to anesthesia

At the completion of the operation, one must either remove the patient's hypnoanesthesia or set a time limit for the termination of the posthypnotic anesthesia. It is possible that four days later the patient may wind up in the hospital with an abscess because he has had no warning of discomfort. If, for any reason, patients are sent out of the office with a posthypnotic anesthesia, a specific time limit must be set: ". . . and your jaw can continue to stay as numb as it is now until you walk in here tomorrow morning."

For pleasant memories

Suggestions may be given in regard to pleasant memories of the dental experience. The patient who is in a deep trance may have a spontaneous amnesia, with no memory of anything that occurred and that fact may disturb him. He or she would really like to know what happened during the elapsed time. The following statement is offered for that particular situation, especially where the situation may have some traumatic aspects—an especially unpleasant bit of surgery, gross tooth reductions, or the like. The patient can be assured, "Now isn't this a pleasant way to have dentistry done? This is really like a dream. Sometimes it is difficult to remember dreams, even just after you waken, isn't it? Well, this may fade away from you like a dream and you may forget about the dream, but I would like you to remember the pleasant part. It has been pleasant, hasn't it? You will remember the pleasant part for me, won't you? I will appreciate it if you will remember the pleasant part."

Promising to remember the pleasant part gives the patient the permission to forget those things that he does not want to remember.

For recall or return appointment

Patients can be told that when they receive the dentist's communication verbally, by telephone, or in the mail, it will serve as a reminder to them of the very pleasant experience they had in the dental office. "It is a pleasant situation, isn't it? Wouldn't you like to remember that? You will remember that the next time you receive the communication, whatever sort it may be."

Protecting patient from unqualified hypnotists

Some patients who have learned to enter hypnosis readily may be imposed upon by friends, entertainers, or charlatans for questionable purposes. The following statement may help to protect the patient:

"You have been a very good patient. Don't you think that you should restrict your use of hypnosis to medical, dental, or scientific purposes?" (Patient agrees.) "I would feel better if you would promise me that you will enter hypnosis only for proper purposes and only with properly qualified persons." (Patient promises.)

The above is more likely to be effective than would an

authoritarian prohibition of the use of hypnosis in which specific instances or persons are proscribed.

Special problems

THE EMOTIONAL PATIENT AND THE DENTIST

If the patient has a problem that involves psychotherapy, has had a record of psychotic episodes, or seems to be prepsychotic, it would be wise to avoid using hypnosis with him until clearance is obtained from the psychotherapist. How can the prepsychotic patient be recognized? Though it is sometimes difficult to be certain about such patients, it is best not to attempt hypnosis on those who behave strangely, who laugh when there is nothing to laugh about, cry when there is nothing to cry about, who are completely at odds with their environment and everyone in it.

THE STAGE HYPNOTIST

The stage hypnotist creates a situation in which he may arouse patient negativism. The patient sees a subject being made to feel ants crawling up his legs and acting in ways calculated to amuse an audience. When this patient comes to the dental office, his attitude is likely to be, "None of that stuff for me. I've seen it and I don't like it." The likelihood of this patient's availing himself of a therapeutic aid that may have been exceedingly helpful to him may be lost. We need to protect the therapeutic use of hypnosis. A promise obtained from the patient that he will use his abilities for constructive purposes and not for entertainment should be obtained on a permissive and voluntary basis.

Although the Roman Catholic Church approves the use of hypnosis for necessary therapeutic purposes, it absolutely forbids its use for entertainment. If the patient is a Roman Catholic, one may therefore secure his cooperation easily.

CONTROL OVER THE LAY USE OF HYPNOSIS

In some communities it occasionally happens that youngsters of junior high and high school age become interested in hypnosis, distribute literature on the subject, and practice it in large groups. The parents may become concerned and call on professional men for help with the problem. One of the things the parents should be told is that no amount of professional knowledge of hypnosis is going to substitute for parental discipline. One constructive approach that physicians, dentists, and psychologists can make is to go to their libraries and request that books on hypnosis, trance induction techniques, and the like be kept on a restricted shelf. Their use should be limited to adults only. Concerning the 25¢ and 35¢ books that one can buy on hypnosis, there appears to be no easy answer. The local Better Business Bureau, Chamber of Commerce, or some similar agency might want to cooperate in trying to keep them out of the community. Such books are not illegal; about all that can be done is to ask for cooperation from the stationery store owners in not stocking these items.

MEDICOLEGAL LIABILITY

Malpractice insurance companies recognize hypnosis today as a legitimate, therapeutic technique. But the dentist who uses hypnosis for a nondental situation, to cure a stomach ache or to do psychotherapy for a nondental problem, may find himself in serious difficulties in the event of litigation. The underwriters may say, "Yes, we protect you in the use of hypnosis, but not in a situation that does not involve the practice of dentistry." It is inadvisable to experiment with patients in the office, eliciting phenomena, just to see how deep a trance can be obtained with them. Suggestions should be limited to those necessary for the trance induction and those necessary for accomplishing therapeutic purpose. If these precautions are observed, there will be no difficulties, either interpersonally or interprofessionally, with colleagues in the allied professional fields, or medicolegally.

The liability insurance companies provide no difference in premiums for those who employ hypnosis. Hypnosis is accepted by the insurance companies as a legitimate dental adjunct, as long as it is connected with the practice of dentistry.

Suggested office procedures

KEEPING RECORDS

Elaborate hypnotic records are not necessary, but marking the patient's record card with pertinent bits of information is helpful. An "H" could designate the use of a hypnotic technique. "L," "M," or "D" could indicate depth of trance. Notations of the likes and dislikes of the patient and material described by him in visual imagery should be noted. Information of this sort is useful in re-establishing rapport with the patient after unusually long intervals between visits.

RECORDING OTHER HYPNOTIC INFORMATION

Other pertinent information should, of course, also be noted. If the patient is a child and the "Sleep Game" approach has been used, that fact should be recorded. It is also frequently helpful to note particular interests of the patient. One dentist has an eleven-year-old patient who is a very competent bowler. Another child likes to see Mickey Mouse in purple buttons. Another wants to be a space cadet. These pertinent facts, jotted down in a couple of words, often afford a cue with which satisfactory interpersonal relationships can be re-established quickly.

Cards are also useful in furnishing information concerning patient referrals. If an old patient refers an acquaintance, the referring individual is recorded on both the new and the old patient's cards. A glance at the cards reminds the dentist to ask about the other patient and helps him to build up the little ties that make interpersonal relationships much stronger and more pleasant.

MEMO CARDS FOR BEGINNERS

One dentist devised a system that he used early in his hypnotic practice. He had two 5×7 inch cards put together with Scotch tape. One was the record card. On the other, he outlined his preparation: the suggestions he might make to the patient—the need to be attentive, the explanation that hypnosis is not sleep, and so on, and his plans for terminating the trance. He also outlined the hand levitation method, the eye fixation language, and the coin technique.

If such cards are used, they should be kept where the patient cannot see the dentist reaching for them. If a little help is needed when eye closure has been obtained, one can readily use the cards. The chances are, however, that a dentist will soon find them unnecessary. With experience, one learns not to fit the patient into the framework of a stereotyped set of instructions, but rather to fit ideas and techniques to the individual patient. The preparation of such a card is a good exercise for beginners, however, even when it is not actually used.

Hypnosis in pedodontia

SUGGESTIONS IN THE DENTAL CARE OF CHILDREN

From the very beginning, activity is directed to establishing rapport with the child. A child must be made to feel accepted and important almost immediately. Remarks of a complimentary nature, such as, "What a pretty dress!" "How nice your hair looks!" are a start in this direction.

From this point, efforts are aimed toward orienting the patient to the physical environment of the office. The child is introduced to the "elevator" (the motorized dental chair). The parent or guardian is seated in the chair and the child is taught to operate the pedals that raise and lower the chair. It is then his turn to be seated. In most instances, he seats himself willingly in a chair that he has learned to operate.

The subject of counting is introduced. "Can you count?" the child is asked. The dentist opens his mouth and asks the patient to count his teeth. If he cannot count, he is asked to look at the dentist's teeth. Permission is then obtained to count or look at his teeth. This is usually granted by the voluntary opening of the patient's mouth. Progress is being made. A child has seated himself in a dentist's chair and is opening his mouth voluntarily for a dental examination.

The next step is to introduce the youngster to the "washing machine," which is the water-cooling apparatus attached to the handpiece. "Teeth become dirty and decayed. This is how we clean them." The control is pressed and water is allowed to spray on the patient's hand. Then he is asked to open his mouth. Water is sprayed from the attachment into the mouth. A round stone in the handpiece is gently revolved around a carious tooth. "That was kind of fun, wasn't it?"

Now the child might be told, "It is time to learn about the Sleep Game. That is a lot of fun. It is a game where one closes the eyes and pretends to be asleep. In the pretend sleep, a child can watch a movie or television, or anything that he enjoys. Any child can learn how to play. Before playing the game, he must learn how to empty his mouth of the washing-machine water while his eyes are closed."

The child learns how the "water-pistol" (water syringe) works. He is asked to close his eyes and to keep them closed. The left hand is placed on the edge of the "sink" (cuspidor). The mouth is filled with water. The instruction is given to bend over the sink, but not to empty until told. When the head is over the center of the bowl, he is told to empty his mouth. "That's fine!" Then he is told, "Now lean back, keeping your eyes closed. We are going to see how smart you are. This time when I fill your mouth, lean over and empty it without my telling you when." It is gratifying that patients, so oriented, never miss the bowl even with their eyes closed; those with eyes wide open often miss the bowl and spatter the nurse, the walls, and the equipment.

Before starting the Sleep Game, the child's preferences in regard to movies, television programs and other pleasure activities are discussed. The usual routine is to encourage him to think of a technicolor cartoon on a movie screen and of the accompanying music. But any imagery the patient elects to produce is used. He is then instructed: "Now close your eyes and keep them closed. Soon you will see that movie sharply and clearly. As the picture gets better, the hand gets light and starts to go up (lift the hand). The higher the hand goes, the better the picture gets. When your hand gets to your face, the picture will be perfect. That's fine. Keep your eyes closed. Keep watching the picture and listening to the music. Mark time to the music with your finger."

Some children take a little time starting the imagery. For these, the following is added: "Perhaps you'll see just a dot at first; then perhaps eyes and a mouth; then some whole people and animals." If the hand does not start to rise rather soon, pick it up gently at the wrist with the tips of the thumb and middle finger. Repeat the suggestions of lightness until there is enough catalepsy to keep the hand raised.

By this time the patient is extremely relaxed, and/or hypnotized, and/or dissociated. If operative procedure is anticipated, such as an extraction or caries excavation, the site of an intended injection will have been painted with such a topical anesthetic as Xylocain ointment. Pushing a thumbnail into the gum tissue, one can say, "This pinches but it doesn't bother you, does it?" The patient may agree or he may say that he feels it. Counter with, "Yes, you feel it, but the hurt is gone." This is persisted in until the patient agrees that he feels it, but that it does not matter. At that time, the injection is made and that, too, does not matter. The dentist now has an anesthetized and hypnotized patient. There is no situation more ideal for effecting dental procedures with mutual satisfaction to doctor and patient.

PARENTAL OBJECTIONS TO HYPNOSIS

The dentist may occasionally encounter parents who are emphatically opposed to the use of hypnosis for themselves or their children. Their wishes should be entirely respected and no effort made to hypnotize the child.

PARENTS' PRESENCE DURING HYPNOSIS

As a general rule, the presence of parents is contraindicated. One dentist had a boy of about seventeen in the chair. He asked the mother if she would like to watch the trance induction. The boy started to go into an excellent trance —there was no question about his being a good subject. All of a sudden, the mother said, "Tsk, tsk, tsk," and that was the end of the trance. If one wishes after the child has been induced, he can call the mother into the office and say, "Would you like to come in for just a moment and see how nicely Johnny is sitting here?" Then she can be very much impressed with the way the situation has been handled. But she will not see the actual induction.

Another point of view is that the parent should be permitted in the operating room as long as the child does not use the parent's presence to control the situation. A parent's presence is often supportive for the very young child and parents are favorably impressed by the kindness and understanding of the dentist, necessary in the relationship that results in relaxed states and/or hypnosis.

CASE OF RICKIE M.

As part of the usual procedure in treating one eleven-year-old boy, everyone was excluded from the situation except two professional associates. Some time later the mother, who had accompanied the patient to the office, said, "Doctor, I'm going to criticize you a little bit and I hope you won't feel offended, but I don't think it was nice of you at all to exclude me from the situation." She was asked what she meant and she said, "Well, you just told Rickie that only a dentist or a physician would be able to hypnotize him and I've just about finished with my course in hypnosis and I want to be able to help Rickie." The dentist then learned that she was taking a course from a stage hypnotist, in order to be able to do psychotherapy on her son. In this case it seemed that it was the mother, rather than the son, who needed the psychotherapy.

MOTIVATING COOPERATION IN CHILDREN

Many techniques can be used to elicit the child's cooperation. In working with one little girl who presented quite a problem, the dentist got along pretty well but the patient was obviously not very happy. He finally drew two faces on her appointment slip, one of them frowning, with the corners of the mouth turned down; the other smiling, with the corners of the mouth turned up. He explained, "The children who get along best get prizes. I've got a box full of rings and awards for good children. Now this is the way the good children look and this is the way the others look. I want you to put your name under the one that you're going to be the next time you come here. Don't tell me which one it is now." The next time she had her name under the smiling face, but she had a frown on her own face as she got into the chair. The dentist stood off and said, "Do you know how you really look? Not like the smiling one, but like this." He tried to imitate the facial expression. Her mouth turned up the other way and he continued, "Keep those corners up now; you look a lot better; you really look awful the other way, but beautiful this way."

TWO INDUCTION TECHNIQUES FOR CHILDREN

Variation of coin technique

Variations of the coin technique are frequently successful with children. One colleague makes a few little marks with a ball point or a crayon on the thumbnail of the child. The marks resemble a face and furnish motivation for the youngster to fix his eyes on his thumb. Another dentist uses stars, red, gold, yellow, blue, the kind the child gets for a good report card, attaches them to the thumbnail and uses them as a fixation point.

Prayer technique

One rather religious colleague uses prayer with children very successfully as a help in inducing hypnosis, especially when he knows the child does say prayers and comes from a religious family. He says, "Now clasp your hands together, Johnny, and close your eyes and pray that Doctor Jones will be guided by the Lord to make his hands gentle and to keep you from being hurt." This suggestion was published in one of the dental bulletins and several dentists have written in to say, "That prayer really does bring results."

HANDLING FEES FOR CHILDREN

The following statement may be made to the parents: "I don't charge any more for children than I do for adults." This startles the parents, because somehow or other they have the feeling that when the dentist works on deciduous teeth, which will be lost in a few years, he should not charge as high a fee as for the permanent teeth. General experience has shown that work with children takes as long as, or even longer than, similar work on adults. There should be equivalent compensation.

The exaggerated gag reflex

Control or elimination of the exaggerated gag reflex may be approached from three different levels of suggestive therapy: (1) authoritative waking suggestion; (2) symptom removal by hypnotherapeutic suggestion; (3) treatment of cause by brief hypnoanalysis.

Some patients will respond to only one of these approaches. Others will fail to respond to one approach while responding to the others. There are those who will react favorably to all of them. Still others will resist therapy at any level. The approaches mentioned will be successful with patients whose gagging symptom is based on an established habit pattern remaining after the original need for the symptom has disappeared. If there is any other basis for the symptom, the patient will probably resist treatment.

The authoritative waking approach may be used when the purpose is to control the exaggerated gagging reflex for brief periods ranging from five to ten minutes in duration. The control afforded in this technique may facilitate or make possible throat examinations, the taking of dental impressions, registrations for dental prosthetics, intraoral radiography, local anesthesia, and many other treatments.

The antigagging instructions used in implementing this technique is effective in only about 50 per cent of the cases unless it is preceded by instruction in breath control and unless it offers a patient a rationale for the procedure. Adding the breathing instructions and the rationale that it is impossible to gag while holding one's breath raises the success of the treatment to over 90 per cent.

VERBALIZATION

DOCTOR

I am going to show you a method for controlling your gagging. So that this method may be successful, you will have to prove to yourself that you cannot hold your breath and gag at the same time. The first step is to be able to recognize when you are no longer holding your breath. Take a deep breath and hold it. Make your abdominal muscles as tight as you can. Feel the tensions in your chest. The moment you begin to feel the least bit of easing in your chest of your abdominal muscles, you are leaking breath.

Let us measure the time you can hold your breath. As soon as you have taken a deep breath and can feel the tightness in your chest and abdomen, stretch out your arm. As soon as your chest or abdomen begins to ease up, drop your arm. I will time you. (*Doctor measures time arm was stretched out.*) That's fine. Your arm was up for 15 seconds. If what I said before is true, you should be able to keep from gagging for at least 15 seconds. Take a deep breath and hold your chest tight while I test with this tongue blade."

The doctor tests gag reflex while instructing the patient to hold his abdomen tight, tight, tight! It may take two or three trials before the patient learns that he does not gag until his breath starts to leak. He is asked if he is convinced that there are certain conditions under which gagging is **not** only unnecessary but actually impossible.

The patient must be thoroughly satisfied about this before the next step is taken. If the patient is taller than the doctor, he is seated and the doctor stands facing him. If the patient is the same size or shorter, they both stand. The doctor places his hands on the patient's shoulder and stares at the base of his nose. The following instructions are then given:

> You are now ready to lose your exaggerated gagging reflex. Follow my instructions exactly. Look straight into my eyes without wavering. If you take your eyes away from mine, we will have to start over from the beginning. (*Patient fixes his eyes on doctor's eyes.*) Take a deep breath and hold it until I count to five. Real deep, chest tight. Hold it! One—hold it! Two—tight! Three—hold it! Four —hold it! Five. Now, let it out and relax your abdomen. Your gag is gone. To make sure, we will do it once more. That's part of the system. Keep looking at my eyes. Take a deep breath and hold it until I count to five. Chest tight! One! Two! Three! Four! Five! Let it go. The harder you try to gag, the more difficult it becomes. Try to gag and take pleasure in failing. (*The patient finds that he cannot gag.*)

The doctor must speak authoritatively and convincingly. Any doubt within himself may be transmitted to the patient. In carrying out this technique, the doctor must be sure to look at the base of the patient's nose. Some doctors have been known to go into a trance while looking into the patient's eyes.

After the medical or dental treatment has been accomplished, instructions may be given for the future. If gagging threatens, one need only hold one's breath as long as possible, let it go, take another deep breath, and so on, continuing in this way indefinitely, until the emergency is over.

Gagging denture wearers who have been instructed in this technique may be taken to a mirror and advised as follows:

> Look into the mirror. There is your patient. You are his doctor. Practice this method I have shown you three times every day until the gagging is completely under control. You will find that the need to practice will gradually disappear.

SYMPTOM REMOVAL BY HYPNOTHERAPEUTIC SUGGESTION

Obtain a hypnosis as deep as the patient is willing to produce. The deeper stages are preferable, but a medium stage is adequate. When hypnosis has been achieved, the procedure may follow two directions:

Prestige suggestion

The patient is told that gagging results from tensions, and that because he is now relaxed, he need no longer gag; that he may try to gag, but the more he tries, the more difficult it becomes; or, he may simply be instructed to stop the unnecessary part of the gagging.

Transfer of anesthesia

A more positive and more successful technique is the one employing transfer of anesthesia. The patient is taught to develop hypnoanesthesia and to transfer it from one part of the body to another. He is then instructed to anesthetize those tissues which, when stimulated formerly, provoked gagging. He is informed that he cannot gag because of the anesthesia. The suggestions are made that he has now learned to control his gagging; that to be able to gag is normal; but that he will, henceforth, no longer need to gag unnecessarily.

Whenever a symptom has been removed by suggestion, the possibility should be raised that because of habit, the patient may feel a need to manifest the symptom at some time in the future. The patient will usually accept the suggestion that when such an event occurs, it might be preferable to manifest some other symptom instead. Such a symptom could be the anesthetizing of one of the toes. In this way, the patient may improve his situation by trading his annoying symptom for something innocuous.

TREATMENT OF CAUSE BY BRIEF HYPNOANALYSIS

Age regressions should be avoided by therapists untrained in the handling of repressed materials or those unequipped to cope with manifestations of hysterical behavior.

Stimulating recall or revivifying the past, while keeping the patient in contact with the therapist and the present, is within the scope of the abilities and educational level of all. Furthermore, there is an advantage in that lighter stages of hypnosis are often adequate for this procedure.

The deepest hypnosis of which the patient is capable is achieved. He is then asked to relax with his hands on his thighs. He is told that questions are going to be asked, to which he does not know the answers on a conscious level. His unconscious mind knows the answers and will be able to respond. The method of response is as follows. When the answer to the question is "Yes," the right index finger will rise. When the answer is "No," the left index finger will rise. An "I don't know" will be indicated by the lifting of the right thumb. Answers in any other category, such as "I don't care to say" or "This is not the time to tell" will be indicated by the raising of the left thumb. The patient is instructed to make no conscious responses and to make no effort to move his fingers or thumbs. These movements should come by a process of unconscious levitation.

The first question is a test question. "Are you in a trance?" The response should either be a "Yes" or a "No." The character of the response is observed. A rapid movement is usually associated with conscious level. A slow, quivering, characteristically hypnotic movement is associated with subconscious level response. An "I don't know" is a conscious level response.

The next question: "Is the original cause of your exaggerated gagging something that you are willing to discuss with me here, and at this time?" Only a "Yes" or "No" answer is acceptable.

If the answer is "No," the next question is, "Is the cause of your gagging something that you are willing to think about without telling me about it, or discussing it with me?" If the answer to this question is "No," then the matter should be dropped or the case referred to a psychiatrist or psychologist. If the answer to this or the preceding question is "Yes," we may proceed as follows:

"Is that something that happened before you were ten years old?" ANS. "Yes." "Did it happen before you were five?" ANS. "No." "Did it happen before you were seven?" ANS. "No." "Did it happen before you were eight?" ANS. "Yes." "Did it happen when you were seven?" ANS. "Yes."

The suggestion is then made to relax completely. The patient is told that very soon there will flash across his mind the knowledge we seek. When the insight has come, he is asked if he cares to tell about it. There must be no insistence. No matter what the patient decides, it can be pointed out that it is something that happened to a seven-year-old that started the trouble. There was a good reason to gag then. But he is now no longer the seven-year-old who needed to gag. The exaggerated gagging has become an unnecessary habit. He is asked if he is willing to give up the unnecessary part of his gagging. When these suggestions are accepted, the patient is cured.

Before the patient is dismissed, the possibility of symptom substitution is discussed. The same procedure is followed as for the patient whose symptoms have been attacked directly. (See Symptom Removal by Hypnotherapeutic Suggestion.)

These methods have been tested clinically on more than one hundred subjects. Success has been achieved in 90 per cent of the cases. Although follow-ups have not been made, more than thirty subjects have voluntarily reported, at intervals of from seven months to three years after treatment, that they were still free of gagging.

Many initially stimulating factors were mentioned. These included painful dentistry, tonsillectomies, careless throat examinations, bad-tasting medicines, etc.

The method described has been an example of uncovering techniques. Investigation of the causal mechanisms with other symptoms may be pursued in much the same manner. Too much emphasis cannot be placed on the importance of permissiveness in the approach. If the symptom is one on which the patient relies for his adjustments to reality, or one associated with knowledge he cannot face at conscious level, he should not be coerced into cooperation. Such coercion may lead to hysteria or other embarrassments. One should always respect the patient's needs.

Demonstration 15: GAGGING CURE

PREPARING THE PATIENT

DOCTOR S (*demonstrating*)

Are you at all hesitant about being in front of an audience? You realize that this is not a showplace; we are all a group of doctors who are here for a serious purpose. Now, may I refer to you as Bill? You have troubles, do you?

SUBJECT

I have a gagging reflex.

DOCTOR S (*demonstrating*)

Would you care to show us just how much trouble you have?

SUBJECT

Not at all, you mean me personally?

DOCTOR S (*demonstrating*)

Yes, you can make your own trouble. I want to help you out of trouble, not to get you in trouble.

SUBJECT

I have trouble enough, but it is a rash man who puts his finger in my mouth.

DOCTOR S (*demonstrating*)

Well, I won't be then. (*Checks reflex.*) That's trouble, isn't it?

SUBJECT

You're right. That's trouble.

DOCTOR S (*demonstrating*)

How about x-rays, dental x-rays?

SUBJECT

Impossible.

DOCTOR S (*demonstrating*)

Impressions of any kind?

SUBJECT

Never had any.

DOCTOR S (*demonstrating*)

And tooth brushing—pretty rough, huh?

SUBJECT

Yes.

DOCTOR s (*demonstrating*)

Do you know anything about hypnosis, Bill?

SUBJECT

Only what I've learned from general reading. That's all.

DOCTOR s (*demonstrating*)

There is one aspect of hypnosis of which we here disapprove entirely. That is its use for entertainment purposes. Some people get a wrong idea of hypnosis and it makes it difficult for them to have it used for their benefit when they really need it. And you can really use it. Do you think so?

SUBJECT

Sure.

DOCTOR s (*demonstrating*)

Do you know something else about hypnosis? The stage hypnotist makes it look as if he has a power over someone else, but if you had attended the meetings here you would have heard us explain that no one really hypnotizes anybody else. We show the patient what it is that he has to do.

If you will allow yourself to go into the hypnotic state, you will find yourself in a very pleasant condition to begin with, and in a condition in which you will be able to help yourself very materially. So you really have a worthwhile purpose. I would not want you to go into a hypnotic state if there were not something useful to accomplish from it. We don't want you to be abused; we don't want you to be amused, and we don't want to entertain anybody. We want to accomplish something for you and, in teaching you how to accomplish something for yourself, these other doctors will be benefited because they have similar problems with other people. You will therefore be making a contribution, not only to your own personal health and welfare, but to the education of men in the therapeutic fields. That is really a worthwhile accomplishment, isn't it?

SUBJECT

Yes.

DOCTOR S (*demonstrating*)

What do you think is going to happen to you when you take yourself into hypnosis? I'll show you how to do that.

SUBJECT

Well, I have no idea except that it has become rather obvious that a person could be hypnotized, for example, by looking at a flickering fire or candle or anything of that nature. Or you can look into your eyes when you shave and find yourself . . .

DOCTOR S (*demonstrating*)

Kind of drifting off?

SUBJECT

Surely.

DOCTOR S (*demonstrating*)

Do you have any idea that a person is unconscious at any time during hypnosis?

SUBJECT

I would think he wouldn't be.

DOCTOR S (*demonstrating*)

That is correct. As a matter of fact, a person who is in the deepest stages of hypnosis is even more alert and capable of using all his mental faculties than in the ordinary so-called waking state. Actually, it is a state of consciousness, not unconsciousness. That is really quite correct and usually the misinformed person has the opposite feeling. It is a pleasure to have you express your knowledge in that regard.

Now I'm going to show you what it is that you have to do to accomplish this and I want you to realize that I am not going to try to amuse anybody, that I am only going to give you those suggestions which are going to help you do this. Any time you do not like what is happening, you can just quit, get up and walk off and it will be perfectly all right. Already you have the feeling that nothing like that is going to happen or else we would not have you here; isn't that right? I want you to know that you have that privilege, that you have that ability, that you have that power. You are going to find what is happening so pleasant, so comfortable, that you are really going to enjoy it.

INDUCTION OF LIGHT TRANCE

DOCTOR s (*demonstrating*)

Now, I said we are going to do a lot of things. Here's one way you can go into the relaxed state. It is called the black-board test and it gives us an idea of how well you are going to be able to do. The way we do this is to ask the patient to make himself as comfortable as possible; to relax as much as possible, realizing that it takes tensions to keep one's legs crossed, to keep one's arms crossed, and we want you to relax as comfortably as you can.

(*to audience*)

You see the indication is already very favorable. This patient is capable of responding to ideas. I did not ask him to uncross his legs; I didn't ask him to uncross his arms, but I indicated a good reason for it. He accepted it; he is capable of responding to ideas and very often it is easy to go into hypnosis with an eye fixation, but it is even as easy and sometimes easier for people to do it in other ways. One way you can do it is by starting off with your eyes closed. Once the eyes are closed, it is very wise to keep them closed until your cooperator, your instructor, indicates that the time has come to change.

Blackboard test

DOCTOR S (*to subject*)

Now, it would be helpful if you would visualize a blackboard, any kind of a blackboard, anywhere, in a schoolroom, at church, in an office, and as soon as you can see it, you can acknowledge it by just nodding your head—as soon as you see that blackboard sharply and clearly. Then at the bottom of that blackboard, you see a tray. Can you see it? In the tray there is a piece of chalk. Do you see that? You can see yourself reaching forward in your visualization and picking up that chalk. You then inscribe a large circle on the blackboard and you put the chalk back where you found it. Right next to it there is an eraser and you pick that up and you erase the circle that you have made, completely erase it. The eraser is then put back in the tray and you see yourself stepping back about two paces and you take a good look at the blackboard. Now, please, Bill, tell me what you see. Look hard, Bill! Do you see that smudge that was left by the erasure of the circle?

SUBJECT

Yes.

Vase of flowers imagery

DOCTOR S (*demonstrating*)

That's fine. Very good, Bill. Now turn your back to the blackboard and you will see in front of you a table piled high with flowers. Tell me, Bill, what colors do you see?

SUBJECT

(*pause*) Yellow and red.

DOCTOR s (*demonstrating*)

That's right. About how many flowers would you say there were approximately?

SUBJECT

About a dozen.

DOCTOR s (*demonstrating*)

That's right. And about how long are the stems, Bill? Show me.

SUBJECT

About fifteen inches.

TRANCE DEEPENING

DOCTOR s (*demonstrating*)

That's right. Now, just turn your back to that and you'll see in front of you just nothing, just a blackness. Just empty your mind of thoughts and relax your mind and your body. Take a deep breath and relax a-l-l o-v-e-r, r-e-l-a-x, r-e-l-a-x. From now on, Bill, you are going to breathe slowly and deeply and every breath you take is going to make you d-e-e-p-e-r and d-e-e-p-e-r relaxed, and you are going to find my voice kind of monotonous and sleep-inducing. It is going to make you sleepy. Any noise or sound that you hear will contribute to your sleepiness and relaxation. Even as I talk to these other doctors, you need pay no attention; just ignore it and become aware of the fact that you are getting sleepier and sleepier, and appreciate the fact that I am telling these doctors how well you have done up to this point.

DOCTOR S (*to audience*)

You noticed that, in the blackboard test, the first indication we got that he was really and truly responding to ideas was when he looked again at the blackboard and saw the smudge. Until we called it to his attention, he had not seen anything. At the point when the patient has turned his back to the table of flowers, he is usually in a light trance. I think this patient is in a deep part of the light trance and that he will go still deeper. We can now start all over again with another procedure or go on to deepen from this point, assuming that the patient is already in a light trance.

DOCTOR S (*to subject*)

As you breathe slowly and deeply, Bill, you will begin to appreciate a drowsy, dreamy feeling as if you were floating in a cloud and at the same time sinking deeper and deeper into that cloud. You can feel a heaviness creeping up all over your body, because it takes tensions to move a muscle, it takes tensions to wink an eyelash, it takes tensions to move a finger. You feel so good. You don't want anything to change the way you feel. You let your whole body and your arms appreciate the feeling of heaviness and you won't mind my doing whatever is necessary to contribute to this situation. I'll hold onto your arm here as it continues to feel heavier and h-e-a-v-i-e-r and you can really feel the heaviness in it. As I manipulate your hand here, you can let it go limp. That's it. That's it! Just let it hang limp and loose. It is really heavy. As I drop it, Bill, you can let it drop to your lap, breathing heavy, heavy, heavy. Think of nothing and do nothing.

Hand levitation

DOCTOR S (*demonstrating*)

And now, Bill, I would like you to appreciate the sensations and feelings that you have in your hands and your fingers, with the realization that every individual finger has a sense of feeling separate and apart from every other finger. As you pay attention to that, you can feel the pressure of your body, through your hands, through the cloth into the palms of your hands, and into your fingertips. You can feel your fingers moving somewhat in both your left hand and your right hand, and pretty soon one finger is going to make a demonstrative movement, such as a jerky movement away from your trousers leg, or away from the other fingers. You can enjoy the prospect of which finger it is going to be. You can think about it and ponder about it, and soon you will know because that finger is going to make a jerky movement. Will it be on the left hand or will it be on the right hand?

You can just think about it. Will it be the index finger or will it be the thumb moving away? I've kind of got an idea it's going to be the index finger of the right hand, but it doesn't have to be. It did move before a little bit, and you were probably aware of it. One of these fingers is going to make a demonstrative movement. Let it, Bill. Don't stop it. Let it make the movement. It seems to want to be both the middle finger and the index finger of the right hand, and you can let that movement get more and more pronounced, and soon that feeling of lightness will cause the finger to lift, lift, lift, and then that feeling will radiate into the other fingers, and then into the palm of the hand, and to the wrist. Soon there will be a feeling of lightness in your entire hand and arm and fingers. You can have a feeling that there is a rope tied around that wrist, lifting, lifting your arm, pulling it up, up, up.

Broadening the task

DOCTOR S (*demonstrating*)

It is pleasant for you to contemplate that, and as that is happening, your subconscious mind is taking care of it; you can pay attention to your right hand. With your left hand, press down against your leg. As your left hand presses down, your right hand gets lighter and lighter. Your left hand presses down; your right gets l-i-g-h-t-e-r and l-i-g-h-t-e-r. The more pressure you apply with your left hand, the lighter your right hand gets. You enjoy that and allow your right hand to go up, up, up, as your left hand goes down, down, down. The right hand goes up, up, lifting, lifting, and you r-e-a-l-l-y enjoy that sensation. Let it go; don't try to prevent it. Don't try to help it, but go along with it, because you really are going to enjoy what happens as a result of this.

Use of imagery

DOCTOR S (*demonstrating*)

You can imagine that there is a rope tied around the wrist and someone is pulling up on that rope, pulling, pulling, pulling, and that wrist and arm and hand get lighter and lighter and that pull gets stronger and stronger. Enjoy that sensation as it goes up, up, up. Doing fine! Eventually, that arm is going to bend at the elbow, Bill, and as it bends at the elbow, that bending will bring your hand toward your face.

Setting goal of deep hypnosis

DOCTOR S (*demonstrating*)

Now your subconscious mind knows how fast you need to go. When your hand touches your face, you will be in a deep state of hypnosis. When you are ready for it, and not until then, Bill, will your hand touch your face. But you do want that to happen; I want it, because we are going to accomplish much that will be of benefit to you when we get there, Bill. And your hand continues to rise, because you *really* want it to, do you not? You don't need to do anything about it, because your subconscious wants it to and will do all the work.

There is no particular rush about it, but you will be surprised that it is going to develop soon, very soon, even sooner than you think. That pull gets stronger and stronger, as if there were a shackle around your wrist, really pulling and lifting. And feel that pull! Enjoy it. Enjoy the sensation that this is something that you are producing with your own subconscious mind.

Complimenting patient

DOCTOR S (*demonstrating*)

The best way to help is to help oneself, isn't it? Doing fine, Bill! Doing very, very fine! Now you are far enough advanced to where it really doesn't make any difference whether your hand continues to your face or drops back to your lap. When your hand touches your face, you can be in a deep hypnosis, or when your hand touches your trousers leg, you can be in a deep hypnotic state. Most people like to complete the levitation by raising the hand to the face and allowing it to go back to the lap as the hypnosis deepens. It doesn't matter what you do. Maybe you find it difficult to lift your hand, but you can try. I think you really can do it if you want to. You may find it difficult, but not so difficult that you can't conquer that resistance. You really are making progress, aren't you?

DOCTOR S (*to audience*)

When the patient makes progress, as it is evident that Bill is doing, one must be sure to compliment him, to give him a figurative pat on the back. He is doing it all, and *he* deserves the credit. The only credit that I will deserve is that which enables me, as therapist, to recognize what it is that he is doing, and enables me to help him do what it is that he needs to do. Bill knows, even though I haven't said it, that I am complimenting him. The indirection of that suggestion may be more pleasing to him than if I actually said,

"Thank you, Bill. You too, realize that I said it both ways, directly and indirectly."

DOCTOR S (*to subject*)

And, Bill, it's surprising to you that it is happening even faster than you thought possible. At first it seemed difficult and, even now, it seems difficult, but less difficult. Easier now. Soon, very soon, because you are more than halfway there, you can just relax completely and deeply. Melting into the chair, going into a deep state of hypnotic sleep or relaxation. As close to real sleep as it is possible to get and yet remain conscious, hear the sound of my voice, cooperate in the activity necessary for you to accomplish our ultimate objective.

The state of hypnosis is only going to be utilized to help you with a specific problem. The state of hypnosis is a very normal thing. Most of us are in it and out of it some time or another in a very light way. But you are going to be able to accomplish it in a very ultimate and deep way. Shortly, very soon! And it is a pleasure for me to see the hand getting closer and closer and nearer and nearer. You are doing wonderfully well, Bill, and when your hand touches your face, you will really be deeply relaxed. Doing very well!

Although there is no real hurry, the sooner you do accomplish the hypnosis, the sooner we will be able to tackle the problem for which the hypnosis has been induced. I don't want to rush you. But I want you to think about the fact that the sooner this is accomplished, the sooner we will be able to get at that problem. You are making an excellent subject for teaching purposes, as well as being able to utilize this for your own benefit.

Whether I talk to you or not, that hand moves closer and closer. Anything can contribute now to making you relax more deeply—sounds, noises, quiet. Sometimes quiet helps one to take oneself into sleep. If this isn't working fast enough to suit you, there's more than one way of getting your hand and face together. If the mountain won't come to Mohammed, Mohammed can come to the mountain, you know. Your head can begin to nod toward your hand.

HAND LEVITATION AS DEEPENING DEVICE

Hand dropping

DOCTOR S (*demonstrating*)

As you go deeper and deeper, your arm gets so heavy, and as it gets heavy, you cannot hold it up. As it drops down to your lap, it takes you deeper and deeper. And when your hand makes contact with your trouser leg, it takes you as far as you can possibly be and still remain awake and conscious and hear the sound of my voice. It is such a friendly sensation as you go deeper and deeper relaxed. D-e-e-p-e-r and d-e-e-p-e-r relaxed.

Catalepsy

DOCTOR S (*demonstrating*)

Now, Bill, your whole body is heavy with relaxation, except your left arm here which becomes stiff and rigid like an iron bar. Really stiff and rigid, with your fingers outstretched and tension going into your elbow and into your wrist and to your finger tips. Make it so stiff and rigid that you cannot bend it at any joint. Stiff, stiff and rigid so that you cannot bend it at any joint. Stiff, stiff and rigid, so strong that when I try to push it down to your left, you can resist me. You increase that resistance. Keep on increasing it now. Don't allow it to ease up. Keep on increasing that resistance to my pushing your arm down until I count to three. At the count of three, you suddenly let go that resistance to my pushing your arm down, then melt into the chair as if you were butter melting into a hot skillet, as if you were a rubber band that had been stretched out and suddenly let go. That quickly do you melt into the chair as you quickly let go the resistance. But until that time, you INCREASE the resistance. Increasing it, increasing it, until I count to three. At the count of three, you let it go and go deeply asleep in this hypnotic type of sleep in which you are still conscious. But keep on resisting it now. Keep it up, keep it up, keep it up! Even while I count. But at the count of three, suddenly let it go. One—two—three! Let go. Quick. Deep, deep, deeply relax and breathe slowly and deeply now. With each breath that you take, go deeper and deeper and deeper relaxed. As I let your hand go, you can let it take you deeper and deeper relaxed.

DOCTOR S (*to audience*)

I found it necessary here to elicit catalepsy and then discharge the tensions, in order to deepen the hypnosis. Distractions during the levitation interfered with the deepening process.

Posthypnotic suggestion

DOCTOR S (*to subject*)

Bill, your eyes are closed and I would like you to keep them closed until I ask you to open them. When I ask you to open them, you will have no difficulty in doing so and you will feel wide awake, sharp and alert, having enjoyed everything about this procedure, but until I ask you to do so, you are to keep your eyes closed. Please, I would appreciate the knowledge that you will keep your eyes closed, under all circumstances, until I ask you to open them. (*Patient nods affirmatively.*)

Now pay attention, please. I am going to give you further instructions, so that you may learn how to do this better, quicker, going deeper each time you need to do it, so that you can do this with your doctor when it is necessary for other purposes. But you are going to have to follow my instructions as I give them to you, immediately, precisely, exactly as I give them to you. Fine, very fine! You have been most cooperative and I want to thank you very much.

Glove anesthesia of one hand

DOCTOR S (*to subject*)

I would like to call to your attention a phenomenon that is known in the medical literature as "glove anesthesia." That means a complete numbness of a glovelike nature in which there is a total anesthesia surrounding your hand; if it happens to your foot, it is called "boot anesthesia" or "shoe anesthesia." I would like you to imagine that we are injecting a very powerful local anesthetic from which you can get all the benefits but none of the discomforts. You can feel the distentions and the pushing of tissue and a tingling feeling or a glovelike feeling, or a dead, numb, wooden feeling—some kind of a feeling that is comparable to the sensations of a chemical anesthetic. As soon as you become aware of a difference between your right and your left hands, acknowledge that by raising this finger here—the index finger of your left hand. Fine. Now pay attention. I am going to count to five. With each count, it gets deeper and more profound, so that at the count of five, it is completely numb and anesthetic. When we test it, you may feel pressures but no discomfort. One—numb; two—numb, getting more numb, and pay attention and enjoy that feeling of heaviness and numbness; three—numb and still getting more numb; four—and at the next count, completely numb; five—as numb as it needs to be.

Complementary hypersensitivity of other hand

DOCTOR S (*to subject*)

Now your left hand can be numb and anesthetic; your right hand, however, is getting supersensitive. When I test it with this instrument, it will seem that it is unusually sensitive to pain. As I test it, it is going to feel like the jab of an ice pick. Pay attention. (*Test first in sensitive hand and note withdrawal response. Then test in other hand and obtain recognition for difference.*)

Transfer of anesthesia

DOCTOR S (*to subject*)

Now here is what I would like to have you do. I would like to have you put the palm of your hand against the side of your face. The anesthetic hand, your left hand, you press against the side of your face and, as I count five, you will find the anesthetic running out of your hand and into your jaw. As it gets to your jaw, it will go all over, especially on the palate and on the tongue. You will have an anesthetic jaw, an anesthetic head, so to speak, and that is also going to serve a useful purpose. At the count of five, the anesthetic will be transferred from your left hand to your head and you will drop your hand to your lap as a sign to me that the transfer has been accomplished. All right, Bill?

One—leaving your hand; two—entering your head; three —almost all gone from your hand; four—almost all in your jaw; five. Fine, fine!

TRANCE UTILIZATION

DOCTOR S (*to subject*)

I'd like to have you consider this, Bill. Your ability to gag with anything in your mouth is due to the fact that you can feel a ticklishness and a sensitiveness, but with your jaw anesthetized, you will be unable to feel that. With that anesthetic, you can, while you have the anesthetic, eliminate the gagging. It's that simple.

Symptomatic relief

DOCTOR S (*to subject*)

Would you like to try it out and show that you have done so? This is on the symptomatic level. Here is a mirror. You stay deeply relaxed, but that does not mean you are asleep. It means that you can talk to me, that you can cooperate with me, but you can remain deeply relaxed. As a matter of fact, you could even open your eyes and stay in this hypnotic type of sleep, but you might perhaps be distracted. For today, let it suffice that you sleep with your eyes closed. If you want to, you can open them—if you want to. Meantime, you yourself were able to make yourself gag. Now you made yourself anesthetic; now you can try to make yourself gag, but you know that you can't do it. You know what I mean? The harder you try, the more difficult it becomes because you are anesthetic.

Show the people that you are trying but that you can't. Isn't that wonderful, Bill? Now, should you need your throat examined, should you need x-rays, should you need impressions taken, should you really need to get back there with your toothbrush and brush your teeth, you can really do it, can't you?

I am going to show you how you can go back into this state easily and quickly, how you anesthetize your jaws and thereby not only eliminate the gagging, but eliminate the discomfort of other dental procedures, such as tooth extractions, drillings, cleanings and the like. That's a very pleasant thing to contemplate, isn't it, Bill? You have accomplished that rather quickly and easily. Aren't you proud of yourself? Just keep that anesthesia there as long as you like, and just show these people that you can't gag, won't you, Bill?

This is what we call symptom removal, Bill. It means that we have cured the symptom. But there is probably a reason for your gagging. That sounds reasonable, doesn't it? You, at a conscious level, don't necessarily know at this time the reason for your gagging. Perhaps it might be useful to find out why, but we don't have to do that. It would be more important first to find out when you first developed this exaggerated reflex and then we can determine why later. Is that satisfactory to you?

Probing for causation

DOCTOR S (*to subject*)

Just keep your hands down here and let us use these fingers for response mechanisms. I am going to ask you questions to which you don't know the answers, so don't make any attempt at answering them. But your subconscious mind knows the answers. Let your subconscious mind do the responding. I am going to teach you now.

STIMULATING RECALL BY FINGER QUESTIONING

DOCTOR S (*to subject*)

This finger on the left hand is "yes"; this one is "no"; this is "I don't know"; that one is, "I'd rather not say." Bill, the thing that most commonly causes gagging like this to persist at a later age, when it is no longer necessary, is something of a disagreeable nature that happened in early childhood. It could be something like taking medicine; something like a tonsillectomy—something of that nature. Just being frightened at the same time that you were swallowing something may have done this. Now I am not trying to suggest these things to have you give me one of them as a reason, but your subconscious mind knows whether or not it is something that happened in childhood. I am talking now directly to your subconscious mind; it will answer yes or no. Is it something that happened in your childhood? That answer is "yes." Fine.

Is it something that your subconscious is willing to have you discuss with me, here in this situation? Yes!

Is it something that happened before you were fifteen? The answer is "yes."

Is it something that happened before you were ten? The answer is "yes."

Is it something that happened before you were five? That answer is, "I don't know."

Did it happen before you were nine? You don't know.

Did it happen after you were five? Yes.

Did it happen after you were six? You don't know.

Did it happen before you were six? Yes.

Then it happened after five? Yes.

Did it happen before seven? Yes.

Did it happen while you were six years of age? You don't know.

Well, it happened before seven and after five. That's close enough, Bill.

Now, is it something that your subconscious mind is willing for you to discuss with me, a stranger, and in front of other strangers? It is? Fine!

RECALL

DOCTOR S (*to subject*)

Now, just think back and think back, and soon you will be able to feel and see yourself re-experiencing in your mind's eye as if there were a little boy in front of you, somewhere between the ages of five and seven, and you see that little boy in front of you sharp and clear. He is a good-looking little boy, isn't he? You can see him now in front of you? Fine! He is suffering now, isn't he? Something in his throat? Is it an illness? Is it something in his throat?

All right, you just watch the situation and you will soon begin to recall what it is—this fact that the subconscious tells us is responsible for that gagging. You will be able to tell us about it, and if your subconscious mind wants you to, and is willing to tell it to strangers, and I am as friendly a stranger as you are ever likely to meet, you can do so, and tell it to us. Would you like to do that for us?

SUBJECT

Excessive dosage of castor oil.

DOCTOR S (*demonstrating*)

Fine! All right!

Evaluation of trauma

DOCTOR S (*demonstrating*)

You are a grown man now, and not that boy between five and seven years of age, are you not? You know that subconsciously the thought was so traumatic to you that your conscious mind just did not want to countenance it. In order to prevent yourself from getting that sensation of castor oil, every time you had something in your mouth you started to gag. Your body and your subconscious mind tried to be kind to you by giving you a defense mechanism. But, after all, you have been using a machine gun to defend a situation that needs only a water pistol, isn't that right? Now that you know what it was that caused your gagging, are you satisfied that you no longer need to use it as a defense mechanism? Now when we terminate the hypnosis and terminate the anesthesia, there will no longer be any need for you to gag—with an anesthesia in your mouth or without one. Do you accept that? Good!

Evaluation of need for symptom

DOCTOR S (*demonstrating*)

Supposing your subconscious mind feels that it still needs that symptom; supposing instead of gagging, the tip of this finger gets numb. All right? Now, I also want you to pay attention to this: That tip of your finger can get numb any time your subconscious mind needs you to be protected, and you can use *this* as a protection instead of gagging. Is that satisfactory?

Then you can start thinking in your subconscious mind about how often you need to use this defense mechanism. Would once a month be all right? If you used it once every six months, or every two months, or every four months, would that be agreeable? You probably will never use it, but if you do, the periods in which you may use it will be further and further apart.

TESTING OF THE CURE

DOCTOR S (*demonstrating*)

So that you can continue to avail yourself of hypnosis, Bill, I would like you to show that you have no longer any need of excessive gagging. Stay in hypnosis but release the anesthesia from all over your body. Is the anesthesia gone now? I would like to test that by putting a little probe in your mouth. I'll be gentle because I know there is no longer any anesthesia, but I just want to demonstrate that there is no more anesthesia. Just over here—it is going to hurt—it is going to hurt. Did that hurt? Now, you no longer need to gag because there is no longer any reason for it. You are not that little boy who had the castor oil; all of that was a long time ago. Show us that you don't gag. You can keep it that way, waking, sleeping, or any other way, Bill.

REINDUCTION CUES AND TRANSFERENCE OF RAPPORT

DOCTOR S (*demonstrating*)

Now, Bill, every time you enter hypnosis, you enter more quickly and more deeply. This pressure on your right shoulder can be a signal for you to go back into this deep hypnotic state. In the deep hypnotic state, you can do anything that your doctor asks you to. He will never ask you to do anything that is unnecessary. He asks only that you do those things that are needful, desirable, and helpful to the situation at hand. This pressure on the left shoulder can be a signal that will allow you to awaken quickly, comfortably, and to be alert. You respond just a little differently to this signal (right shoulder) than to this signal (left shoulder). This one you respond to quickly; this one you take your time about; you awaken feeling sharp, alert, fresh, normal, and wonderful in every respect. We are going to practice that a few times, shall we? Then you will practice with your doctor, so that you and he can know that it works just as well with him as it does with me. Let us try the waking signal. (*The patient arouses.*)

POSTHYPNOTIC TESTING OF RESULTS

DOCTOR S (*demonstrating*)

You can go quickly into a deeply relaxed state and enjoy dentistry as you never thought possible before. Remember how you used to gag? It is a thing of the past now, isn't it?

SUBJECT

It's a difficult thing not to remember the possibilities.

DOCTOR S (*demonstrating*)

Would you like to show us what you have accomplished?

SUBJECT

Sure, I'd like to. Certainly, by all means. (*Mirror is passed over hard palate to tonsils.*)

DOCTOR S (*demonstrating*)

Is there anyone here who doubts it? Do you doubt it, Bill?

SUBJECT

No, I've experienced it for years. There is no doubt in my mind that my gagging has stopped.

DOCTOR S (*demonstrating*)

Isn't it pleasant to know that going into hypnosis is an accomplishment of the individual, not of anyone else? In other words, I didn't force you into it. Actually, you were just guided to where you needed to go. Now that I have shown you how, I can be far away and you can work with your doctor or any other doctor. But don't you think it would be a good idea if your knowledge of this were kept restricted to its therapeutic use, that you would never allow yourself to be the butt of entertainment at a party or used by an amateur or by a stage hypnotist? I would feel very happy if I could get an assurance from you that that will be the case. Fine.

11
Hypnosis in Psychology

Both hypnosis and psychology are fields that are wider than any specialty. Psychologists share the study of hypnosis with physicians and dentists, in particular. On the academic side, they share psychology with sociologists, neurophysiologists, psychiatrists, and many other specialists. The distinguishing mark of the psychologist is his interest in mental and emotional processes, whether theoretical, experimental, or applied. In the practical use of hypnosis, his place is close to the psychiatrist in clinical areas, but independent in his dealings with the dynamics of subjective and behavioral processes. A number of psychiatrists are also psychologists.

The demonstration that follows is again an example of the induction technique. The subject is Doctor C, who assisted in a previous induction demonstration (Demonstration 10). This affords an opportunity for follow-up and for contrast, as well as for elaboration of the guiding factors involved in both instances. Matters of dynamics, considerations in clinical observation of the subject or patient, and specialized techniques will be discussed on a general basis.

Demonstration 16

SUBJECTIVE RECALL FOR PRIOR HYPNOSIS

DOCTOR C (*demonstrating*)

I'd like to ask Doctor C for his comments on what happened last week. I have in mind going through the same sort of thing again.

SUBJECT

Well, I haven't thought much about this since last week. I remember that I sat here and you had me hold my fingers in this fashion (*Index finger and thumb separated*). You had me look at them, and then slowly close them. By the time they were closed, I imagine I was in a light state of trance, because I felt sleepy and I wanted to close my eyes because I felt it was more comfortable to close my eyes. And then you did a hand levitation. As a matter of fact, you did two hand levitations. Then you asked me where I thought my right hand was in relation to my nose and where I thought my left hand was in relation to my nose, and I flunked that one, I guess.

DOCTOR C (*demonstrating*)

No.

SUBJECT

No? (*Laughs*) However, I do recall that it was a pleasant sensation and I was rather reluctant to come out of the trance. I think that's when I realized it was the deepest I had ever been in a trance. I have been in a light trance before in practice sessions. Also, one doctor did a hand levitation demonstration with me in San Francisco, in my first contact with hypnosis. Last week is, I should say, probably the third time that anybody has worked with me in hypnosis, and I feel that I was able to go into a much deeper state than of course I could at the start. Is that the type of thing that you wanted?

DOCTOR C (*demonstrating*)

Yes. Do you have any comments?

SUBJECT

Well, I don't know that I have any particular comments about it. Of course, my interest is increasing in it.

DOCTOR C (*demonstrating*)

Thank you, Doctor.

REPETITION OF INDUCTION (FINGER-THUMB JUXTAPOSITION)

DOCTOR C (*to subject*)

Now, if I may, I would like to try the same procedure again, bringing my fingers together and letting you watch them. (*Right index finger and thumb permitted to go together automatically during these comments.*) And now, Doctor C, I'd like to have you relax as I discuss with the group the sort of things that have happened.

RATIONALE FOR FINGER-THUMB BY HYPNOTIST

DOCTOR C (*to audience*)

Last time, as I was bringing my fingers together, I discovered that they were held apart, with a definite feeling of resistance to juxtaposition. At that time, I had told Doctor C that he would relax. I therefore felt that he was working in reverse to my suggestion. It was an intuitive awareness. I was reading directly to his unconscious from my unconscious, as it were, with the sensation that my fingers were pulling apart. I then reversed matters to say that things would become clearer to him. Some persons wish to become more aware, to have things more definite, not to relinquish control or awareness; it was on that basis that I reversed the technique. Obviously, no one else was aware of this, because no one else could see the feelings in my hand or in my fingers. Yet, I am sure that unconsciously at least, Doctor C responded very definitely and very strongly to that shift in approach.

DOCTOR C (*to subject*)

And now, would you care to try levitation of either or both hands?

DOCTOR C (*to audience*)

Levitation could, of course, include lifting of the arm, lifting of the hand, motion of any finger, and also any other indication of relaxation or emotional reaction in the individual. These comments that I am making could be interfering to some degree. Not being somnambulistic, the subject could respond to them. Actually, the "explanation" about levitation was also a series of indirect suggestions for possible modes of hypnotic response on the part of the subject.

DOCTOR C *(to subject)*

> Those deep breaths are good. . . . And every breath you take, you find that you can relax more and more completely, but the relaxation is on your own terms, whatever you wish, whatever you feel is appropriate.

MODERATE TRANCE

DOCTOR C *(to audience)*

The closing of the eyes, as you know, removes external distraction. *(Indirect recognition of subject's progress.)* Now, regardless of superficial evidence, at this moment, Doctor C is in a moderate trance.

DOCTOR C *(to subject)*

> A good, deep breath, relaxing, relaxing, relaxing, still deeper and now in a moderate but somewhat deeper trance. . . . Getting closer and closer to a full-scale trance. There are momentary excursions into a deep trance. . . . Just relax, let yourself go, and remain in that trance. That's better. Now you can go indefinitely deeper.

DOCTOR C *(to audience)*

Telling the subject his actual progress, when the statements are correct, is very impressive to him and greatly facilitates the induction. For these purposes we do not need a stuporous trance.

DOCTOR C *(to subject)*

> You can go deeper and deeper moment by moment, enjoy-

ing the experience, comprehending it, becoming accustomed to it. It's entirely your choice what you wish to do with this trance, whether to relax, to remember things, forget things, think of things, or to wonder about any number of things. . . . Now, Doctor, for a few minutes I will exchange comments with the audience, leaving you free to carry on your own line of thought, but also to record for your future reference anything that was discussed.

USE OF FINGER-THUMB TECHNIQUE

QUESTION

Does it make any difference whether your fingers are close to the side, or the palm is upward?

ANSWER

When patients use the fingers themselves, the gravity works against the force if the hand is palm upward. It is a more spectacular performance. Any position is perfectly adequate, however.

INTUITIVE JUDGING OF TRANCE DEPTH

QUESTION

What criteria are you using for checking depth of trance?

ANSWER

Strictly intuition. I ask questions of my own fingers, numbering the thumb one, little finger five, on a one to five scale. One is the waking state, and five is over the edge into a deep trance. And I ask my unconscious periodically how deep the effect is. It's a matter of testing one's own hunches or intuitions. That, of course, is a matter of experience and practice.

QUESTION

Then would you say there is rapport on the so-called unconscious level?

ANSWER

Yes, I do feel that there is rapport on an unconscious level.

DEEPENING TRANCE

DOCTOR C (*demonstrating*)

Now, Doctor C, is there anything that you would like to do with hypnosis?

SUBJECT

Well, it would be interesting to me if I could go into a deeper trance.

DOCTOR C (*demonstrating*)

All right, how deep do you think it is now?

SUBJECT

I feel a tension in the right arm, but it has a numb feeling when you touch it. I mean it doesn't have the sensation it would ordinarily have if you touched it.

DOCTOR C (*demonstrating*)

Well, that sensation actually was the cord from the microphone. (*Sacrifice of impressiveness of sensation for sake of future better rapport with subject.*) . . . And now, how did that feel? (*Arm was passive, but not cataleptic.*)

SUBJECT

Very light, as though it could come up very easily.

DOCTOR C (*demonstrating*)

All right, we'll let it drop again. Now, what else do you have in mind.

GLOVE ANESTHESIA SUGGESTED BY SUBJECT

SUBJECT

(*Deep breaths.*) I believe I would like to have you try a glove anesthesia.

DOCTOR C (*demonstrating*)

All right. Which hand?

SUBJECT

The right would be perfectly satisfactory.

DOCTOR C (*demonstrating*)

Good. In that case, let's draw the line for the anesthesia right at your cuff line. When that anesthesia is complete, your left forefinger will go up as high as it possibly can. (*Turning of full control over to subject.*) In the meantime, I will talk to the audience. When the finger is high enough, either you or one of the audience will remind me.

USE OF CHALLENGES

QUESTION

What would happen if you tried some so-called test procedures at this stage, challenging him? Supposing you were to tell him, "Now, Doctor, you cannot open your eyes," what do you suppose would happen?

ANSWER

Working in a clinical way, I tend not to do that because I

am interested in future benefits and values for the patient. I may cajole or tease, or otherwise engender doubts in the person about the depth of the effect, the results, the direction of procedures, but only in terms of a long-range plan, so that the depth is not too important. I can gauge light, medium, deep without difficulty. This demonstration, of course, illustrates a consistently passive approach.

PROVING DEPTH OF TRANCE

QUESTION

But in terms of people who tend to doubt the matter of an individual's depth, I might say right now that I'm not sure I agree with you that he is in a medium trance or a deep trance. What could you do to prove it to me?

DOCTOR C (*demonstrating*)

If I were setting out to prove depth, I would first of all use a subject who was not too good. I would use one where the conflict (or resistance) was obvious. Working with patients, I am not concerned about that. I may have a person in a deep trance and, if he chooses to think that he is not, what does it matter? I still get results. At certain times, by questioning it is possible to get a person to go into deeper and deeper effects. Presently I'll show you with Doctor C the sort of thing that can be done.

DIRECT SUGGESTION BETTER FOR ANESTHESIA

QUESTION

Can't you get a quicker anesthesia in the hand by doing a direct suggestion?

ANSWER

I could get it more quickly by direct suggestion, but I prefer to allow a period of assimilation where the patient himself does it directly to himself and then signals me the result. This is not the usual posthypnotic suggestion; it is the result of suggestion within the trance state. When the subject is somnambulistic, specialized procedures may be used to achieve dissociation and consequent anesthesia, which the subject does not expect.

(*to subject*)

I notice that the finger *is* lifting, lifting quite adequately. (*Failure to test the glove anesthesia at this point builds up motivations on the part of the subject, as will be seen later.*)

(*to audience*)

The whole question of deciding the depth of hypnosis is a very difficult one. With my patients or subjects I speak about a deep effect, and leave the question of just how deep that is entirely to the individual. In the long run, a deep effect is a deep effect. It is very difficult to quantify from one person to another.

General remarks

DOCTOR C (*demonstrating*)

Let me interrupt the clinical part of the session, Doctor C, and let you go back to your seat and I will talk in a more general sense. But some time in the next fifteen or twenty minutes you may have a visual sensation that will be so clear to you that you will wish to tell about it. Either you will volunteer or someone near you will notice and remind me to ask you about it.

LEVELS OF THERAPY

DOCTOR C (*to audience*)

One can operate at roughly three levels of therapy. First, there is the commonsense dealing with situations on a superficial level. This includes such things as indecision about jobs, conflict with in-laws, and other common stress situations, as well as the therapy of habits. This level of therapy is also used with patients who cannot or will not tolerate the eliciting of unconscious material. The second level is intermediate, dealing with personality problems, such as hostilities, fears, or guilts that derive from relatively simple sources and do not cripple the individual very much. The third level is that of depth psychotherapy, where the individual seeks to improve his adjustment and level of functioning to a degree higher than he has ever attained in the past. In contrast, intermediate level therapy is directed at enabling the patient to regain his former level of functioning.

It has been my practice to leave the decision as to level up to the patient. I feel that I do not have the right to trap a patient into longer or more strenuous efforts without his consent, or even better, his active desire to work at a deeper level. Unless the patient decides at the outset that he wants depth therapy, he is started at the superficial level and remains at it until matters are resolved, or it is evident that a deeper approach will be required. By an indirect approach, such as the one demonstrated for indirect permissive therapy, the patient is given the opportunity to approach his problems more seriously. Again, however, when he reaches a point of diminishing returns, or feels that his problems are well enough under control to be able to proceed on his own, he is at liberty to terminate or interrupt therapy. With this orientation, only a small percentage of people, perhaps one in thirty, go on to a depth of therapy that is equivalent to psychoanalysis.

In the more superficial type of therapy, one can use hypnosis in a somewhat exploratory way. This will ordinarily meet the needs of the dentist and general practitioner. With the more advanced techniques, especially those for depth therapy, it is risky to use a technique until one is certain of what he is doing. If one hypnotizes and then wonders, "Now, what do I do next?" it is wiser to wake the patient and start again after having assessed the situation more completely. The more experience one has with hypnosis and various types of therapy, the better the results will be. In terms of experience, one should be willing to think of five years of experience before going on to some of the deeper or even quicker techniques. This is not to say that the physician working for anesthesia, or the dentist, or the obstetrician should not use many of the techniques that have been described; they are effective in a limited situation. The concern that is expressed is more in terms of the intensive use of the psychologic or the psychotherapeutic or probing techniques relating to cause, psychogenesis, etc., of deep-seated maladaptive processes.

DEVICES

Finger-thumb juxtaposition

Now as to devices, one of them has already been shown, i.e., the finger and thumb juxtaposition, which the therapist can use, which the patient can himself use and which can be effectively utilized for hypnosis, for relaxation, for concentration, for going to sleep, and for expressing the percentage of progress and actual progress in working out a problem.

Finger questioning

Another device—one where the therapist snaps his fingers and asks questions—is termed "finger questioning." Some subjects will hear answers that pop into their minds. Others may respond with "Yes" (index finger); "No" (middle finger), "Don't know" (thumb); and "Can't answer," or "Wrong question" (ring finger). Assigning numbers or percentages to the fingers is also a form of questioning. When using a 1 to 5 scale for depth of hypnosis, it is well to be prepared for a number from 1 to 5 that really means 5 plus the specified number. In the introduction to numbering, 5 is indicated as the beginning of deep states, which gives the implication that higher numbers are possible. When it seems that the patient is deeper than the number he gives would indicate, he can be asked, "Is that 2 (or whatever number he gave), or is it 2 plus 5?" Finger responses are then desirable, assigning, say, the index finger for the number he gave, and the middle finger for that number plus 5. When this is done, and the higher figure is obtained by ideomotor activity, the patient is very much impressed and becomes more accessible to deeper stages.

Finger questioning with percentages has also been employed, getting the patient to think of the numbers. (It is amazing to have someone come out with a figure like 37 per cent and stick by that 37 per cent just as strongly as if there were no doubt in his mind whatsoever.) The limit of accuracy is not known, but it is frequently extremely accurate. (When one gets two or three persons, already competent hypnotic subjects, and each one of them aims for a figure about someone else and all the figures agree, that's impressive.)

Hand levitation and hand conflict

One way of using hand levitation is to combine it with hand conflict. The patient has been raising his hand, and may have slowed down about halfway. He can then be told that his hand will remain up until he is convinced that he is deeply hypnotized or reaches the point where he is deeply hypnotized. Any resistances or misgivings are then focused into a conflict about letting the hand drop again. This conflict is heightened by the effects of gravity, which can become an insidious factor in convincing the patient that effects are deeper than he believes they are. The use of one hand for lifting up and the other for pressing down has already been demonstrated.

CONFUSION IN THERAPY

Confusion therapy is often useful in later stages. It does not necessarily depend on hypnosis. A patient comes in and he is absolutely sure that things are a certain way. Since they are not actually, one proceeds to confuse him, as utterly and as systematically as possible. Just as soon as he feels he knows where he stands, something is said to unsettle him again. Ultimately, he feels so completely confused that he goes home and straightens things out on his own. It is an excellent technique. Admittedly, it is very uncomfortable and patients do not like it, but it works.

PUTTING CONFLICTS IN THE DEEP FREEZE

The following approach can be used more generally. A person comes in. He shows some conflict, some difficulty. He is told that he can put the problem in the deep freeze—under hypnosis, that is—to be dealt with at a time when it is convenient, or when he is with a person or in a situation where it is appropriate.

Demonstration 16 (Part 2)

DOCTOR C (*demonstrating*)

And now, what about Doctor C? . . . Would you care to come up here again? What comments do you have?

RAPPORT REACTION

SUBJECT

Well, I had a very strange feeling come over me just now as you turned and looked at me. It's kind of hard to explain how it is. Something happened the minute you turned to me and smiled. I haven't noticed any anesthesia in this hand yet and I have been watching for that. I think that's about all I have observed since I left the stand. (*Subject shows no interest in general discussion. He also demonstrates that the rapport of the initial trance is easily evoked.*)

AURAL EFFECTS IN HYPNOSIS

DOCTOR C (*demonstrating*)

Do you think that you could have gone into a trance? (*Actually, he had never roused from the original trance and wasn't asked to.*)

SUBJECT

You mean when you first looked at me? I think I could have gone completely asleep if you hadn't asked me to come up here.

DOCTOR C (*demonstrating*)

That brings up the whole question of interruptions and diversion. This is a different situation. In an ordinary clinical situation, I certainly would not have interrupted Doctor C in that manner. You will find also that the interruptions that do not bother the therapist and have no personal significance for the patient, will have little effect on induction or later trance states. The patient can also be reassured about his ability to pick up after interruptions and will be able to do so. Of course, the present hypnotic situation has not been terminated, but if it had been we would still find that for a period, perhaps until he went to sleep tonight, Doctor C could be accessible to rehypnosis. This aura or aftereffect is a common phenomenon. (See Postscript to Demonstration, below.)

VISUALIZATION SOUGHT, BUT SUBJECT NOT READY

SUBJECT

I'm rather enjoying it. (*Laughs.*) You can demonstrate some more phenomena with me. I'd enjoy having you do it.

DOCTOR C (*demonstrating*)

Well, let's see what the audience has to say. What shall I demonstrate?

QUESTION

How about his vision?

ANSWER

Do you have any picture impressions? . . . None. My own approach is not to try to push these things over on a person unless he is willing.

NATURE OF INTUITION

QUESTION

Do you have a definition for intuition, and how do you produce it?

ANSWER

I have no idea in the world how I produce intuition. I think Theodor Reik describes it rather well in his book, *Listening with the Third Ear*. But I simply take advantage of it; I don't think I produce it.

QUESTION

When you do this, are you in very close rapport with your patient?

ANSWER

I think that in intuition there is a tremendously strong rapport with the patient.

PREOCCUPATION OF THE SUBJECT WITH THE HYPNOSIS

DOCTOR C (*to subject*)

What is happening now?

SUBJECT

Well, I'm just watching my fingernail here.

DOCTOR C (*demonstrating*)

Is anything else happening?

SUBJECT

No, I'm not conscious of anything taking place.

DOCTOR C (*demonstrating*)

And where are we at this moment?

SUBJECT

Mmm . . . We're in the Coral Room on the *Ocean Monarch*.

DOCTOR C (*demonstrating*)

Would you have expected any other place?

SUBJECT

No.

DOCTOR C (*demonstrating*)

Have you been paying attention to what I have been talking about?

SUBJECT

Mmm . . . Vaguely.

QUESTION OF FUTURE RECALL

DOCTOR C (*demonstrating*)

Do you think you will remember all of it?

SUBJECT

No.

DOCTOR C (*demonstrating*)

Now, that could be negative hallucination or it could simply be unawareness of the unconscious.

QUESTION

If he decided to remember, how would he recall?

ANSWER

Probably as, "This is something I have forgotten, but now I remember it." It's a lot easier to remember something and know that you had forgotten it than to forget something and know what you have forgotten! In other words, when a patient comes up with amnesia, how does he know he has it? We go by negative evidence.

QUESTION

Would Doctor C be able to use a trance to recall this session?

ANSWER

That would depend entirely upon his own goals. I'm sure that he has the capacity. It is a matter of motivation, and then the question of whether he would wish to remember it today or tomorrow, next week, next year, and whether he wants to remember it permanently, or to forget it from time to time. There are any number of possibilities. He will select his own.

SPONTANEOUS DEEPENING OF TRANCE

DOCTOR C (*demonstrating*)

How deep is the effect now?

SUBJECT

Well, I think it's deepening. I feel more comfortable with my eyes closed; I've been watching the right foot of the third man in line here and he disturbs me when he moves it. However, he shifts it once in a while, then I have to pick it up again. (*Description of lag in response.*)

DOCTOR C (*demonstrating*)

Do you expect him to remain motionless?

SUBJECT

(*Laughs.*) Well, he should for my convenience!

DOCTOR C (*demonstrating*)

That's true. And if he doesn't, you just close your eyes. Perhaps you'd like to rest for a while, then awaken feeling quite refreshed, knowing that you can go still deeper at any time in the future, at your own convenience, and according to your needs and desires.

INACTIVE OR INDIRECT APPROACH

QUESTION

I was wondering if you'd use this inactive approach in most of your therapy.

ANSWER

Therapy is different with every patient.

QUESTION

I mean, if you're going to use a hypnotic technique, do you simply use this indirect approach for the induction procedures? After the patient is already conditioned and in later sessions, do you use a more active approach?

ANSWER

I can't give any definite answer, because my procedures are always in transition. I go through periods when I use cues for hypnosis with all my patients, and others when I simply ask them to go into hypnosis on a conscious, intentional basis, by agreement; sometimes I suggest it, sometimes they suggest it. But, even in the hypnotic procedures, we might go through quite a give-and-take process. It doesn't matter whether it is for probing or for trying to integrate the material. I can't give a clear-cut answer because there is no clear-cut procedure. This mode of varying procedures is experimental in nature. It is also an excellent means for broadening the bases for observation of hypnotic and therapeutic processes.

QUESTION

But you don't usually take most of the hour with the patient drifting into and out of hypnosis?

ANSWER

No, I don't put the patient into the hypnosis, work for a deep trance, then bring him in and out, except for purposes of training and of deepening the effects. Ordinarily, if the patient comes out, it is because of traumatic material. Then I decide whether or not to reinduce the hypnosis. I work for deep effects in the first place, then utilize the material at an unconscious level particularly. However, I do not seek hypnosis for all of any session, or even for all sessions, since the revaluation of traumatic material needs to be done both in the conscious state and in the unconscious state, separately as well as in coordination or conjunction.

QUESTION

Then actually in the initial stages, you can't possibly be quite as inactive and permissive as here?

ANSWER

No. In a hypnotic session, I will usually devote only five or ten minutes to induction attempts. For demonstration purposes and research, I may use a much longer period of time and I adopt a more passive approach.

PRESENTING HYPNOSIS TO THE PATIENT

QUESTION

Realizing that most people know little or nothing about hypnosis, or that their knowledge is limited to the performance of a stage hypnotist, you would not proceed this way in your first session, would you?

ANSWER

I vary my presentation of hypnosis to patients. There was a time when I would discuss it one week and try the next week, attempting to bring up all possible resistances to see how they would be resolved. I don't work that way any more. I approach some patients without any warning at all, bring up the question, and see whether they will go into a quick trance or not. With others, I go more slowly.

QUESTION

Well, would you help them into it the first time? How will they know how to direct themselves as to what they do in order to assume that state? Do you put them into hypnosis one time at least, so that they know what to expect, and then let them go on from there, or what?

ANSWER

Well, how does a person know what to expect in hypnosis? Either he watches someone else or he can be assured that hypnosis is a state everyone gets into on many occasions, that he can do it on his own, or be induced by one of the procedures already demonstrated. Actually, the unconscious does know what is required in hypnosis. If you analyze some of the techniques, you will recognize that they really do not instruct the patient in what he is to feel, but rather lead him into a pattern of behavior that enables him to assume the appropriate attitudes for induction of hypnosis.

DOCTOR C (*to subject*)

And just keep on, keep on breathing deeper and deeper and more easily. . . . Your hands can raise or drop as they choose. (*Subject had initiated levitation on his own. A rather marked tremor was observed in the right forearm.*)

SIGNIFICANCE OF TREMOR

QUESTION

Does his tremor signify resistance?

ANSWER

The tremor could signify resistance, except that there is no particular suggestion from me, so that it is probably a reaction of some kind to some subjective impression. At least, that is what I feel right now.

DOCTOR C (*demonstrating*)

Doctor, is this tremor anything that you wish or feel you should discuss?

SUBJECT

(*Sighs.*) No, it's, maybe it's just that I had too much coffee. (*Laughs.*) I never shake this badly with it, I'm sure.

DOCTOR C (*demonstrating*)

You never shake this badly? I think we should leave it at that. (*In a demonstration the individual's rights are protected, even when it may actually be that there is no reason for concern. It seems likely that the tremor was related to fatigue effects, but there was no point in stirring up reactions that might persist.*)

Now, you can release it and, if you wish to come out of the hypnosis feeling fine, this would be a good time for it. . . .

TRAINED SUBJECT'S AWARENESS OF DEMONSTRATION SUBJECT'S STATUS

QUESTION

Is the patient going deeper now? I can feel a deeper effect in myself.

ANSWER

He could be going deeper. (*Diversion in order not to prolong demonstration.*) Sometimes a person will stay at an even keel when a disturbance occurs. At other times, it fosters deeper effects. The jerky pattern of easing of the tremor is rather typical.

INQUIRY ABOUT DEPTH

QUESTION

Will you check him for depth?

DOCTOR C (*demonstrating*)

On the one to five plus scale, how deep are you now?

SUBJECT

(*Deep breath.*) There isn't any number that comes to me, but I have a peculiar feeling, a cold feeling, all over my body, just as if I've been suddenly put into a draft. My limbs and whole body feel cold.

DOCTOR C (*demonstrating*)

Does that mean you are in a relatively deep trance?

SUBJECT

Evidently I must be. (*Deep breathing. His desire to remain in the trance was obvious. Depth at this point was 4, bordering on 5.*)

WAKENING SUGGESTIONS

DOCTOR C (*demonstrating*)

I think we have worked long enough on this trance, so that we ought to let you rest from it. Now, come on out of the trance at your own pace. Unconsciously, you can give yourself any posthypnotic suggestions that you would like for your own benefit.

(*to audience*)

You will notice that the tremor redeveloped when the question of depth was raised.

(to subject)

Just let yourself come wide awake, feeling fine. When you walk back to your chair, you will find that you are completely out of the trance.

PROTECTING THE INDIVIDUAL

QUESTION

Could you use a deepening process to find out the etiology of this?

ANSWER

I would not use any probing in a situation of this sort.

QUESTION

By that statement, do you mean here in this situation?

ANSWER

Not in a demonstration situation.

QUESTION

In a private situation you could?

ANSWER

Yes, although that depends on the person's preference at all times.

INSISTENCE ON SUBJECT AWAKENING

DOCTOR C *(demonstrating)*

Doctor, are you ready to waken fully now?

SUBJECT

(Sighs.)

DOCTOR C *(demonstrating)*

You will have noted a slight catalepsy just now when I lifted the left arm. (*Depth of 5 at this point.*) Now your left arm can relax completely. I'd like to have you wake up, and thanks very much for your assistance.

POSTSCRIPT TO DEMONSTRATION

After the demonstration was over and while the audience was breaking up, the subject once again reverted to a trance, clearly enjoying the experience. This was called to the attention of the demonstrating doctor, who was prevailed upon to demonstrate catalepsy and to elicit the glove anesthesia, which the patient had wished to experience. Demonstration subjects, like patients, are often so pleased at their ability to achieve a deep trance for the first time that they are unwilling to give it up.

The role of posthypnotic suggestion was evident in the subject doctor's reactions. He had been told that he could go back into a trance readily, that he could make any posthypnotic suggestions he wished, and that the anesthesia would develop when he was ready for it. He was thus left free to initiate such behavior on his own or to seek assistance if he wanted it. His knowledge of the work the demonstrating physician did with catalepsy and anesthesia and the fact that he had seen a demonstration of this work fortified the subject. His desire for experiencing added phenomena was whetted by the demonstration, and the passivity of the approach left him with a real readiness to enter into them. Capitalizing on a subject's readiness is particularly useful with the resistive subject or the overanxious one.

References of Interest

Adler, M. H. and Secunda, L.: An indirect technique to induce hypnosis. *J. Nerv. & Ment. Dis.*, 1947, 106, 190-193.

Aldrich, C. Knight: *Psychiatry for the family physician:* McGraw Hill, 1954.

Alexander, F. and French, T. M.: *Psychoanalytic therapy,* New York: Ronald Press, 1946.

American Journal of Clinical Hypnosis, 32 West Cypress Street, Phoenix, Arizona.

Barety, A.: *Le magnétisme animal étudié sous le nom de force neurique rayonnante et circulante,* Paris: O. Douin, 1887.

Barker, N. and Burgwin, S.: Brain wave patterns during hypnosis, hypnotic sleep, and normal sleep. *Arch. Neurol. Psychiat.*, 1949, 62, 412-420.

Barker, R. G., Dembo, and Lewin, K.: Frustration and regression: an experiment with young children. Studies in topological and vector psychology. II. *University of Iowa studies in child welfare, Vol. 18, No. 1 University of Iowa Studies No. 386.* Iowa City: University of Iowa Press, 1941.

Baruk, H. and Massaut, C.: Action physiologique experimentale et clinique du scopochloralose. *Ann. Med. Psychol.*, 1936, 94, 702-712.

Baudouin, C.: *Suggestion and autosuggestion,* London: George Allen and Unwin, Ltd., 1920.

Bernheim, H.: *Suggestive therapeutics* (1886). New York: London Book Co., 1947.

Braid, J.: *Neurypnology: or the rationale of nervous sleep considered in relation with animal magnetism,* London: John Churchill, 1843.

———: *Braid on hypnotism:* Julian Press, Inc., 1960.

Bramwell, J. Milne: *Hypnotism: its history, practice and theory:* Julian Press, Inc., 1959.

Chertok: L.: *Psychosomatic methods in painless childbirth:* Pergamon Press, 1959.

Cooper & Erickson: *Time distortion in hypnosis:* Williams & Wilkins, 1959.

Dorcus, R. M.: *Hypnosis and its therapeutic applications.* New York: McGraw Hill, 1956.

English & English: *Comprehensive dictionary of psychological and psychoanalytical terms:* Longsman, Green & Co., 1958.

Erickson, Milton H.: Hypnosis: A general review. *Dis. Nerv. Syst.,* 1941, 2, 13-18.

————: Deep hypnosis and its induction, Chapter in (106).

————: An experimental demonstration of the psychopathology of every day life. *Psychoanal. Quart.,* 1939, 8, 338-353.

————: The method employed to formulate a complex story for the induction of an experimental neurosis in a hypnotic subject. *J. Gen. Psychol.,* 1944, 31, 67-84.

————: A study of clinical and experimental findings on hypnotic deafness: I. Clinical experimentation and findings. *J. Gen. Psychol.,* 1938, 19, 127-150; II. Experimental findings with a conditioned response technique. *J. Gen. Psychol.,* 1938, 19, 151-167.

————: The development of an actual limited obsessional hysterical state in a normal hypnotic subject. *J. Clin. Exper. Hypnosis,* 1954, 2, 27-41.

————: Special techniques of brief hypnotherapy. *J. Clin. Exper. Hypnosis,* 1954, 2, 102-129.

————: The induction of color blindness by a technique of hypnotic suggestion. *J. Gen. Psychol.,* 1939, 20, 61-89.

———— & Erickson, E. M.: Concerning the nature and character of post-hypnotic behavior. *J. Gen. Psychol.,* 1941, 24, 95-133.

———— & ————, E. M.: Hypnotic investigation of psychosomatic phenomena: I. Psychosomatic interrelationships studied by experimental hypnosis. *Psychosom. Med.,* 1943, 5, 51-58.

———— & Kubie, L. S.: The successful treatment of a case of acute hysterical depression by a return under hypnosis to a critical phase of childhood. *Psychoanal. Quarter.,* 1941, 10, 583-609.

————: Possible detrimental effects from experimental hypnosis. *J. Abnorm. & Soc. Psychol.,* 1932, 27, 3, 321-327.

————: The investigation of a specific amnesia. *Brit. J. Med. Psychol.,* 1933, 13, 2, 143-150.

———— & Hoskins, R. G. et al. A cooperative research in schizophrenia. *Arch. Neurol. & Psychiat.,* 1933, 30, 388-401.

————: The concomitance of organic and psychological changes during marked improvement in schizophrenia: a case analysis. *Amer. J. of Psychiat.,* 1934, 13, 6, 1349-1357.

———— & Huston, P. E. & Shakow, David: A study of hypnotically induced complexes by means of the Luria technique. *J. Gen. Psychol.,* 1934, 11, 65-97.

————: A brief survey of hypnotism. *Med. Rec.,* 1934, 160, 11, 609-613.

————: A study of an experimental neurosis hypnotically induced in a case of ejaculatio praecox. *Brit. J. Med. Psychol.,* 1935, 15, 1, 34-50.

————: The experimental demonstration of unconscious mentation by automatic writing. *Psychoanalytic Quar.,* 1937, 6, 4, 513-529.

————: Development of apparent unconsciousness during hypnotic reliving of a traumatic experience. *Arch. Neurol. & Psychiat.,* 1937, 38, 6, 1282-1288.

———— & ————, E. M.: The hypnotic induction of hallucinatory color vision followed by pseudo-negative after-images. *J. Exper. Psychol.,* 1938, 22, 6, 581-588.

———— & Kubie, L. S.: The use of automatic drawing in the interpretation and relief of a state of acute obsessional depression. *Psychoanalytic Quar.,* 1938, 7, 4, 443-466.

————: The application of hypnosis to psychiatry. *Med. Rec.,* 1939, 150, 2, 60-63.

————: An experimental investigation of the possible anti-social use of hypnosis. *Psychiat.,* 1939, 2, 3, 391-414.

————: Demonstration of mental mechanisms by hypnosis. *Arch. Neurol. & Psychiat.,* 1939, 62, 2, 367-370.

———— & Kubie, L. S.: The translation of the cryptic automatic writing of one hypnotic subject by another in a trance-like dissociated state. *Psychoanalytic Quar.,* 1940, 9, 1, 51-63.

————: Hypnosis: a general review. *Diseases of the Nervous System*, 1941, 2, 1, 13-18.

———— & Brickner, Richard M.: The development of aphasia-like reactions from hypnotically induced amnesias: experimental observations and a detailed case report. *Psychosomatic Med.*, 1943, 5, 1, 59-66.

————: A controlled experimental use of hypnotic regression in the therapy of an acquired food intolerance. *Psychosomatic Med.*, 1943, 5, 1, 67-70.

————: Experimentally elicited salivary and related responses to hypnotic visual hallucinations confirmed by personality reactions. *Psychosomatic Med.*, 5, 2, 185-187.

———— & Hill, Lewis B.: Unconscious mental activity in hypnosis—psychoanalytic implications. *Psychoanalytic Quar.*, 1944, 13, 1, 60-78.

————: An experimental investigation of the hypnotic subject's apparent ability to become unaware of stimuli. *J. Gen. Psychol.*, 1944, 31, 191-212.

————: Hypnotic techniques for the therapy of acute psychiatric disturbances in war. *Amer. J. Psychiat.*, 1945, 101, 5, 668-672.

————: The therapy of a psychosomatic headache. *J. Clin. & Exper. Hypnosis*, 1954, 2, 1, 27-41.

———— & Rosen, Harold: The hypnotic and hypnotherapeutic investigation and determination of symptom-function. *J. Clin. & Exper. Hypnosis*, 1954, 2, 3, 201-219.

————: A clinical note on indirect hypnotic therapy. *J. Clin. & Exper. Hypnosis*, 1954, 2, 3, 171-174.

————: Pseudo-orientation in time as a hypnotherapeutic procedure. *J. Clin. & Exper. Hypnosis*, 1954, 2, 4, 261-283.

————: Self-exploration in the hypnotic state. *J. Clin. & Exper. Hypnosis*, 1955, 3, 1.

————: Naturalistic techniques of hypnosis. *American Journal of Clinical Hypnosis*, 1958, 1, 1, 3-8.

————: Pediatric hypnotherapy. *American Journal of Clinical Hypnosis*, 1958, 1, 1, 25-29.

———— & ————, E. M.: Further considerations of time distortion: subjective time condensation as distinct from time expansion. *American Journal of Clinical Hypnosis*, 1958, 1, 2, 83-88.

————: Hypnosis in painful terminal illness. *American Journal of Clinical Hypnosis*, 1959, 1, 3, 117-121.

————: Breast development possibly influenced by hypnosis: two instances and the psychotherapeutic results. *American Journal of Clinical Hypnosis*, 1960, 2, 3, 157-159.

————: Psychogenic alteration of menstrual functioning. *American Journal of Clinical Hypnosis*, 1960, 2, 4, 227-231.

————: Book review: Marmer's hypnosis in anesthesiology. *American Journal of Clinical Hypnosis*, 1960, 3, 1, 63.

Esdaile, James: *Hypnosis in medicine and surgery*. Julian Press, Inc., 1957.

Estabrooks, G. H.: *Hypnotism*. E. P. Dutton & Co., Inc., 1957.

Freytag, Fredericka F.: *The hypno-analysis of an anxiety hysteria*. Julian Press, Inc., 1959.

Gorton, Bernard E. M.D.: The physiology of hypnosis. *Psychiat. Quart.*, 1949, *23*, 317-343, 457-485.

————: Physiologic aspects of hypnosis. In *hypnosis in modern medicine*, (J. Schneck, Ed.), 246-280. Springfield, C. C. Thomas, 1953.

————: *The annual review of hypnosis literature*. (With Kline, M. V., Haggerty, A. D. and Guze, H.) Volumes I and II (Combined) 1950-51. New York, The Woodrow Press, 1953.

————: The method of Schultz, "autogenic training." In Weitzenhoffer, A. M. *General techniques of hypnotism*, New York, Grune and Stratton, 1957.

————: Autogenic training. *Am. J. Clin. Hypnosis*, 1959, 2, 31-41.

Heron, W. T.: Hypnosis and dentistry. *Northwest Dentistry*, 1949, 28, 154-158.

———— & Abramson, Milton: An objective evaluation of hypnosis in obstetrics. *American Journal of Obstetrics and Gynecology*, 1950, 59, 1069-1074.

————: Dental hypnosis and personality. *Personality*, 1950, 1, 349-354.

————: Hypnosis as a factor in the production and detection of crime. *The British Journal of Medical Hypnotism,* 1952, 1-15.

————, & Abramson, M.: Hypnosis in obstetrics. *Experimental Hypnosis* (Ed. LeCron, L. M.), New York: Macmillan, 1952.

————: Hypnosis and psychology. *Northwest Dentistry,* 1954, 33, 215-220.

————: Hypnosis as an anesthetic. *British Journal of Medical Hypnotism,* 1955, 6, 20-26.

————: Principles of hypnosis. *Southern Medical Journal,* 1955, 48, 307-310.

————: *Clinical applications of suggestion and hypnosis.* Springfield, Ill.: Chas. C. Thomas, 1957.

————: An old art returns to dentistry. *Seminars on Hypnosis,* 1958.

———— & Hershman, Seymour: An old art returns to medicine. *Seminars on Hypnosis,* 1958.

————: Instruction in hypnosis. *Hypnosis in Modern Medicine,* Chap. 11, (Ed. Schneck, J. M.) (2nd edition), Springfield, Ill.: Chas. C. Thomas, 1959.

————: Hypnosis in medicine. *Minnesota Medicine,* 1959, 42, 941-943.

————: The psychology of hypnosis. *Journal of the American Academy of General Practice,* 1959, 20, 92-101.

Hershman, Seymour: Hypnosis in the treatment of obesity. *J. Clin. & Exper. Hypnosis,* 1955, 3, 3.

————: Hypnosis and excessive smoking. *J. Clin. & Exper. Hypnosis,* 1956, 4, 1.

————: Hypnosis in medicine and surgery. *Journal of the Arkansas Medical Society,* 1957.

————: Use of hypnosis in obstetrics. *Northwest Medicine,* 1959.

———— & Heron, William T.: An old art returns to medicine, *Seminars on Hypnosis,* 1958.

————: Is modern medical and dental hypnosis hazardous? *American Journal of Clinical Hypnosis,* In Press.

Hull, C. L.: *Hypnosis and suggestibility. An experimental approach,* New York: D. Appleton-Century Co., 1933.

Krebs, Stanley L.: *Fundamental principles of hypnosis*. Julian Press, Inc., 1957.

Kubie, L. S. & Margolin, S.: The process of hypnotism and the nature of the hypnotic state. *Amer. J. Psychiat.*, 1944, 100, 611-622.

Kuhn & Russo: *Modern hypnotism*. New York Psych. Library Pub., 1947.

LeCron, L. M.: *Experimental hypnosis*. New York: Macmillan Co., 1952.

LeCron, L. M. & Bordeaux, J.: *Hypnotism today*. New York: Grune and Stratton Inc., 1947.

Mann, H. Group hypnosis in the treatment of obesity. *Am. J. Clinical Hypnosis*, 1959, 1, 114-116.

Mann, H. Hypnotherapy in habit disorders. *Am. J. Clinical Hypnosis*, 1961, 3, 123-126.

Moll, A.: *Hypnotism*. London: Walter-Scot, 1890.

———: *The study of hypnosis*. Julian Press, Inc., 1958.

Pattie, F. A. A report of attempts to produce uniocular blindness by hypnotic suggestion. *Brit. J. Med. Psychol.*, 1935, 15, 230-241.

———. The genuineness of hypnotically produced anesthesia of the skin. *Amer. J. Psychol.*, 1937, 49, 435-443.

———. The production of blisters by hypnotic suggestion: a review. *J. Abn. Soc. Psychol.*, 1941, 36, 62-72.

———. Some American contributions to the science of hypnosis. *Amer. Scholar*, 1943, 12, 444-454.

———. The genuineness of unilateral deafness produced by hypnosis. *Amer. J. Psychol.*, 1950, 63, 84-86.

———. The effect of hypnotically induced hostility on Rorschach responses. *J. Clin. Psychol.*, 1954, 10, 161-164.

———. Theories of hypnosis. In R. M. Dorcus (Ed.), *Hypnosis and its therapeutic applications*. New York: McGraw-Hill, 1956. Pp. 1/1-1/30.

Methods of induction, susceptibility of subjects, and criteria of hypnosis. In R. M. Dorcus (Ed.), *Hypnosis and its therapeutic applications*. New York: McGraw-Hill, 1956. Pp. 2/1-2/24.

————. The genuineness of some hypnotic phenomena. In R. M. Dorcus (Ed.), *Hypnosis and its therapeutic applications.* New York: McGraw-Hill, 1956. Pp. 6/1-6/18.

————. Mesmer's medical dissertation and its debt to Mead's "De imperio solis ac lunae." *J. Hist. Med. all. Sci.,* 1956, 11, 275-287.

————. (with F. Kodman). Hypnotherapy of psychogenic hearing loss in children. *Amer. J. Clin. Hypnosis,* 1958, 1, 9-13.

Reiss, Robert & Scheerer, Martin: *Memory and hypnotic age regression.* International University Press, 1959.

Schilder, P.: *The nature of hypnosis* (1921, 1926). New York: International Universities Press, 1956.

Schultz & Luthe: *Autogenic training:* Grune & Stratton, 1959.

Secter, I. I.: Gagging controlled through hypnosis. *Dent. Survey,* 1952, 28, 1366-1367.

————: Hypnosis. *Dent. Items Interest,* 1953, 75, 160-167.

————: We don't have to be disliked. *Dent. Survey,* 1953, 29, 322-324.

————: A practical attitude towards hypnosis in dentistry. *Cal. Mag.,* 1954, 15, No. 7, 8-9.

————: Considerations in resistances to initial inductions of hypnosis. *J. Clin. Exper. Hypnosis,* 1957, 5, 77-81.

————: Suggestion in the dental care of children. *J. Hypnosis Psychol. Dentistry,* 1958, 1, No. 4, 10-11.

————: The psychologically oriented dentist, an editorial. *American Journal of Clinical Hypnosis,* 1959, 2, 1-2.

————: Conserving time in patient orientation. *J. Hypnosis Psychol. Dentistry,* 1957, 1, No. 3, 4-5.

————: Some notes on controlling the exaggerated gag reflex. *American Journal of Clinical Hypnosis,* 1960, 2, 149-153.

————: Hypnotizability as a function of attitude towards hypnosis. *American Journal of Clinical Hypnosis,* 1960, 3.

————: Some notes on T.A.T. card 12m as a predictor of hypnotizability. *American Journal of Clinical Hypnosis,* 1961, In Press.

————: Some notes on personality factors as related to hypnotizability. *American Journal of Clinical Hypnosis,* 1961, In Press.

————: Tongue thrust and nail biting simultaneously treated during hypnosis. *American Journal of Clinical Hypnosis,* 1961, In Press.

———— & Heron, W. T. Hypnotherapy for relief of pain. *Dent. Items Interest,* 1953, 75, 391-393.

———— & Cochran, J. L. Restoration by hypnotherapy of loss of the sense of taste. *J. Nervous Ment. Disease,* 1956, 123, 296-298.

———— & Heron, W. T. Clinical applications of hypnosis in dentistry. *Dent. Survey,* 1954, 30, 331-333.

Sidis, B.: *The Psychology of suggestion.* New York: D. Appleton Co., 1910.

Weitzenhoffer, A. M.: *Hypnotism: an objective study in suggestibility.* New York: John Wiley and Sons, Inc., 1953.

————: *General techniques of hypnotism.* Grune & Stratton, 1957.

Wolberg, Lewis: *Medical hypnosis*—Volume 1 and 2: Grune & Stratton, 1948.

Index